Illness and Irony

Illness and Irony
On the Ambiguity of Suffering in Culture

Edited by

Michael Lambek and Paul Antze

Berghahn Books
New York • Oxford

First published in 2003 by

Berghahn Books

Social Analysis, Volume 47, Issue 2, Summer 2003

Paperback edition published in 2004 by

Berghahn Books

www.berghahnbooks.com

Library of Congress Cataloging-in-Publication Data

A C.I.P. catalogue record for this book is
available from the Library of Congress.

ISBN 1-57181-674-7 (pbk)

Printed in the United States on acid-free paper.

Contents

Acknowledgments

Earlier versions of several of these essays were presented at a panel we organized for the annual meeting of the Canadian Anthropology Society (CASCA) in Montreal, May 2001. Deidre Rose, Jean-Michel Vidal, and Donna Young also contributed stimulating presentations on that occasion. Lawrence Cohen and Vincent Crapanzano joined us later and were very gracious about the severe time constraints we imposed upon them. We thank all of our contributors for participating in a venture that must often have seemed ambiguous. Thanks, too, are due to the anonymous reviewers of the individual papers, to Shawn Kendrick for excellent editing, and to Vivian Berghahn and Kingsley Garbett for their patience.

We wish to thank our respective families—Jackie Solway and Nadia and Simon Lambek, and Rosemary Jeanes Antze and Emily and Bridget Antze—for their suitably ironic appreciation and support of our work. Michael also thanks Anne Goldstein for supplying, at the eleventh hour, the essay by Virginia Woolf.

INTRODUCTION
Irony and Illness—Recognition and Refusal

Michael Lambek

> Frasier: Until you got here, things were going fine.
> Bulldog: Yeah, well things seem to have changed. What do you
> eggheads call that—irony?

Proponents of irony can hardly propose a definite theory or even a definitive introduction to their subject. Here we intend merely to review the impetus for our volume and the suggestions we gave our bemused contributors.[1]

This project began when one of us chanced upon the brilliant discussion of Socratic and Platonic irony by Alexander Nehamas in his book *The Art of Living* (1998). Nehamas invokes Thomas Mann's portrait of illness in *The Magic Mountain* (1995 [1924]) but without developing a general discussion of the relationship between illness and irony. As anthropologists who have spent considerable time thinking about issues of illness, selfhood, and agency in their relationship both to local practices and to dominant theories—in short, to culture—it seemed that here was rich terrain to explore. Our interest increased as we came to realize that were we forced to sum up the aim of the book we had previously edited together, *Tense Past* (Antze and Lambek 1996), we would call it an exposition of the overliteralization of memory in certain contemporary discourses. That is to say, *Tense Past* explores accounts and practices of memory that appear to be characterized by an absence of irony. In this new volume we want to restore irony to its place. We do so by turning not to memory per se (though it is hardly irrelevant to our subject) but rather to illness and therapy, broadly conceived.

We begin with two hunches: first, that there is often something in the situation of illness that resembles irony or that brings the recognition of irony to the fore; and, second, that therapeutic practices and discourses can be described and distinguished according to the degree to which they recognize or refuse irony. Irony might be an inevitable part of encounters that get classified as therapeutic or forensic. But it might equally well be threatening to the kind of expert professionalism that is a significant feature of these domains at present, especially in the United States where there is a bias toward literalism in both the

Notes for this section begin on page 16.

church and the law (Crapanzano 2000). Neither scientific expertise nor bureaucratic or legalistic rationalization will find in irony a happy bedfellow.

Since Freud, theories of illness and therapy have included the possibility that
sufferers are complicit in their conditions. This "idealism of the pathological, if
not to say pathological idealism," to paraphrase Thomas Mann (1995 [1924]:
645), is replete with the possibilities of irony—irony of both (Sophoclean) tragic
inevitability and (Socratic) self-recognition. Irony is more characteristic of psychoanalytic thought (at its best) and possibly of certain non-Western or coun-
terhegemonic therapeutic and discursive forms than it is of biomedicine, which
takes pathology literally. Indeed, one way to phrase the distinction between 'illness' and 'disease', so fruitfully explored by Arthur Kleinman and his associ-
ates (Hahn 1995; Kleinman 1980; Kleinman, Eisenberg, and Good 1978), would
be to suggest that 'disease' refers to a literalization of phenomena whose experience is always culturally, socially, and psychologically mediated and hence
open to interpretation ('illness'). The contributors to this collection explore
some of the ways in which illness and therapy may be characterized by irony
(or ironically) as sites at which ironies of the human condition are produced,
encountered, acknowledged, and possibly recognized, clarified, understood,
and deployed—or conversely discounted and overlooked in favor of more literal
readings. How might such sites offer privileged access for exploring questions
of human agency, dignity, and accountability more generally? What might we
learn from illness and therapy about the place for irony in theory?

The Scope of Irony

We hesitate either to define irony or to offer an extended review of available
definitions and discussions. Irony can be located in many ways—as a feature of
the world, as a rhetorical trope, as a kind of attitude. Moreover, the objects of
irony are infinite—knowledge, truth, and Enlightenment reason being among
the most notable. Anthropologists wishing an overview of the place of irony in
their subject and discipline can turn to *Irony in Action*, a set of smart and
engaging essays edited by Fernandez and Huber (2001) that appeared while our
collection was in gestation. That volume also provides extensive bibliography.

We begin by making a rough distinction between irony of commission and
irony of recognition. The former is rhetorical irony—intentional and 'made'; the
latter is situational—interpreted and 'found'. We recognize that the two are
complementary and often indistinguishable in practice, but we draw the distinction precisely in order to offset the assumption—evident in many studies of
irony and in early responses by colleagues to our work—that irony is properly
to be consigned to the rhetorical, as an intentional mode of presentation.

As a prototypical instance of the former, we can think of the wink that accompanies an ostensibly straightforward utterance and intimates that the performer
means something else and is playing with the audience. Such coyness stands in
contrast to tragic irony, in which people say or do things that actually reverse their

intentions. In trying to escape his fate, Oedipus moves toward it. The audience realizes the irony, but the character does not. Here, to be sure, the playwright is deliberately portraying irony (though that is different, perhaps, from *being* ironic). However, the larger point is that psychic and social life are composed of multiple dramatic situations (of small and large scale) that are not pre-scripted by a play-wright (though local theodicies may ascribe events to such a hand) and in which the irony of the protagonists' situation slowly dawns on them.

Hegel's irony of history draws from the tragic form and gets refracted in Freudian and Marxist versions. Indeed, the unconscious in psychoanalysis can be understood more like the second kind of irony—less as an explanation for ostensibly unintentional acts or utterances than as paradigmatic of fate itself, of the partial and gradual recognition of how, at the moment we think we are act-ing most as ourselves or being most agentive, we are actually caught up by something else. Irony, in our usage, centers on such recognition of the funda-mental undecidability of agency and intention in (internal) psychological and (external) historico-material contexts.

It follows that although we have contrasted irony with literalness, we do not view irony as necessarily opposed to either sincerity or seriousness. The human subjects described in our essays are both sincere and serious, and so are the authors of the essays. Irony may be playful,[2] but in our approach we do not consider it to be cynical, detached, or frivolous. We connect irony to something more deeply felt, some inner recognition about the contingency of truth. We think of irony as a stance that gives ambiguity, perspective, plurality, contra-diction, and uncertainty their due.

We do not wish to claim that irony is an exclusively postmodern phenome-non nor even to make a particular association between irony and the present historical situation. As Hutcheon remarks of the twentieth century, "ours joins just about every other century in wanting to call itself the 'age of irony,' and the recurrence of that historical claim in itself might well support the contention of contemporary theorists from Jacques Derrida to Kenneth Burke that irony is inherent in signification, in its deferrals and in its negations" (1994: 9). We would broaden the implicitly Occidental reference to argue that irony is char-acteristic of cultural production in the entire range of societies with which anthropologists have worked. Indeed, if modernity is sometimes characterized by overly literal and earnest discursivity, there is much (so-called) premodern or extramodern irony around. Far from being exclusively postmodern and cyn-ical, irony is highlighted in the religions (or 'worldviews') of many small-scale and non-Western societies.[3] Irony speaks to, of, and from the human condition. One might even argue that it is a feature intrinsic to consciousness—inherent in signification, as Hutcheon suggests—and that humans are continuously reminded of it.[4] This is partly a matter that the said is always accompanied by the unsaid (Tyler 1978), but more deeply that consciousness so often entails a recognition of its own limits.

Such limits have to do, in part, with the vehicles of consciousness, namely, culture. Thus, Rorty proposes that irony in a general sense entails the recognition and acceptance of contingency, of our historical and cultural situatedness: "I use 'ironist' to name the sort of person who faces up to the contingency of his or her own most central beliefs and desires—someone sufficiently historicist and nominalist to have abandoned the idea that those central beliefs and desires refer back to something beyond the reach of time and chance" (1989: xv).

By this count, irony is superior to most theoretical enthusiasms and metaphysical presumptions—more cautious, reserved, distant, wise. And by this count, most anthropologists would be ironists, at least in their public professions. But if anthropologists are ironists to a degree, they have sometimes distinguished themselves from their subjects by implying that the latter are not. We anthropologists often portray our subjects as earnestly committed to specific ways of life, to realizing and affirming certain truths that they 'hold self-evident'. If the search for universal truth, and hence the absence of irony in Rorty's sense, has been characteristic of philosophy from Plato to Kant, so too does the commitment to local truths appear in the classic portraits of ethnography, from Malinowski's passionate Trobrianders, and Evans-Pritchard's rational Azande through most recent work. It has been a deep assumption of anthropologists that the people we study hold nonrelativist commitments to the worlds they live in. Most exceptions to this have been people depicted as living through situations of rapid change, especially those generated by colonial and postcolonial encounters.

As Rorty compellingly remarks—and it is interesting that no anthropologist has been able to put it so strongly:

> Ironism ... results from awareness of the power of redescription. But most people do not want to be redescribed. They want to be taken on their own terms—taken seriously just as they are and just as they talk. The ironist tells them that the language they speak is up for grabs by her and her kind. There is something potentially very cruel about that claim. For the best way to cause people long-lasting pain is to humiliate them by making the things that seemed most important to them look futile, obsolete, and powerless. Consider what happens when a child's precious possessions—the little things around which he weaves fantasies that make him a little different from all other children—are redescribed as 'trash,' and thrown away. Or consider what happens when these possessions are made to look ridiculous alongside the possessions of another, richer child. Something like that presumably happens to a primitive culture when it is conquered by a more advanced one. The same sort of thing sometimes happens to nonintellectuals in the presence of intellectuals ... The redescribing ironist, by threatening one's final vocabulary, and thus one's ability to make sense of oneself in one's own terms rather than hers, suggests that one's self and one's world are futile, obsolete, *powerless*. Redescription often humiliates. (Rorty 1989: 89–90)

Of course, Rorty's analogy with children is suspect, as is his use of evolutionary terminology. Our ethnographic subjects (whoever they are) are generally not portrayed as being in doubt, as undecided, watchful, disinterested, and so forth. But it *is* to be doubted that they really are so different from ourselves (or so similar to one another) on this score. It is to be doubted that they do not venture their own redescriptions. It would be equally problematic were we to portray our subjects entirely in our own image, to mistake a specifically anthropological ironical stance for a generally human one.

Irony, we venture, is not pervasive, nor is it discrete—a virtue, or vice, restricted to ourselves. Instead, it is likely to be among the philosophical or existential stances available everywhere, part of the human repertoire. It is also something that is difficult, if not impossible, to sustain all of the time. Common sense, certainty, assurance must intervene. We think that there are certain moments in life and certain experiences that are likely to be more demanding or more enabling of irony than others. Among these is illness. Illness provides a condition (or set of conditions) in which irony rises readily to the surface. It does so in the experience of sufferers, in the theories of those attempting to understand illness, and in the practices of those attempting to alleviate it, whether by prevention or cure.

Voice, Text, and Agency

The term 'irony' comes to us from the classical Greeks. Indeed, there are at least two quite distinct forms in Greek thought and literature. First is the irony of Sophoclean drama. This is tragic irony in which fate creeps inevitably upon its protagonists despite their earnest endeavors to avoid it. The spectators know what must happen, but the characters refuse to acknowledge or accept it, and in that space is irony. Second is Socratic irony. This is Socrates' rhetorical stance with his students and interlocutors, turning questions back upon the questioners and forcing people to think for themselves and recognize how poorly they can rationalize their assumptions about how the world works.

What do these two forms have in common? In both instances irony realizes the limitations and ambiguity of praxis. Thought and agency run up against constraints, external ones of fate and circumstance and internal ones of ignorance, confusion, and contradiction. External and internal constraints on knowledge force us to speak with an assurance we do not have. Irony is a recognition of this fact.

As Paul Antze describes in his chapter, Freud is indebted to both versions of classical irony. Freud's Oedipus complex and his understanding of psychic conflict draw from the Sophoclean sense of fate. Neurosis offers a challenge to the idea of free agency. And one could say that the form of psychoanalytic therapy Freud originated—with its emphasis on patients learning to listen to themselves—is a particular development of the Socratic method.

In this volume we think of irony as a function of the recognition of the inherent incompleteness of any particular form of knowledge or segment of discourse. Irony thus bears an interesting relationship to heteroglossia, the juxtaposition of multiple voices. Kenneth Burke famously saw irony as the outcome of a dramatic, multivoiced situation in which each character offers a perspective and comments on the others: "The dialectic of this participation produces (in the observer who considers the whole from the standpoint of the participation of all the terms rather than from the standpoint of any one participant) a 'resultant certainty' of a different quality, necessarily ironic, since it requires that all the sub-certainties be considered as neither true nor false, but *contributory*" (1945: 513). In other words, for Burke, every drama contains a Rashomon quality.[5] But most heteroglossic situations are not explicitly constructed as drama or literature. Irony here is the recognition that some of the potentially participatory voices or meanings are silent, missing, unheard, or not fully articulate, and that voices or utterances appearing to speak for totality or truth offer only single perspectives. Hence, irony understands that the 'whole' of which Burke speaks is grasped at best only partially and, as Burke suggests, only ever as the emergent dialectical product of multiple voices that are each, taken individually, neither true nor false per se.[6]

Where literary critics speak to the irony of texts, their insights can be expanded to situations and to "meaningful action considered as a text" (Ricoeur 1971). The text metaphor has been brilliantly developed in anthropology, notably by Geertz (1973b), but also, of course, by means of structuralism, thus enabling the discovery or application of diverse literary devices and rhetorical tropes, including irony, in a variety of places. These range from religion to bureaucracy (Fernandez 1982; Herzfeld 1997) and include forms of therapy (Lévi-Strauss 1963 [1949]) and our very conceptualizations of specific illnesses (Sontag 1977). Indeed, notwithstanding Sontag's passionate argument against metaphor, many medical anthropologists would contend that it is impossible to think of illness except by means of tropes. Progress occurs by merely replacing one metaphor with a less inadequate one, in a kind of trajectory that Rorty (1989), for one, would apply to human history more generally. History, he argues, is the replacement of dead metaphors (turned literal) with fresh ones. Yet much human thought is characterized by "the disposition to use the language of our ancestors, to worship the corpses of their metaphors" (ibid.: 21). Rorty is, by his own admission, an ironist.

Critics of the interpretive approach to culture and action have incorrectly attributed to its method a misplaced concreteness, as though 'text' itself had become a dead metaphor and as though 'texts' and their interpretations were fixed in their frames for all time. But interpretivists themselves are generally not so literal-minded; they have been aware both of the irony inherent in any invocation or structuring of text[7] and of processes of framing, structuration, composition, entextualization, and their converse—that is, of the ways in which ideas, conversations, and actions coalesce as texts and the ways texts dissolve. They have been concerned, as well, with the multiple kinds of relations texts can have with what is conceptualized as lying outside of them—with authors, readers, other texts, modes of transmission, and so forth (e.g., Becker 1979). As the partiality of various kinds of relations increases, so the possibilities for irony multiply.

If we can move from attending to multiple voices inside the text—literarily or literally conceived—to the broader world of action, so can we turn these insights inward, applying them to the mind. Here, Freud, with his notions of internal conflict, ambivalence, and contradiction, has been essential. In one line of development, irony has come to do with the implicit recognition of the limits of moral agency, a reminder of the lurking presence of the unpredictable and the unpredicatable unconscious, of what Jonathan Lear (2000) calls the "remainder of life." As such, irony is not only a way of interpreting others or a rhetorical means of representing oneself to others, but also a dimension of how one understands oneself and the larger existential situation.

What, then, is the relationship of irony to agency and to responsibility? Both Freud and Foucault challenge the idea of autonomous agency and demonstrate its limits, thereby pointing to an ironic view of the world in which persons are understood primarily as subjects. But what if we turn this back and start with the subject as knowing ironist? Self-irony implies both a more knowing person and a more naive one. Is being knowledgeable about one's own ignorance— being cognizant of one's own limitations, subjection, and uncertainty—itself not a kind of agency? Or a first step in constituting such agency? What are the limits of (literalist) naiveté and enthusiasm on the one side and (ironic) detachment on the other?

If irony recognizes constraint, it does not negate the idea of agency. Rhetorical irony contextualizes, placing both the author and recipient at a certain distance from the utterance—not so far removed that they stand at the Archimedean point, not so close that they are oblivious, but at reasonable arm's length. Irony thereby offers room for maneuver, interrogating or putting into quotation predictable categories and distinctions.

Theodicy and Irony

Attending to irony directs us to the large questions that Weber placed under the term 'theodicy' and that have formed a leitmotif in anthropological classics, such as those by Evans-Pritchard, Fortes, and Geertz. In *Witchcraft, Oracles and Magic among the Azande* (1937), Evans-Pritchard argued that the diagnosis of witchcraft served to answer the 'why me?' existential questions that science and medicine evade. Although Evans-Pritchard did not quite say so, perhaps we can imagine the Azande of central Africa accepting witchcraft with a kind of ironic shrug. One cannot know who is the witch, or where and when a witch will strike next. One cannot even know whether one is a witch oneself, or whether one may be accused of being one. Witchcraft, in Evans-Pritchard's argument, is supposed to remove uncertainty. It does so with respect to specific events, for example, why *this* granary fell while *my* mother was sitting under it. But it raises a good deal of uncertainty more generally: Who are the witches among us? Why, really, do they act as they do? What, actually, am *I* capable of doing?

In his aptly titled and brilliantly conceived essay *Oedipus and Job in West Africa*, Fortes (1983; cf. 1987) explores how the Tallensi of northern Ghana address the uncertainties of existence and, most compellingly, how they understand the reality of 'spoiled lives'. He thus provides an ethnopsychological account of agency and its tribulations. In many West African societies, the personal experience of having a number of offspring die in infancy or early childhood is explained in terms of mischievous or troublesome spirits who continue deliberately to die quickly and to be reborn in order to vex their parents. This is an example of what Fortes refers to as prenatal destiny or fate. How can one be sure that one has such a child, or that it may choose to stay on this time? How do such children understand themselves? Such anguish and puzzlement are evoked, ironically, by a number of West African writers, for example, by Achebe in his classic novel of precolonial Iboland, *Things Fall Apart* (1959).[8]

Geertz (1966) summed up the question of theodicy by suggesting that any religion worthy of the name ought to be able to address the fundamental human questions of perplexity, suffering, and injustice. But as he pointed out, religion must do so without succumbing to the thought that these are fundamentally characteristic of the world as a whole. Thus, while Geertz goes on to suggest, in the manner of Ruth Benedict, that each religion will have its particular emotional tone or style—one quiescent, another activist, and so forth—implicitly he is arguing that all must recognize an ironic sense in which between the surface events of life and the depths of causation there is some kind of slippage or gap, one that escapes both our direct knowledge and our control.

One of the ways to keep understandings from collapsing in on themselves is through irony, through the uncertainty of holding things in a double vision, and through keeping what is said and what is unsaid in some uneasy but lively tension with one another. In many smaller-scale societies this is done through a play with secrecy, as in masking, initiation, and the like; here, ambiguity resists reduction, and representation is never limited to reference.[9] Knowing or suspecting that there is something beneath the surface of things, while recognizing, equally, that one cannot know fully what that something is, epitomizes an ironic attitude. We go on living our lives and enacting our dramas even though we are aware that fate may be leading us in an entirely different direction. And we assume the superficiality of perplexity, suffering, and injustice even though we cannot directly perceive their contraries. As Mary Scoggin puts it: "Irony is a reflection of the imperfection of the human world, the practical recognition of contradiction between, as Kierkegaard would have it, essence and phenomenon, and irony can even be prized as a path to reflection, demonstrating the human capacity for learning virtue" (2001: 147). Indeed, Kierkegaard's "leap of faith" begins from irony.

The tension produced by irony is a dynamic one, especially when there is no strong cultural impatience with ambiguity and when truth is seen not as what lies beneath the mask (or outside the cave and beyond the fire) so much as what is produced by means of it. The point about irony that is often forgotten is that it need not invite a kind of hermeneutics of suspicion, a peeling back of the surface of the 'said' to discover what is really meant underneath, so much as an expression or recognition of the fact that meaning is not so simply divided into discrete levels.

We may conceal these discrepancies—and indeed we must, through most of our waking, commonsense lives[10]—but certain events, such as medical emergencies, throw them into sharp relief. Indeed, for middle-class Westerners, at least, medical events are likely to be major provocations of uncertainty and existential challenge. For Virginia Woolf, the condition of being ill provided a kind of privileged perspective. Illness offers rich new forms of experience, but it also reveals the hollowness of the everyday world:

> There is, let us confess it (and illness is the great confessional), a childish outspokenness in illness; things are said, truths blurted out, which the cautious respectability of health conceals ... in health the general pretense must be kept up and the effort renewed—to communicate, to civilise, to share, to cultivate the desert, educate the native, to work together by day and by night to sport. In illness this make-believe ceases ... we cease to be soldiers in the army of the upright. (Woolf 2002 [1930, 1926]: 11–12)

Attributing Irony

Modernity itself is sometimes characterized by its literalism, its will to truth, and the earnest pursuit of its meta-narratives. But as Woolf illustrates, irony, too, is found in high modernism. A famous example is Thomas Mann's *The Magic Mountain*, a novel replete with irony about illness and therapy, suffering and recovery. Mann's "perfectly ordinary" protagonist arrives at the sanatorium ostensibly healthy—or is he?—and ends up succumbing lethargically to the regime, staying seven years, only to leave it for the real site of death and suffering that Europe becomes during World War I. Among his companions at the sanatorium is a man who is unequivocally ill with tuberculosis but passionate about life and politics. Yet this man, Settembrini, does not escape Mann's irony either. He is engaged in contributing to a vast scholarly project "which is to bear the title *The Sociology of Suffering* ... an encyclopedia of some twenty or so volumes that will list and discuss all conceivable instances of human suffering, from the most personal and intimate to the large-scale conflicts of groups that arise out of class hostility and international strife" (Mann 1995 [1924]: 242). This is an ambition that might give pause to driven academics, especially perhaps to some of those who participate in the medical anthropology of social distress characteristic of certain inhabitants of that Magic Mountain located on the banks of the Charles.[11]

That was meant ironically, of course.

But then, perhaps, so is this.

Here we get to the rub of irony, to some of the ways it irritates. I mention only two. The scope of Mann's irony embraces scholars no less than sufferers or the projects of therapy. Epistemologically, irony subverts encyclopedic projects.[12] Ethically, it resists easy attributions of accountability. Did I just make fun of someone or did I not? Was it malicious or was it not? Was that really 'me' speaking anyway? Was it a mere rhetorical tactic, a staged voice? And, notoriously, is there a continuous and consistent 'I' speaking in every instance? Since writing the above, I have discovered the remark by Arthur Kleinman that "to create a universal science of human suffering ... would be archly ironic" (1995: 118).[13]

Irony blurs or complicates easy distinctions—between truth and falsity, sense and reference, objectification and empathy, the literal and the allegorical. Irony thereby foregrounds undecidability, ambiguity, indeterminacy, though as Hutcheon points out, it cannot be reduced to them because it always has an 'edge' (1994: 33) and is weighted in favor of the unsaid (ibid.: 37). It thus confounds determinism and reduction and offers a resistance against both overly literal and, we suppose, overly metaphorized or overly allegorized readings. Determinism and reductionism may be the products of monologic voices, of hegemonic ideologies and practices, bureaucratic rationalizations, overly objectifying intellectual schemes, or overly naturalizing discursive processes. But irony also undercuts the determinacy and reductionism inherent in ideas of autonomous agency, free will, subjectivity, and rational choice. It cuts both ways.

This is perhaps where irony becomes most interesting or most attractive in the present political and cultural climate. Sophoclean irony underlines the fallibility of the individual human struggle against fate; Socratic irony points to the limitations of assumed self-knowledge. In both forms, irony contextualizes and compromises naive notions of agency. Yet in neither the tragic nor the philosophical form is agency, struggle, or the quest for knowledge renounced.

"True irony," Kenneth Burke succinctly remarks (1945: 514), "is not 'superior to the enemy.'" Indeed, it is characterized by humility, "based upon a sense of fundamental kinship with the enemy, as one *needs* him, is *indebted* to him, is not merely outside him as an observer but contains him *within*, being consubstantial with him."

Such consubstantiality becomes particularly salient when we think about illness. However, it is hardly what comes to mind when we think of postmodern irony today. We might clarify the difference by reference to Linda Hutcheon's admirable book *Irony's Edge*. Hutcheon (1994: 2) begins with the following questions: "Why should anyone want to use this strange mode of discourse where you say something you don't actually mean and expect people to understand not only what you actually do mean but also your attitude toward it? How do you decide if an utterance is ironic?" These questions are not equivalent. We suggest that *what irony frequently throws into question is intentionality itself*. It is not so obvious either that all ironies are intentional or that there is a clear separation between what you actually mean and what you don't actually mean, or that you have a clear and single attitude toward it or know yourself what it means. All this makes an answer to the second question concerning the interpretation of irony even more problematic than Hutcheon suggests. If irony is not always an intentional 'discursive strategy', its reception cannot be interpreted in straightforward terms of successful comprehension or misfire (ibid.: 3).

Whether grasping a given utterance or text as ironic requires inference on the part of the interpreter, as Hutcheon argues, the weight placed on the intentionality of the ironist can be exaggerated. This may be especially the case when utterances or acts are formed within particular cultural modes, idioms, discursive practices, or genres that are already constituted by means of irony or in which irony is already embedded. In his essay in this volume, Lambek argues that spirit possession is such a mode. Andrew Lakoff suggests in his contribution that attributions of mind under various forms of psychiatric practice or pharmaceutical regimes may be another.

Hutcheon rightly gives great weight to the reception of irony and to the intentionality of the interpreter or community of interpreters. Post-Freudian and post-Marxian hermeneutics can hardly operate without suspicion that there is more than meets the eye, more than one message being offered, though of course this is true of any act of communication and not simply irony. To interpret a message as ironic may be to say something about the agency or consciousness of the speaker or performer. But perhaps we need to ask as well where and how such intentions and interpretations get suppressed, as they may in spirit possession or in psychiatry (or, for that matter, in politics). Moreover, reception can itself adopt an implicit or proto-ironic mode in which the listener is hearing two messages without necessarily being fully aware of it. One thinks here of Bateson's (1972) double bind in which the meta-message contradicts or overrides the message, but not all such situations need be pathological.

An anthropological study must give as much weight to the irony or literalism of interpretation as it does to that of the original production. For example, however the authors of the Bible intended their texts to be understood, the question is how literally generations of Jews and Christians have read them. The possibility for disjuncture raises some fascinating questions. If it were established that certain biblical passages were meant metaphorically by their authors, would a literal reading now have to accept that? Would it be more 'literal' to remain faithful to an author's ironic intentions or to disregard them in favor of a literal reading of the text itself? Would the latter reading be a special form of irony despite itself? These questions may not be quite so hypothetical when we move from biblical exegesis to medical diagnosis.

In any case, we must always question reflexively whether there is any irony in our own interpretations of the acts and utterances of other people as ironic or as unironic. And this includes, recursively, our interpretations of the interpretations of the local interpreters and pronouncers of irony.

Hutcheon makes the disclaimer that her concern "is simply with verbal and structural ironies, rather than situational irony, cosmic irony, the irony of fate, and so on" (op. cit.: 3). That makes good heuristic sense for a literary critic, but it is not certain that these various forms of irony can be so easily distinguished. One reason that Hutcheon, along with many other cultural critics and theorists, can do this is that they are working primarily with 'high culture', or at least with highly framed texts and performances. Even when their subject slips into popular production or reception, they are concerned with deliberate works of art or representation, whereas anthropologists are plunged in the thick of life and in arenas where art, praxis, and judgment are not so easily distinguished.

In sum, it may be that the overdose of postmodern irony itself needs to be 'ironized'. To the extent that postmodern irony has served as a form of conceit—of *knowing* conceit, of knowing both sides, of superiority to the enemy— it needs to be balanced with the irony that admits of not knowing, or rather, of not knowing definitively. Of course, we need to be aware of the conceit of ignorance as well.

Refractions of Agency: Illness and Irony

One arena where distinctions of text and practice, of verbal and situational ironies, are blurred is that of illness and the social responses it generates. Thus, we add to Hutcheon's exposition and elaboration of the political dimension of irony in art, literature, and museum display the medical arena and the field of self-irony or ironic self-recognition, as well as the recognition of being caught in situations that themselves might be described by either protagonists or outsiders as 'ironic'.[14] Irony comes to the fore in illness, and one of the arenas in which it is frequently uncovered, invoked, or displayed is therapy (healing). Therapy here is understood as a kind of performance or sequence of performances, but performances that, as Victor Turner (1967) so effectively showed, are always situationally located. Addressing illness requires objectified theories, established modes of performance, and sustained situational judgment on the part of ill people and their families and therapists, as well as their professional and institutional communities, and, increasingly, the public as mediated by the media, the judicial system, bioethics, and various other forms of discursive and disciplinary practices. One of the critical questions is the balance of literalism and irony in these theories, performances, interpretations, mediations, and judgments.

Non-Western therapy often offers its patient an ironic perspective, or at least draws upon the resources and richness of irony. Such a positive reminder of the value of uncertainty stands in striking opposition to the central goals of Western medicine and many of its clients, who demand certainty and satisfaction. An appreciation for the limits of what we can know and say and do and expect is sometimes suppressed or refused in biomedicine and its social institutionalization. One could almost say that the demand for certainty is the pathology or limit of biomedicine.

Is psychoanalysis an antidote? Well, sometimes, and especially when linked to art or surrealism, or simply in the double relationship—transferential and empathic—between analyst and patient (assuming it does not stray exclusively to one side). But psychoanalysis also strains toward certainty, and there is probably nothing sillier than psychoanalytic literalism. Especially in North America, psychoanalysis has been subsumed by the dominant cultural expectations of certainty, monologic explanation, complete knowledge, and fully effective and efficient intervention. Lakoff's essay indicates some of the problems in quite a different cultural milieu. Both inside and outside psychoanalysis, the irony inherent in fantasy can be refused and fantasy taken too literally.[15]

A sense of irony may also undercut the highly idealized Western notion of individuated agency as freedom. Contributors examine agency with reference to lived practice and cultural constructs in a variety of settings, attending to the ways in which both inner and outer constraints come to the fore and are variously acknowledged and transcended. Thus, they address cases in which illness or moral engagements and commitments point up the possibly paradoxical character of individuated agency and hence the importance of irony as a neglected element in anthropological theories of the person. Some of the essays also suggest that the attribution of agency is relative and that it may be understood relationally rather than as the product or expression of an autonomous (possessive) individual.

However, we do not emphasize here the role of irony as justification for either a detached, apolitical stance or an interested, political one. From the perspective of sufferers, the point of irony is less to conceal suffering or to displace it than simply to recognize things as they are. We think there is often a fine line between tragic and comic interpretations of the recognition of the limits of moral agency. Irony can serve as a transfer point between tragedy and comedy. One question that we suggested contributors might consider—a challenge taken up by Anne Meneley—is what turns irony in one direction or the other? When does the despair of Job give way to what Laura Bohannan (Bowen 1964) memorably called a "return to laughter"? With respect to illness, one can abhor or appreciate the Rabelaisian effects of bodily or mental breakdown and the collapse of personal agency. Why not celebrate the carnivalesque or grasp the comic dimension of suffering? When is the situation seen as one of tragic linear inevitability and when of comic indeterminacy? What possibilities do forms of therapy provide for recognizing or moving between these alternatives? What contexts enable the presence of multiple and incomplete interpretations?

Both illness and the cultivation of moral discipline provide sites at which agency and its limits are addressed by human subjects and hence become explicit for anthropologists. Indeed, often it is their intersection that is critical. This is evident in our first contribution, Meneley's ethnographically rich interpretation of fright illness among Muslim women of Zabid, Yemen. Here, the ability to laugh at one's distraught behavior—to turn trauma into comedy—indicates a return to the sense of shame that is such a positively valued and necessary attribute of selfhood. Meneley shows clearly how virtuous behavior entails being neither too removed and stoic nor too passionate in one's responses to illness, death, and other forms of suffering. To take fright at the afflictions of others is a sign of love but possibly also of dependence or weakness. Drawing on the work of psychoanalyst Roy Schafer, Meneley shows how exemplary Zabidi women move beyond tragedy and comedy and achieve an 'ironic' acceptance of fate.

Michael Lambek follows a similar trajectory to Meneley insofar as he examines the creative and ethical potential of cultural idioms. Thinking back on years of work on spirit possession among Malagasy speakers of Mayotte, an island in the western Indian Ocean, and reflecting in particular on the case of a young man from Mayotte who was struck with rheumatism by a spirit while serving as a recruit in the French army, Lambek argues that spirit possession is "intrinsically ironic." The scenario is one in which the irony is deeply embodied, symptomatically more than discursively expressed, and neither deliberate nor explicitly self-conscious. Lambek relates the case to theories of self-deception and agency and suggests that other forms of illness, such as hysteria—as expressed by the patients of Freud and Breuer—might be redescribed as ironic, as being sick in an ironic mode.

Janice Boddy turns her eye to colonial practices, specifically the attempt of the British to eradicate extreme forms of female circumcision in the Sudan during the 1920s and 1930s. Boddy illustrates the ironies that inevitably arise in the encounter of cultural difference inflected by strongly unequal power relations, as well as the historical ironies of the consequences of intervention and 're-description'. She charts the story of Mabel Wolff, first matron at the Midwives Training School in Omdurman, whose attempts (along with those of her sister) to reduce the harm of circumcision had the effect of partially medicalizing it. As Boddy notes: "Expressing scientific ideas in vernacular terms is no transparent business." Moreover, colonial motives were themselves complex and contradictory; not only was the Wolffs' pragmatism heavily inflected by cultural biases, but they had to struggle for professional legitimation with both their Sudanese clientele and the British government itself.

Andrew Lakoff takes us to the heart of the paradoxes of psychiatric attributions of selfhood as psychoanalysis is confronted by recent advances in psychopharmacology. Drawing on his ethnographic research in a pair of psychiatric wards in a hospital in Buenos Aires, Lakoff demonstrates how the debate within psychiatry—recently captured for the United States in Tanya Luhrmann's aptly titled *Of 2 Minds* (2000)—plays out in Argentina. There are multiple ironies here. Lakoff describes the extraordinary situation in which the men's ward of the hospital is run by biomedically oriented psychiatrists while the women's ward is staffed by Lacanian psychoanalysts. He explores the ensuing debates and contradictions, seeing their roots in the sociopolitical context no less than in the distinctive epistemologies and in the nature of mind itself. Whereas the Lacanians are able to come to an accommodation in practice, for many doctors the two approaches are incommensurable in theory. For the Lacanians, pharmacology simply cannot address questions of subjectivity. And in certain instances, resolutions that work for the Lacanian practitioners not only deny the insights of their patients but appear to have iatrogenic consequences.

In his chapter, Paul Antze takes up several issues raised provisionally in this introduction, providing a deep appreciation of the depth of irony in psychoanalysis as Freud developed it over the length of his career. In particular, Antze is able to clarify distinct but complementary models or interpretive strategies within Freud, according to the form of irony on which they draw. Antze traces a conceptual distinction between rhetorical (or strategic) and dramatic irony from the Greeks and then shows the shift in the weight they provide to Freud's interpretations as he moves from the cases reported in *Studies on Hysteria*

(Freud and Breuer 1895) through *Dora* (Freud 1905) to the mature case histories (Freud 1909, 1918).[16] Among other things, then, Antze takes up the question raised in Lambek's chapter concerning the sense in which hysteria might be redescribed as irony and illuminates both the manner in which Freud saw it at the time of his original studies and how it could be viewed by means of his later work.

Finally, in a rich and wide-ranging series of reflections, Lawrence Cohen asks how irony, especially in its Socratic form, might enable us to move beyond simplistic answers to the troubling questions that senility poses for culture. Here he draws on Nehamas's understanding of Socratic irony as a signifying practice in which overt meanings point not to their opposites but rather to an unknown "something else," which nonetheless engenders an ethical life. Cohen considers the possibility that such an attitude might offer a way beyond the exclusionary logic that characterizes most responses, both lay and expert, to senile dementia. He argues that a Socratic refusal of certainty might support more open-ended ways of listening to dementia while still taking its biology seriously. He concludes with a highly suggestive discussion of Socrates as a figure whose old age raises doubts about the meaning of old age itself.

In the chapters that follow we will see several senses in which the 'I' of irony and the 'I' of illness may be compared.

Conclusion

"Most people either value irony too much or fear it too much," observes Lionel Trilling. "Both the excessive valuation and the excessive fear of irony lead us to misconceive the part it can play in the intellectual and moral life" (2000: 292). This collection does not simply either value or fear irony but asks what the recognition of irony suggests for a deeper theoretical (and not *simply* ironic) understanding of the human social condition and being in the world. We ask: How does irony coalesce into illness? How does illness expose the ironies of human agency and self-realization?

Insofar as our own stance is one of irony, we would like to think that it shares an affinity with the irony of Jane Austen, which Trilling describes as

> a method of comprehension. It perceives the world through an awareness of its contradictions, paradoxes, and anomalies. It is by no means detached. It is partisan with generosity of spirit—it is on the side of 'life', of 'affirmation'. But it is preoccupied not only with the charm of the expansive virtues but also with the cost at which they are to be gained and exercised. This cost is regarded as being at once ridiculously high and perfectly fair. (Trilling 2000 [1954]: 293)

Having explored in *Tense Past* some of the consequences of taking memory literally, we now consider whether a distinction between the literal and the ironic offers a purchase for distinguishing certain non-Western discursive forms from biomedicine as well as for distinguishing positions and movements within the latter. Conversely, we turn to irony less to celebrate its 'edginess' than to explore the ways in which illness and treatment open up or foreclose spaces for the recognition of irony or the irony of recognition. Of course, we cannot take the distinction between literalism and irony itself fully literally. We understand irony in both its Socratic form as the recognition of the inability to reach full knowledge and its Sophoclean form of not knowing where we are heading. Irony is thus both an element of self-knowledge and a perspective on it. Illness and treatment sometimes either ignore or objectify and exaggerate the will and agency of sufferers. But in other contexts they 'ironize' agency, offering up recognition of the extent to which we both are and are not the authors of our own dilemmas, and can and cannot reach understanding or do something about our condition. We ask additionally how such different positions are reached and evaluated.

We do not wish simply to celebrate irony but advocate maintaining a balance between perspectivism and a working stability of language and meaning. Philosophers of irony interpret it with respect to their own domains and hence, while they see it challenging grandiose abstractions such as Truth, risk giving it a certain grandiosity and abstraction of its own. But irony need not be all or nothing; it need not challenge every truth or reject every resting place. It, too, may be perspectival.

In sum, we are reaching toward an ethics of irony.

NOTES

1. Although Lambek is listed as the author of this introduction, the ideas were developed in close conversation with co-editor, Paul Antze, to whom Lambek is much indebted for intellectual and psychological support. Hence, the pronoun "we" is used throughout, though at times the reference expands to include the other contributors and at times the implied readers. Unlike the case in Malagasy, English does not distinguish between the inclusive and exclusive first person plural—thereby perhaps gaining a vehicle for irony.
2. We venture that not all irony is playful. However, it may well be, depending on definitions, that all play is, in part or at some level, ironic.
3. Of course the difficulty in recognizing irony is only enhanced for the anthropologist working in a foreign culture. Just as many early anthropologists often interpreted the representations of non-Western religions too literally, so the reverse is also possible.
4. Think of the use by Geertz (after Ryle) of the wink to illustrate signification.
5. We refer to the famous Japanese film *Rashomon* (directed by Akira Kurosawa) in which the same 'event' is played from the view of several protagonists. Another famous literary example of perspectivism is Lawrence Durrell's *The Alexandria Quartet* (1977), in which each of the first three volumes offers a picture of events as seen by three distinct narrators. Bakhtin (1981) argues that all novels, however many the narrators, are polyphonic insofar as one can distinguish author, narrator, and the distinctive voices of each character. Each of these functions can, in turn be further broken down.

6. Lambek (2002) has applied this Burkean perspective to the polyphonic construction of history by means of the spirits and spirit mediums of a set of distinct ancestors among Sakalava of Madagascar.
7. Rowe refers to the 1949 essay "Irony as a Principle of Structure" in which Cleanth Brooks argued that irony was a principle of literary structure insofar as a text had "to distinguish its own special language from that of ordinary experience" (Rowe 1995: 32).
8. Comparison might be made to the irony invoked in narratives of pregnancy loss in North America (Layne 1996).
9. See, among many other instances, Losche (2001).
10. For Rorty, "The opposite of irony is common sense" (1989: 74).
11. See Das et al. (2000, 2001); Kleinman et al. (1997).
12. But it does not necessarily decide between such projects and either of the two alternative forms of moral inquiry (genealogy and tradition) identified by MacIntyre (1990).
13. This may be interpreted as an ironic appreciation of the Harvard project by its chief architect, although it is unclear from the typesetting whether it is to be attributed to one voice or two, namely, Arthur and Joan Kleinman. I believe that Kleinman's view of irony approximates the one advocated here insofar as he cites Max Scheler to the effect that irony stands with endurance, aspiration, and humor as one of the "transcendent responses" to the resistances humans face in the course of their lives (Kleinman 1995: 119).
14. We note that illness recurs as a kind of leitmotif through Burke's primarily literary examples.
15. A striking example is the current epidemic of witchcraft accusations against children in Kinshasa, as reported and analyzed by De Boeck (2000, 2003).
16. For the full references to these works, see the list following Antze's chapter.

REFERENCES

Achebe, C. 1959. *Things Fall Apart*. New York: Ballantine.

Antze, P., and M. Lambek. 1996. *Tense Past: Cultural Essays in Trauma and Memory*. New York: Routledge.

Bakhtin, M. M. 1981. *The Dialogic Imagination: Four Essays by M. M. Bakhtin*. Edited by M. Holquist. Translated by C. Emerson and M. Holquist. Austin: University of Texas Press.

Bateson, G. 1972. *Steps to an Ecology of Mind*. New York: Ballantine.

Becker, A. 1979. "Text-Building, Epistemology, and Aesthetics in Javanese Shadow Theater." Pp. 211–243 in *The Imagination of Reality*, edited by A. L. Becker and A. A. Yengoyan. Norwood, N.J.: Ablex.

Bowen, E. S. [L. Bohannan]. 1964. *Return to Laughter*. Garden City, N.Y.: Doubleday.

Burke, K. 1945. "Four Master Tropes." Pp. 503–517 in K. Burke, *A Grammar of Motives*. New York: Prentice-Hall.

Crapanzano, V. 2000. *Serving the Word: Literalism in America from the Pulpit to the Bench*. New York: New Press.

Das, V., et al., eds. 2000. *Violence and Subjectivity*. Berkeley: University of California Press.

———. 2001. *Remaking a World: Violence, Social Suffering and Recovery*. Berkeley: University of California Press.

De Boeck, F. 2000. "Le 'deuxième monde' et les 'enfants-sorciers' en République Démocratique du Congo." *Politique Africaine* 80:32–57.

———. 2003. "Kinshasa: Tales of the 'Invisible City' and the Second World." In *Under Siege: Four African Cities—Freetown, Johannesburg, Kinshasa, Lagos*, edited by Okwui Enwezor et al. Documenta11, Platform 4. Kassel: Hatje Cantz Verlag.

Durrell, L. 1977. *The Alexandria Quartet*. London: Faber and Faber.

Evans-Pritchard, E. E. 1937. *Witchcraft, Oracles and Magic among the Azande*. Oxford: Clarendon Press.

Fernandez, J. 1982. *Bwiti: An Ethnography of the Religious Imagination in Africa*. Princeton: Princeton University Press.

Fernandez, J., and M. T. Huber, eds. 2001. *Irony in Action: Anthropology, Practice, and the Moral Imagination*. Chicago: University of Chicago Press.

Fortes, M. 1983 [1959]. *Oedipus and Job in West African Religion*. Cambridge: Cambridge University Press.

———. 1987. *Religion, Morality and the Person: Essays on Tallensi Religion*. Cambridge: Cambridge University Press.

Geertz, C. 1966. "Religion as a Cultural System." Pp. 1–46 in *Anthropological Approaches to the Study of Religion*, edited by M. Banton. London: Tavistock Publications. [Reprinted in Geertz 1973a]

———. 1973a. *The Interpretation of Cultures*. New York: Basic Books.

———. 1973b. "Deep Play: Notes on the Balinese Cockfight." In C. Geertz, *The Interpretation of Cultures*. New York: Basic Books.

Hahn, R. 1995. *Sickness and Healing: An Anthropological Perspective*. New Haven: Yale University Press.

Herzfeld, M. 1997. *Cultural Intimacy: Social Poetics in the Nation-State*. New York: Routledge.

Hutcheon, L. 1994. *Irony's Edge: The Theory and Politics of Irony*. London: Routledge.

Kleinman, A. 1980. *Patients and Healers in the Context of Culture*. Berkeley: University of California Press.

———. 1995. "Suffering and Its Professional Transformation: Toward an Ethnography of Interpersonal Experience." Pp. 95–119 in A. Kleinman, *Writing at the Margin: Discourse between Anthropology and Medicine*. Berkeley: University of California Press.

Kleinman, A., L. Eisenberg, and B. J. Good. 1978. "Culture, Illness, and Care: Clinical Lessons from Anthropologic and Cross-cultural Research." *Annals of Internal Medicine* 88:251–258.

Kleinman, A., et al., eds. 1997. *Social Suffering*. Berkeley: University of California Press.

Lambek, M. 2002. *The Weight of the Past: Living with History in Mahajanga, Madagascar*. New York: Palgrave-Macmillan.

Layne, L. 1996. "'Never Such Innocence Again': Irony, Nature, and Technoscience in Narratives of Pregnancy Loss." Pp. 131–152 in *Comparative Studies in Pregnancy Loss*, edited by R. Cecil. Oxford: Berg.

Lear, J. 2000. *Happiness, Death, and the Remainder of Life*. Cambridge: Harvard University Press.

Lévi-Strauss, C. 1963 [1949]. "The Effectiveness of Symbols." Pp. 181–201 in C. Lévi-Strauss, *Structural Anthropology I*, translated by Claire Jacobson and Brooke Grundfest Schoepf. Garden City, N.Y.: Doubleday.

Losche, D. 2001. "What Makes the Anthropologist Laugh? The Abelam, Irony, and Me." Pp. 103–117 in *Irony in Action*, edited by J. Fernandez and M. T. Huber. Chicago: University of Chicago Press.

Luhrmann, T. M. 2000. *Of 2 Minds: The Growing Disorder in American Psychiatry*. New York: Knopf.

MacIntyre, A. 1990. *Three Rival Versions of Moral Enquiry: Encyclopedia, Genealogy, Tradition*. London: Duckworth.

Mann, T. 1995 [1924]. *The Magic Mountain*. Translated by J. E. Woods. New York: Knopf.

Nehamas, A. 1998. *The Art of Living: Socratic Reflections from Plato to Foucault*. Berkeley: University of California Press.

Ricoeur, P. 1971. "The Model of the Text: Meaningful Action Considered as a Text." *Social Research* 38:529–562.

Rorty, R. 1989. *Contingency, Irony, and Solidarity*. Cambridge: Cambridge University Press.

Rowe, J. C. 1995. "Structure." In *Critical Terms for Literary Study*, edited by F. Lentricchia and T. McLaughlin. 2nd ed. Chicago: Chicago University Press.

Scoggin, M. 2001. "Wine in the Writing, Truth in the Rhetoric: Three Levels of Irony in a Chinese Essay Genre." Pp. 145–171 in *Irony in Action*, edited by J. Fernandez and M. T. Huber. Chicago: University of Chicago Press.

Sontag, S. 1977. *Illness as Metaphor*. New York: Farrar, Straus, Giroux.

Trilling, L. 2000 [1954]. "Mansfield Park." Pp. 292–310 in L. Trilling, *The Obligation to Be Intelligent: Selected Essays*, edited by L. Wieseltier. New York: Farrar, Straus, Giroux.

Turner, V. 1967. *The Forest of Symbols: Aspects of Ndembu Ritual*. Ithaca: Cornell University Press.

Tyler, S. 1978. *The Said and the Unsaid*. New York: Academic Press.

Woolf, V. 2002 [1930, 1926]. *On Being Ill*. Introduction by Hermione Lee. Ashfield, Mass.: Paris Press.

Chapter 1

SCARED SICK OR SILLY?

Anne Meneley

Irony is not the property of a particular age, as many have argued. Rather, as Michael Lambek claims, "Irony speaks to, of, or from the human condition." He further suggests that the realm of illness and therapy may be a space where the ironies of the human condition can be explored, particularly in non-Western discursive forms that do not depend on the literalism of biomedicine. This chapter explores a malady called 'fright' (*faja`a*), which is central to the contemplation of life's existential dilemmas as they are envisioned by the pious community of Shafi`i Muslims in the town of Zabid in Yemen. Fright is caused by a severe emotional shock (*sadma*), usually as a result of sudden, unexpected harm coming to oneself or a loved one. Fright is thought to cause the recipient's soul (*ruh*) to shake, leaving the sufferer vulnerable to a variety of other illnesses. It is an affliction through which individuals—sufferers, diagnosticians, supporters, onlookers—implicitly explore the limits of agency and confirm or question dominant frames of causality. The practices surrounding fright illness are evaluative, involving reflection and judgment of the stimulus and symptoms. Although biomedicine is enormously popular and highly valued in

Notes for this chapter begin on page 38.

Yemen, fright is not an affliction that is understood causally in biomedical terms, nor is it amenable to treatment by biomedical means. Fright illness sits uncomfortably within a monotheistic Muslim framework, which posits that 'everything is from God' (*kullu min Allah*), questioning as it does the will of God when misfortune visits people. Fright is also the subject for rich narratives in which averted tragedy is told in a comic mode, as Zabidis contemplate the power of fate, the limits of human agency, and the often embarrassing comportment of the badly frightened.

Psychoanalysis, cultural anthropology, and Yemeni discourses about fright share a certain methodological space in the sense that the raw data for all three are meanings and subjective experiences. Like psychoanalysis, fright illness is used to understand self and relationships to others, and structures narratives of personal histories by which one presents oneself to others. Lambek highlights the fact that psychoanalytic thought and non-Western therapeutic discourses may share the characteristics of irony. In fright illness, as in the psychoanalytic vision described by Roy Schafer (1976), comic, tragic, and ironic visions are apparent. By visions, Schafer means "judgments partly rooted in subjectivity, that is, in acts of imagination and articles of faith, which, however illuminating and complex they may be, necessarily involve looking at reality from certain angles and not others" (1976: 23). I explore here the different modes of reacting to or coping with fright.

The narratives on which this essay is based were gathered during my participant observation research in Zabid, during 1989–1990, and a short visit in 1999. Zabid is an ancient town on Yemen's coastal plain bordering the Red Sea on the Arabian Peninsula. It is a town long famous for religious scholarship, and while it is no longer the center for Islamic learning that it once was, Zabidis remain proud of their town's history and place a high value on religious learning. My key informants were mainly women, many of them from elite families. They reside in Zabid but own estates in the surrounding river valley, where sharecroppers work their land while handing over half the produce to the landowners. Elite Zabidis uphold strict gender segregation. Women veil before they go out on the street, and any kind of exposure, immodest behavior, or unregulated contact between nonrelated men and women threatens a woman's honorable reputation and that of her family. These elite women's lives in Zabid are characterized by a hectic whirl of visiting, a means by which people acknowledge the moral worth, social respectability, and ranking of each other's families.[1] It was often during these daily visits that narratives about fright were told. Talking in Zabid always seems a bit of a competitive sport; speech is layered, and dull conversations are quickly cut off by an often abrupt change of topic. To hold one's audience, one must be a skilled raconteur. Zabidi women are quick witted, engaging, and often scathingly funny, and it is in this register that fright stories were frequently told.

I begin with an anecdote about my own unusual fright experience in Zabid. One evening, around 8:30, I was walking home from a visit. Women do not usually walk alone in Zabid after dark, but I had been accompanied by a friend to the corner of my street. My house was in sight, so I told my friend I would be fine walking the rest of the short distance alone. I noticed a young teenager who appeared to be around fourteen years of age walking ahead of me; he stopped as I was about to pass him. I moved around him, and he lunged over and pinched me. I responded as I had seen Zabidi women do with cheeky children. I cried "Shame on you!" (*'ayb `alayk*), chastising him for the impropriety of his action and asked him where his father lived. He did not respond, and I whirled around to proceed on my way. In a move I was not at all expecting, he grabbed me and bit me on the shoulder! I screamed and started to run. A neighbor ran out and told me to go into his house to be with his mother and sisters. He chased the boy and then tracked down my husband. I did not feel pain at this point, but had been rendered virtually speechless with shock. When my husband rushed in, I quickly told him in English what had happened, and he exclaimed to our neighbor in Arabic, "He BIT her!"

The news of this incident seemed to go around Zabid at lightning speed. Everyone asked me, "Were you scared [*tafaja`ati*]?" I replied that I had indeed been scared, for reasons quite palpable to them: being touched by a strange man on the street (never mind being bitten by one!) is a serious transgression in Zabid as elsewhere. It is the kind of offense that would usually be punished in Zabid with violence, the woman's male relatives retaliating against the offender for transgressing against her honor and, by extension, theirs. It is also the kind of incident that would be expected to produce a fright in Zabid—not only hurting and shocking one physically, but threatening one's reputation for modesty. My neighbors explained to me that the young man was a crazy man (*majnun*), and that he was always causing his family trouble with his erratic actions. They immediately asked if they should have him beaten for the offense. But then they described his mother as '*miskina*' which means 'poor thing' but also 'sweet and nice'; she was a woman who had already suffered mightily for the actions of her son. Perhaps they told me this to elicit my sympathy, but in any event, it was unnecessary, as my own sense of anthropological self would have suffered, indeed, were one of the Zabidi residents beaten on my behalf. I said that of course I would not want the boy beaten if he was a *majnun* and not fully responsible for his actions. My husband and our neighbors merely accompanied him to his family's house, where his father did not show similar mercy and administered a beating.[2] The neighbors in whose house I had taken refuge were warmly solicitous, bringing me cool water and urging me to sit down and relax. Yet as the other neighbors popped by to see what the fuss was about, my hosts could hardly stop laughing. The Zabidis sympathized with me over my fright, but they also found this incident as funny as I found it cringingly embarrassing. I was not keen to draw yet more attention to this incident, because in every house I was greeted with the same reception that I had received from my neighbors that night. The Zabidis were mostly unaware, I suspect, of the way in which this incident caused a fright to my conceptions of professional narratives of establishing rapport. No anthropological account I had ever come across had regaled the reader with a report of the anthropologist being BITTEN by a native, even a crazy one. To make matters worse, the story was readily transformed as it whipped around Zabid. To my horror, I heard a version that featured the anthropologist biting the *majnun*!

The day after this event, I suffered from terrible cramps, which I attributed to being an unwilling host to a myriad of intestinal parasites, although I also had some dark fears about the gruesome infections that are said to result from human bites. My Zabidi friends, however, inferred a different meaning from my symptoms. They assured me that I was in fact suffering from fright. I was offered the local treatment, which is for someone to catch the afflicted unawares and burn them on the back of the neck with a cigarette or a hot iron branding rod (*misam*). It was explained to me that a bad shock (*sadma*) is thought to cause the soul (*ruh*) to shake. A countershock needed to be applied to balance out the original shock and restore the person to equilibrium. If this is not done, the shocked person leaves herself vulnerable to illness. I declined, not seeing how this treatment, which sounded rather harsh to me, could possibly help my health, and at this point, I was in no mood to be ritually burned for the sake of anthropological knowledge.[3]

The Comic in the Near Tragic

My own fright incident was so distressing to me that I could not see the humor in it for many years. Despite my fears that the incident was evidence of a serious rapport disaster, it actually had a positive effect on my research, opening a watershed of anecdotes about fright illnesses. Everyone started telling me their own fright stories, after roaring with laughter at mine. I was struck by how often Zabidi women told stories of trauma as hilarious anecdotes. Although I could not manage it in this instance, this style appealed to me personally, as I have always thought that the upside of suffering is that it has better anecdote potential than calm contentment. The well-mannered, enjoyable dinner parties or family vacations fade almost immediately, while the harrowing ones live on in retellings.

Yet the stories of trauma told to me in Zabid were often a good deal less amusing than their lighthearted recounting might suggest. For instance, one woman, Fatima, told the story of how her daughter, a toddler not yet two years old, had fallen into a large plastic tub of water prepared for laundry. By the time she got back to the laundry tub, the little girl was lying limp in the water. Fatima screamed but no one came, so she ran to her nearest neighbors and somehow they managed to get the water out of the child's lungs. After the child recovered, Fatima herself started to feel ill. Her aunt burned her several times on the back of her neck with an iron cauterizing rod, and the scars were still livid. Her account of this incident had the group of neighbors who were her audience that evening all in stitches as she described how she beat herself in anguish and even beat the child until the little girl finally cried out, indicating that she was in fact alive. Fatima described herself wandering around like a crazy person (*majnuna*). She told us how fitfully she had slept the night of the incident, jumping up at every little sound that the child made, until her husband teased her that she was like the new mother of a first-born baby. We roared with laughter at her imitation of herself howling for the neighbors, who were themselves present at this retelling and added their own comic snippets about how crazy, indeed, she had been acting. Only later did it strike me how deeply our laughter was at odds with what had, in fact, almost transpired—the death of a child.

One tale of fright inspired another, as I had just discovered. Another woman present at this gathering, Layla, offered the following fright story. A plastic bag had fallen over the face of her sleeping infant, and the baby was discolored and bleeding from the nose by the time she found her. She and a relative massaged the baby for hours until it finally cried. Layla said she could hardly walk for four days, indicating by shaking her hand how badly her legs had been trembling. She, too, had been therapeutically burned.

Shortly afterwards, while visiting the same neighbors who had given me refuge on the evening of the *majnun* bite, I heard the following tale from Halima, the new wife of the eldest son. Like many young brides, she continued to attend high school after her marriage. The high school is located on the outskirts of town, an area in which mangy wild dogs, considered unclean by Muslims, tend to congregate. She told us of her escalating nervousness, describing how she had become convinced that the dogs were following her, until she panicked and started to run. The dogs followed her and began nipping at her *shaydar*, the black enveloping garment that is worn by women when they leave their houses. Halima choked with laughter, tears rolling down her face, and she could hardly sputter out a description of how the skirt of her *shaydar* had started to come off, revealing her dress. She was rescued, in this exposed state, by a male teacher who was a close friend of her husband. We were all laughing at this point, although Halima covered her face in remembered embarrassment as she mentioned her husband's friend. She had suffered from fright, too. although it was not clear what had frightened her more—the dogs or being exposed in front of an associate of her husband, as losing one's *shaydar* in public is considered akin to being naked. I would expect that the latter was in some ways more terrifying in Zabid, given the damage that exposure of one's body does to one's reputation and the particular avoidance of contact between wives and husband's friends.

The fact that these traumatic incidents are often recounted as hilarious anecdotes suggests that Zabidis are employing what Freud calls 'humorous displacement'. The potential tragedy eventually becomes a moment of ironic reflection on the thin line between the comic and the tragic. The behavior of the afflicted at the time of the incident was often transgressive; people appeared crazy, as they beat themselves, an afflicted child, or even a husband. This kind of behavior was held to be a sign of the severity of the shock, which was bad enough to cause one to temporarily lose one's 'reason' (*'aql*), a quality that implies the control of mind and behavior that responsible, sane adults display in the course of everyday life. In the ironic retelling of these stories, it is the embarrassing breaking of the frames, in Goffman's sense, of normal comportment that people find so funny. One can be frightened by a *majnun*, but fright can also make one act like a *majnun*. A diagnosis of fright is necessary to reframe the transgressive comportment so that it is perceived as understandable, given the circumstances, rather than stigma-producing. As Freud notes (1991 [1905]), comic modes can be aggressive, and what is prominent in the comic tellings of fright incidents in Zabid is a scathing self-satirizing, as individuals caricature themselves and their post-shock actions. Being able to produce this kind of comic account is a sign of recovery from shock and any illness that ensued. As one distances oneself from one's own aberrant comportment, an ironic distance from the near tragedy is achieved. The near tragic is displaced by the comic. This process implicitly expresses a giddy relief that individuals, despite their fear, had not had to bravely accept a grave loss as the will of God. The embarrassment individuals display over their silly or transgressive behavior shows a return to shame, which in its positive sense is highly valued in Zabid. Shame or modesty (*istahya'*) refers not only to sexual modesty in terms of dress and gender segregation, but also in a wider sense to the capacity to act with appropriate deference and restraint, a capacity of which Zabidi women are proud.

Diagnosis and Treatment

The kind of crazy behavior exhibited by a shocked person was usually read as a clear sign that a fright illness was inevitably in the offing. Whether the loss of or harm to a loved one turns out to be actual or permanent, the fear generated by the potential loss is dangerous in and of itself. Those badly shocked are often burned immediately as a preventative measure. But sometimes the diagnosis of fright is made retrospectively, as symptoms of illness, vague feelings of nervousness, weakness, and bowel and stomach irritation reported by a sufferer will be traced back to an earlier shock.[4] In the hot climate of Zabid, where intestinal parasites and tropical maladies abound, these symptoms were hardly unusual or specific to fright illnesses. It is the interpretive frame of fright that individuals employ when making particular connections between symptoms and stimuli.

These fright diagnoses are usually made with kin, friends, and neighbors. My landlady, a woman who often appeared to be afraid of nothing or no one, and who was for the most part highly unsympathetic to nervousness or fright illnesses in others, started feeling chronically unwell with several vague symptoms. After lengthy discussions with her daughter and myself, she began to trace the origin of her ill health back to a shock that had occurred a few months earlier. My landlady's great-grandson, a beautiful, buoyant child with an engaging smile, had burned himself quite badly by falling into a bowl of steaming lamb broth as we were all having lunch at her house in honor of the religious festival (*'id*) at the end of Ramadan. She and her daughter decided that she should be burned to counteract the effects of the at this point rather distant shock. The cauterization took place at the home of a part-time specialist. When we arrived, a small iron rod with an oval-shaped head was heating up in hot coals.[5] The specialist quickly touched the rod to the back of my landlady's neck, raising a blister. The specialist continued down the spine, producing seven or eight small cauterizations. It was an informal and brief encounter; we departed after giving her a small fee and exchanging a bit of neighborhood news.

Another fright incident had a different outcome. I was told a story about a woman married to a successful man in the neighboring city of al-Hudayda; I had met the woman two or three times when she visited her friends in Zabid. Her husband's driver routinely drove her to her visiting engagements in the large city. One day, a man jumped into the car, claimed to be a member of the secret police (*mukhabarat*), and held a gun to her driver's head. The woman was convinced he was a robber or a rapist and threw herself out of the car, which had already begun to move. She feared more what the man had in store for her than death itself. She was badly bruised and mentally quite shaken, according to her friend who told me the story. I asked if the woman had been burned, and the friend sniffed, saying that they were too 'advanced' (*mutaqqaddam*) for the burning treatment, which smacks of backwardness to those who consider themselves modern. Rather than being burned, the young woman was sent to India for a month to rest and recuperate. The etiology and diagnosis—that the woman was suffering from fright resulting from severe shock—remained the same, but the treatment was altered.

Fright, Anger, Love

Fright illnesses are deeply expressive of the relationship between persons and God, but also of the ironies of human engagements with others in the social world. There may be a universal dimension to emotional structures that have to do with the existential dilemmas of human biology, particularly the extended helplessness of human infants and the need to nurture them (Myers 1988). Yet there are also cultural distinctions in the way this universal dilemma is talked about, understood, and resolved. In Zabid, fright illnesses very often cause ironic reflections on the ambiguities, complexities, and suffering that result from love and close connections with others. Fright as an emotion is, like anger, related to love in Zabidi 'structures of feeling' (Williams 1977). Most of the instances of fright described thus far have involved injury not to oneself, but to a close family member. To take fright at the danger or tragedy of relatives is to demonstrate love for them. To be untouched by their misfortune would be an indication of callous disinterest in them. In Zabidi understandings of personhood, individual identities are closely bound up with those of kin, and relationships between kin are ideally characterized by 'love' (*hubb*) and demonstrated through exchanges of both material and moral support. A refusal of either kind of support among kin is a serious transgression that is said to produce 'anger' (*za'al*), and can result in damage to or severance of the relationship. Deliberate actions, such as refusals to help, result in anger on the part of those ignored or spurned. In contrast, situations that produce fright are usually involuntary or accidental. Yet fright is a reaction to a threat to a relationship, a threat to one's own well-being, which is dependent, to a large extent, on the well-being of one's kin.

As noted above, when my landlady's great-grandson had been injured, she had been burned for fright. One evening, my landlady herself became violently ill, losing control of her bladder and throwing up at a party given by neighbors. Her daughter was immediately sent for, and we both sat up with her, afraid that she would not live through the night. In the morning, we all made a fearful trip to the local clinic, where she was given medicine. She began to mend almost immediately, but her daughter, who had been stoic and determined throughout the crisis, had to be immediately burned on our return. An unintended consequence of fright illnesses is an implicit enactment and inculcation of familial solidarity. In Zabid, one's attachment to others, particularly kin, is both a source of strength and an often unnerving vulnerability. Fright illnesses, diagnoses, and treatments are all about this central irony of engagements with others in the social world: those whom one loves the most make one the weakest.

All of the anecdotes told so far have involved women, but that is not only because most of my fieldwork was done with women and I was primarily listening to their stories. I heard much about men in the same way as Zabidi women do: through their husbands. I also heard women talking about their sons and brothers. I do not recall any stories about men or boys being burned for fright, except for one story about an old and frail man who was too ill and nervous about his health to leave the house. Men as well as women are, of course, deeply bound up in familial relationships. Yet I suspect that the vulnerability and dependence expressed in fright illnesses is considered unmanly. As I have argued elsewhere (Meneley 1996), it is primarily women who express and constitute relations of dependence and interdependence, while men, especially heads of households, represent the family as an autonomous unit.

Causality and Complicity

Fright may occur whether or not a tragedy actually occurs. Not all tragedies are averted, and these actualized tragedies are not relayed in a comic mode. Yet all fright illnesses, averted or occurring, are moments of ironic reflection on the way in which destiny slips beyond human control. *Faja`a* is a framework for understanding the misfortunes, tragedies, close calls, or feared disasters that impinge on people's realities or imbed themselves too vividly in their imaginations. Implicit in fright discourses are theories of causality and agency. Talk about fright not only touches upon the miseries and losses that are part of everyday life, but also concerns the individual's subjective awareness and emotional proclivities. The impetus for the shock or fright—a threatened or actual harm done to oneself or a loved one—was held to be external to the sufferers, unexpected and beyond human control. Fright illness is more likely to occur when the shock is sudden and unexpected. The death of a chronically ill older person, for instance, is less likely to produce fright than the death of a young and healthy person. The transgressive behavior brought on by fright illness was in some sense also perceived as beyond the control of the afflicted individual; one temporarily lost one's *'aql* and acted like a *majnun*. Many people experience the occasional fright and most recover from it, after treatment, and the incident becomes a funny anecdote.

Chronically Fright-Prone: Being Weak-Hearted

Zabidis did convey a sense of personal agency in talking about fright; fright as an illness condition was not viewed as inevitable. Freud's famous insight that sufferers are complicit in their conditions was both present and absent in Zabidi talk about fright. This commentary implied some form of responsibility and self-awareness on the part of the individual for being prone to fright. A similar incident might cause one person to experience fright yet not another. For instance, one woman reported getting fright from the aftershocks of the earthquake centered in the highland town of Dhamar in 1982. Yet no one else in Zabid described herself as having been so permanently affected by this natural disaster, which did not result in palpable damage in Zabid. The propensity for fright, or resistance to it, is discussed in terms of a heart metaphor. Those inclined to fright are said to have a 'weak heart' (*qalb da'if*). It was said to be bad or dangerous to be so sensitive as to put oneself at risk. If one had a 'strong heart' (*qalb qawi*) one was able to withstand the unexpected misfortunes in life without giving in to fright. It was not entirely clear to me how one got a strong heart if one had a weak one, although a few times I was urged by strong-hearted women to 'become like me' (*takuni zayyi*). (Here the Zabidis sounded less like Freud and more like my father, with his Alberta 'get a grip' psychology: either you have a grip or you don't, and if you don't have one, get one!)

Those who were particularly prone to fright were often viewed with a whiff of wry contempt by the strong-hearted. While being insensitive to the misfortunes of one's kin was reprehensible, taking fright at large-scale natural disasters or the suffering of strangers was thought to be silly. There was a certain degree of impatient eye-rolling and imitation of the nervously fright-prone behind their backs or sometimes even to their faces. I myself was often criticized for having a 'weak heart' for my propensity to cry when others were crying, which was interpreted by the Zabidis as a dangerous and foolish oversensitivity to the concerns of those distant from me. Yet ironically, my capacity for compassion (*rahma*), evidenced, according to the Zabidis, by the fright I took over my land-lady's illness, was seen as a sign of my humanity, in the sense of decency—something that was always somewhat in doubt. Being a Muslim is so central to local conceptions of moral personhood that my status as a non-Muslim always seemed problematic for the Zabidis.[6] Yet while a good Muslim ought to be sympathetic and acknowledge the loss of others through proper visiting rituals as a condition of moral being in the world, feeling the pain of others' tragedies too strongly or deeply endangers oneself.

Inculcating Fright

The ambivalences inherent in fright discourses are evident in socialization practices. Yemeni children and adults are remarkably fearless in general; cowards are despised, while the weak-hearted are teased. Children are inculcated into fright discourses in various ways. They are socialized through threats designed to induce fright, being routinely threatened with shame (*'ayb*) of the neighbors or some more extreme admonishment. Badly behaved children were, in my presence, routinely chastised with the idea that they better behave, or they would be 'sent to Canada with Anne'. The screams engendered by this threat were not entirely flattering for the anthropologist or for Canada, but caused much hilarity amongst the Yemeni adults. The children's expression of fear was then mocked.

On my second visit to Zabid in 1999, I was staying with a family who had three unmarried, vivacious daughters. Their home, as I recalled from my first visit, was a gathering point for the neighbors, and all day long the house was full of visitors popping by for a glass of tea or a bit of a gossip. One morning when the visiting was in full swing, I received a phone call from a colleague in the capital city; we spoke in English. A neighbor's daughter, aged two, started screaming when she heard me speak. As her mother later explained, the little girl had never heard anything but Arabic, and she had taken a fright at the strange words. In the next few weeks, this story was told over and over again, with the mother bringing the girl to me in front of groups of neighbors and friends who were assembled. When the little girl saw me, she would cover her face with her arms and tremble. Everyone seemed to find this hilarious except for the terrified child and me. Not wanting to upset her further, I refused to speak English in front of her, and kept chastising the women, saying it was 'forbidden' (*haram*) to frighten the child like that. Showing their usual disdain for my opinions on proper child-rearing practices, they persisted despite my urging them to take the poor thing away from me. I was reminded of Zabidi training games in generosity, where the adults would demand that a child share a treat with them, returning it with praise if the child gave it willingly. The 'fright game'[7] is a practice related to instilling the proper affect in the child: she was exposed to something she feared, then her fear was delegitimized by being the source of public hilarity. Shame is much used as a means of conformity, and by the time children are a few years older, they are very sensitive to the pressures of public opinion.

The positive side of fright, which exhibits one's capacity for compassion, especially toward one's kin, is also inculcated through practices. Visiting my landlady on my second trip to Zabid, I was told of a recent tragic car accident involving several families from Zabid. When news of the accident circulated, rumors flew quickly regarding who had been in the cars. My landlady had been told that her grandson—a charming and respected man, beloved by grand-mother, mother, and sister, and the father of fourteen children—had been killed in the accident. Every female member of the family, including the girls under ten years of age, was burned because of the shocking news, even though it turned out not to be true. Implicitly, this prophylactic burning instilled in them the capacity to produce proper affect—to be frightened at harm to their father, and to dread and expect illness as a result.

Fright and Narrating the Self

I have mentioned the propensity for Zabidis to turn their fright experiences into entertaining comic stories, featuring self-satirization. Yet for other individuals, fright becomes a kind of central metaphor through which they understand themselves and their history. Like psychoanalytic talk, talking about fright con-stitutes and communicates a particular view of events, modes of reacting, and a reframing of self and psychic realities. These were women for whom fright ill-nesses spurred by tragedy were key to self-understandings, presentations of self and history to others, and everyday practices. Their affliction—being fright-prone—was a central theme in what Linde (1993) calls 'telling a life'. My friend Magda, among others, was one who had interpreted her reactions to several deaths in her family as preconditions for her own chronic illness.[8]

For these women, the avoidance of situations in which they would be likely to take fright became a central part of their subjective awareness of themselves. Taboo practices that regulate fright become an intimate mode of self-making, as Lambek (1992) argues for taboos in Madagascar. The fright-prone managed their inclination to fright through avoidance. The presence of the strong emo-tion of grief was thought to be dangerous for those vulnerable to fright, unset-tling their already fragile equilibrium. One fright-prone woman told me that she cannot enter the house of a friend who died several years ago. Mourning gath-erings often feature deeply moving keening[9] in the first few days. It is for this reason that those who are prone to fright are not supposed to attend mourning gatherings on the first three days after a death. It is usually mandatory that deaths be acknowledged immediately, so this excusal of the fright-prone from such an important obligation was a notable recognition of fright as a serious affliction. At a mourning gathering for the father of a neighbor, I had noticed one woman gasping and sobbing. I could not figure out why she was crying so hard, since I knew she was not a close relative or even a neighbor. I was told she cried like that at every mourning gathering, still reliving her husband's death of ten years ago; he had had a heart attack while having sex with her, and she had been badly frightened. The woman was not from Zabid, and her propensity to keep on attending funeral gatherings made her seem to the Zabidis to be somehow lacking in sense (*'aql*). The proper way of managing one's tendency to fright, according to the Zabidis, was avoidance. It was the

Zabidi woman who had accompanied this woman, not the woman herself, who was scolded for bringing her.

While keening is not unknown in other parts of Yemen (Makhlouf 1979) or elsewhere in the Middle East (Abu-Lughod 1986) or even in Zabid in the past, wailing at deaths is no longer an acceptable practice in terms of the hegemonic framework of Islam as it is understood in contemporary Zabid. At any mourning gathering where there was keening, there was also a chorus of women urging the mourners to stop their crying and accept the will of God, and hissing 'God forgive this blasphemy' (*istaqfar Allah*). Such behavior was described as 'forbidden' (*haram*), as denying the will of God in deciding who lives and who dies and when and how people die.

Fright Discourses and the Moral Imagination

As noted above, ultimately deaths and misfortunes associated with fright were uneasily situated in religious discourses about causality, whose message is that 'all is from God' (*kullu min allah*). Irony is central to fright illness because it is an unspoken, implicit questioning or even an expression of horror at the will of God. The threat of loss or the loss itself, which results in fright illness, shows how much people want to keep what they have and love. As Hutcheon notes, the defining semantic condition of irony is the power of the unsaid to challenge the said (1994: 59). This conflict was particularly evident in the tragedies that caused a fright from which an individual never recovers.

Stuck in Tragic Mode

In the worst case of fright, one really loses one's grip and becomes a *majnun*. At a party one evening, I noticed a woman in unusually slovenly dress behaving oddly, coming in from the streets with her hair uncovered, an unthinkably immodest act for respectable women. My friends behaved oddly toward her, treating her as they would a child whom they wanted to go away, rather than with the respect that an adult woman deserves. When I asked why she was behaving so strangely, I was told her story: she had taken fright when she lost her children and her gold, two of women's most valued possessions, through divorce, and she had never recovered from a crazy state as others had managed to do. The woman's behavior was explained in this way, but her fate appeared to generate unease rather than compassion. Certain stories such as this one are not presented in a comic mode; the often absurd and embarrassing comportment sparked by shock are not described with humorous ironic distance because the individual does not recover.

On my trip to Zabid in 1999, I was told of central events that had occurred in my absence. Two of these stories involved fright caused by tragic occurrences from which certain individuals had not managed to recover. The first story involves an old woman, Aysha, who was the paternal aunt of a friend of mine. Aysha's brother had died in a freak accident several years before I met them. On my first trip to Zabid, Aysha told me the tale of her brother's death: he had been burned very badly by an exploding propane tank and had died suddenly, horribly, and in much pain. Aysha, two other old aunts, and her brother's widow, Aliya, had been left with one son and three small daughters to raise. When I met them, the children were all teenagers, but Aysha was still prone to fright after this tragic incident and was particularly sensitive to any harm coming to her nephew and nieces, whom she loved intensely and fiercely. Aysha was one of the fright-prone women who was a bit of a figure of talk in our neighborhood. If any of the children were late coming home, she would frantically run to all the neighbors' houses, looking for them. When she found them unharmed, she would give them slaps more theatrical than hurtful, chastising them for frightening her. I got the sense that the neighbors quite enjoyed the drama, given the glee with which they imitated Aysha's frantic states. She was one of the women whose tendency to fright was both tolerated and laughed at.

When I returned to Zabid nine years later, I learned that the family had been struck by another tragedy, again from a freakish accident. Aysha's nephew, the one male left in a family of women, had been in the car accident that had involved several Zabidi families. He had been decapitated while attempting to escape from the wreckage. He left a young widow and a two-year-old boy. I went to offer my respects and found the family still in full mourning over a year after the accident. Aysha was unable to get over the shock of this tragic repetition of her brother's early death. She said to me that she kept asking God why he had not taken her instead of her nephew. She repeated this over and over again; it was one of the few times I ever heard a public and overt questioning of the will of God. The young man's mother, Aliya, looked as if she had aged forty years instead of the nine that had lapsed since I last saw her. Her daughters were in full white mourning dress, as were she and Aysha, yet while they retained some interest in the world, their work as schoolteachers, and the news of the neighborhood, Aysha seemed to have no other topic of conversation than the tragedy. All of the light had gone out of Aliya's eyes, leaving no trace of the quiet determination I remembered in her. Even her small grandson, the only remaining male in a house full of women, seemed to cause her anxiety rather than pleasure, as she shrilly cautioned him not to hurt himself.

Another story also involves a death from which certain individuals seem unable to recover. My first day in Zabid on my return visit, I went immediately to pay a mourning visit to the family of a dear friend, Magda, who had died shortly after I left the field in 1990. It had been nine years since her death, yet her mother, Layla, was still wearing full white mourning clothes. We hugged; I had tears running down my cheeks, but Layla was sobbing. The death was still fresh for me since I felt as if I had not mourned my friend properly, not having returned to Zabid since her death. When I looked up from our tearful embrace, I saw the rest of the family looking on in disapproval or averting their eyes. They were quiet and appeared embarrassed as Layla cried with heavy rasping sobs, saying that she would never forget her daughter. She showed me two small pictures of Magda, one with her brother when she had been a young girl, and another, looking thin and pinched in a passport photo. I could scarcely look at them because I would have cried harder, and I could sense the disapproval of the rest of the women. Layla sadly begged me for pictures of Magda, of which I had none. She seemed to have forgotten that all of the adult women in their family had refused to let their photographs circulate outside of the family. Now the concerns for modesty and familial honor did not seem to resonate with her, so anxious was she for a fragment of her daughter's lost life.

It seemed that we were the only two for whom Magda's death retained some kind of immediacy; everyone else had consigned it to the past and moved on. While I was welcomed with great grace and warmth, the family even remembering and making my favorite Zabidi dish for me, even though it was a dish usually made only during Ramadan, I got the impression that they were not keen to have my presence encourage Layla's demonstrations of grief. Magda's sister, Fawzia, startled me when I saw her, because in profile she looked so much like her sister that for a second I could believe Magda was not dead. Tears filled my eyes as I hugged Fawzia, but she gently told me, "Say thanks be to God [*al hamdulillah*], and he will build us a castle in heaven." It had been Fawzia who had written me the letter telling me of Magda's illness and death; I told her how sad I had been to get her letter. Fawzia did not answer me, or say anything further about Magda, and I could not ask anything without crying. Fawzia chattered on about her job as a schoolteacher; she pointed out her brother's five children who had been born in my absence and generally kept well away from any discussion of Magda, although I knew how close the two sisters had been.

Layla took no part or interest in the conversation about schooling or her grandchildren, but as I was leaving she grabbed my hand and took me to the room where I had spent so much time with Magda. This was the room where I had learned the most about Zabid, and it was the room where Magda had died, in the company of only Layla, her final caregiver in the last days when her body was so covered in sores she could not bear to wear clothes. The room was barely recognizable to me, nor was the house; substantial renovations and additions had been made since my last visit to house Magda's newly married nephews. On my first visit, the others would sit and chat with me if Magda was not home, but everyone acknowledged that I was there primarily to see her, that the two of us were special friends. I felt great affection for her sister and nieces, but without Magda, I no longer felt so much at home in their house as I had before. But it was Layla who was most sadly out of place in her own home. Disinterested in the new renovations and the burgeoning numbers of grandchildren, she, too, no longer seemed to fit in the house.

Layla's continuing grief at the death of her daughter was seen as a questioning of the will of God that was in many ways blasphemous. Ironically, this was the same woman who, in a religious lecture to me ten years earlier, had firmly told me that when one's child dies, one must immediately say '*al hamdulillah*' (thanks be to God). But it was her daughter, Magda's sister, who had managed this difficult task, not her. Layla showed no ironic self-recognition of the distance between her earlier judgmental position and her reaction to her own loss. The reputation of her family was threatened by her inability to recover from the fright that had struck her; it appeared that she was unable to submit to the will of God as a pious Muslim should have done. The other members of the family seemed embarrassed by her excesses, and she seemed to be ostracized in her own home. In a typical Zabidi way, they simply refused to acknowledge what they did not want to hear, so her grief seldom found an audience or recognition. This practice of silencing through lack of recognition was a very effective way of policing the boundaries of hegemonic ideas of appropriate comportment without direct confrontation.

I never heard anyone in Zabid recount the death of a child as an amusing anecdote. This was one loss that was never told in a comedic mode—a loss too enormous and too sad ever to be funny. But children's deaths were all too common in Zabid, and many women bore their losses stoically and recovered enough to take a continuing interest in life and in the remaining members of their families. They seemed to portray what Schafer (1976: 50–55) would call an ironic vision, by means of which individuals are able to actively resign themselves to their fate. Zabidis do this within a religious framework, and there is no space for the kind of questioning of the existence of God that is so common in some societies at times of tragedy. Zabidis do not deny their grief, nor do they forget it. When asked how many children they have, women always include the dead as well as the living, and many of the older women had the experience of having more children die than survive. These women contemplate the ironies of fate, eventually, if not easily, submitting to the will of God in a manner spoken about in terms of 'patience' (*sabr*), encompassing both forbearance and endurance. *Sabr* is, among other things, the capacity to accept the will of God.

The exhortation to say '*al hamdulillah*' at the time of the death of a child is reflective of a position with respect to language that implicitly suggests a connection between words and emotion. This is close to Reddy's (2001) concept of 'navigation of feeling', in which emotions are created in part by the naming of them. This kind of submission to the will of God is a very active one, and is considered in Zabid to be an achievement worthy of social respect in this world and of reward in the afterlife. I stress this aspect of achievement—in the sense of a state of emotion that is actively achieved—to counteract the stereotypes of passive Muslims mindlessly submitting to the will of God. This common misreading of the meaning of submission is deftly critiqued by Asad (1993: 219–220). Passivity is not part of the way submission is perceived in Zabid; submission is an active and often difficult achievement.

The two women described in the above anecdotes had become almost liminal creatures, wearing nothing but white mourning garb and rarely leaving their houses. Their inability to leave off replaying the tragedy made them almost dangerous to the moral reputations of their families and to their own spiritual futures. They were unable to accept the existential dilemmas, the limits of human powers to cure, the unpredictability of freak accidents, and the tragic reversal of the ordinary life course when parents die before children. In Zabid, where children are so valued and important, everyone sympathized with the hardship of a loss of a child, but the longevity and public display of the women's continuing grief made people uneasy because it was such a flagrant transgression of Muslim practices as they are now lived in Zabid.

There is a sense in which individual conformity to religious requirements is necessary for the collective good. For instance, when commenting on a drought that had stricken their region for years, Zabidis said it was the result of people neglecting their prayers. The transgressions of those who refused or were unable to stop grieving seemed antisocial and irresponsible to many. Their lack of ability to recover from their fright meant that they were almost ostracized, the legitimacy of their excessive grief unacknowledged in their social worlds. I found this treatment harsh, especially sympathizing as I did with Magda's mother, and I was uneasy with the community's refusal to acknowledge the depth of her grief. I suspect that aside from the religious transgressions implied by her grief, it also must have been hard for them to witness her pain and tolerate her inability to concern herself with everyday life. She had not, after all, lost everything, but lived with her surviving daughter and son and grandchildren, but she was still so overwhelmed with grief for her dead daughter that she could not seem to come back to the living. Her moral world had failed her in not finding a place for her pain, and she had failed her moral world by not conforming to its often difficult standards.

Conclusion

In some cases, fright is relatively straightforward: the shock is treated with a countershock, the patient recovers, and a funny anecdote is born. The humor inherent in fright narratives is functional in that it helps one 'get a grip' after provoking reflection on the vulnerabilities of loving others and the inevitable suffering in life, thus helping sufferers return to a meaningful engagement in the world. In other cases, a diagnosis will be made retrospectively, and a set of symptoms will be traced back to a particular shock. A burning will be administered in hopes that the afflicted will return to health and hopefully 'return to laughter', to use Bowen's memorable phrase. In some cases, fright becomes part of an interpretive framework for constructing a narrative of personal history, becoming a way of endowing meaning to one's life, requiring certain practices, and a means of extracting socially acknowledged exceptions to appropriate comportment. Finally, there are those who, when facing loss, can never seem to switch from a tragic mode to an ironic mode—not a comic mode, but an accepting ironic mode in Schafer's sense of being self-reflective and resigned in a positive way. This kind of acceptance, required and achieved by many Zabidi women, does not diminish the pain at loss but achieves a prestigious submission to God and a particularly active shaping of emotion into culturally valued forms. Those who cannot come to terms with losses that overwhelm them are, in many ways, set adrift as liminal creatures who in some ways endanger their families and the Zabidi community, as well as their own future in the afterlife. Fright illness expresses what always has to be displaced and not articulated. It questions and frequently expresses horror or terror at the will of God, which often threatens or deals out losses, small or large, that individuals can either bear or become overwhelmed by, depending on their personal capacities to live up to the culturally informed dispositions which allow them to make sense of a world that is, indeed, hard.

Ironies of Anthropological Remembering

I was struck when I began to write this essay about the ironies of anthropological remembering and positioning. Lambek, in his introduction to this volume, uses the example of Burke's notion of irony as "the outcome of a dramatic, multi-voiced situation where each character offers a perspective and comments on the others." In a sense, I as an anthropologist am the one observing and identifying the ironies of Zabidi fright discourses as they comment on, resist, or conform to hegemonic religious interpretations. We find irony in situations we experience in the field by reflecting on the various perspectives voiced and then read against each other, discerning their ambiguities and stating these contradictions in ways that would seem at odds with those of our interlocuters in the field. I suspect that some of my interpretations would even seem blasphemous to the Zabidis, uncomfortable as they were with a notion of religion as an object of study rather than a deeply held belief. But unlike the detached observer in the audience, I was, as critiques of anthropological objectivity have suggested, enmeshed in the dialogues, performances, and events surrounding fright illnesses.

I became very sick midway through my fieldwork and was diagnosed by an American doctor as certainly having malaria, possibly typhoid, and as definitely very run down. He suggested I go back to Canada for treatment, which I did. When I returned to Zabid a month later, I was told by my friends that they had been right: I had been suffering from fright brought on by the *majnun* bite. Being bitten by the *majnun* was one of those field events that I have always considered indelibly etched on my memory, despite having been hitherto repressed in print. But I remembered less well the fright anecdotes of others, so when writing this chapter, I turned to my fieldnotes. I came across my own fright incident by accident and, to my surprise, discovered that I had misremembered the timing. In my memory, the *majnun* bite was almost immediately followed by my return to Canada, quite frighteningly ill. My fieldnotes revealed that, in fact, more than two months—and a great deal of work, recorded in hundreds of pages of fieldnotes—had passed between the two events. Ironically, somewhere between the incident and the time of writing this essay, I had been converted to the Zabidi worldview whereby fright could make one vulnerable to disease. Although I never managed to achieve the ironic distance in the field to allow me to laugh at my predicament and reflect on its meaning, I found I had eventually come to accept the Zabidi diagnosis of my encounter with the *majnun*. Fright discourse had, when I was not paying attention, become part of my own subjective awareness.

ACKNOWLEDGMENTS

This essay is based on a shorter version presented in a session entitled 'Irony and Illness' at the CASCA meetings in Montreal, 4 May 2001. Thanks to Paul Antze and Michael Lambek for organizing an unusually thought-provoking series of papers. Donna Young provided generative and most welcome comments at a crucial moment. Stephen Bocking, an outsider to anthropological discourse, gently forced me to defend my field in ways that were more productive and amusing than one might imagine. Julia Harrison once again proved herself to be a dream colleague by making time when she had none to read this essay with her careful eye. Vaidila Banelis lived with me in Zabid in 1989–1990 and always acts a sounding board for me as I try to remain faithful to our experiences in Zabid. Lindsay DuBois once again managed to squeeze me into her busy schedule. Bruce Grant produced his as always astute comments, this time on the fly between Azerbaijan and Moscow. Thanks are also due to the participants in the Symposium on Contemporary Perspectives in Anthropology in Lafitte, 2002, especially Peter Pels, Brad Weiss, Misty Bastian, Adeline Masquelier, and Todd Sanders. As ever, I appreciate the thoughtful comments and encouragement of Michael Lambek and Paul Antze.

NOTES

1. More details of this elaborate practice are available in Meneley (1996).
2. Months later, I heard that he had pinched another woman and had been severely beaten by her kin.
3. Toward the end of my fieldwork, I was burned on the soles of my feet for a different affliction, *barud*, which literally means 'cold' but refers also to an affliction that involves vague symptoms of stomach upset, tiredness, and nervousness. My case, according to a neighbor, had been brought on by drinking too many sweet and cold drinks. I agreed to the treatment at this point because it no longer seemed that strange to me, and I was too tired to argue, in any event, with the aggressive nurturance of my Zabidi friends.
4. Young suggests that this is also the case in contemporary North American post-traumatic stress diagnoses (1996: 97–98).
5. This iron does not leave very large scars. Occasionally, the burn (*wasim*) is done on the inner forearm. However, I have seen scars the size of a quarter on the chests of women from the surrounding river valley.

6. When I visited the sick or cried when parting from neighbors and friends, women would often murmur 'Islam is in her' (*Islam fi hah*). This seemed to resolve the dilemma of how non-Muslim Westerners, who are assumed to be quite depraved, could possibly behave in a way they considered proper. Especially early in my stay in Zabid, my good behavior—or conformity to their norms of interaction—seemed to strike them as entirely unexpected, although welcomed and much praised.
7. I use the word 'game' for a practice that inculcates certain values in children. The 'play frame' (Bateson 1988) is signaled by a high-pitched tone of voice.
8. Magda was my 'key informant' and best friend in Zabid. Her life story is recounted more fully in Meneley (1998).
9. A form of ritualized crying at death.

REFERENCES

Abu-Lughod, Lila. 1986. *Veiled Sentiments*. Berkeley: University of California Press.
Asad, Talal. 1993. *Genealogies of Religion*. Baltimore: Johns Hopkins University Press.
Bateson, Gregory. 1988. "Play and Paradigm." *Play and Culture* 1:20–27.
Freud, Sigmund. 1991 [1905]. *Jokes and Their Relation to the Unconscious*. New York: Penguin.
Hutcheon, Linda. 1994. *Irony's Edge: The Theory and Politics of Irony*. London: Routledge.
Lambek, Michael. 1992. "Taboo as Cultural Practice among Malagasy Speakers." *Man* 27: 245–266.
Linde, Charlotte. 1993. *Life Stories: The Creation of Coherence*. Oxford: Oxford University Press.
Makhlouf, Carla. 1979. *Changing Veils: Women and Modernization in North Yemen*. Austin: University of Texas Press.
Meneley, Anne. 1996. *Tournaments of Value: Hierarchy and Sociability in a Yemeni Town*. Toronto: University of Toronto Press.
———. 1998. "Analogies and Resonances in the Process of Ethnographic Understanding." *Ethnos* 63, no. 2:202–226.
Myers, Fred. 1988. "The Logic and Meaning of Anger Among Pintupi Aborigines." *Man* 23:589–610.
Reddy, William. 2001. *The Navigation of Feeling: A Framework for the History of the Emotions*. Cambridge: Cambridge University Press.
Schafer, Roy. 1976. *A New Language for Psychoanalysis*. New Haven: Yale University Press.
Williams, Raymond. 1977. *Marxism and Literature*. Oxford: Oxford University Press.
Young, Alan. 1996. "Bodily Memory and Traumatic Memory." Pp. 89–102 in *Tense Past: Cultural Essays in Trauma and Memory*, ed. P. Antze and M. Lambek. London: Routledge.

Chapter 2

RHEUMATIC IRONY
Questions of Agency and Self-deception as Refracted through the Art of Living with Spirits

Michael Lambek

Something that anthropology can be and is about, though it is almost never phrased as such, is the art of living. I borrow this phrase (along with much else) from a recent book of that title by Alexander Nehamas (1998). Nehamas's subject is philosophy and in particular certain heroic philosophers who have seen the artful, and at times agonizing, creation of their own lives as exemplary (his subtitle is *Socratic Reflections from Plato to Foucault*). Anthropologists sometimes discover characters among their subjects who stand out for their genius or the style or emphasis with which they lead their lives, cutting a swathe through convention. But perhaps we learn most by exploring how ordinary people draw on local conventions and idioms in the living of their individual and interrelated lives. Their actions can prove exemplary or edifying when they illustrate the potential of local idioms for generating or articulating insight and movement of general relevance.

I have gradually come to see that one of the things that I have been exploring over the years is the art of living as practiced and demonstrated by spirit mediums in the Malagasy-speaking world of northwestern Madagascar, Mayotte, and, increasingly, France. What has intrigued me is less the ritual of spirit possession or the temporary state of trance than the integration of other voices, other persons, with the self in the construction of a life for oneself and with others—a life (as we say) for better and for worse, in sickness and in health, in good times and bad. That is to say, I have been intrigued with tracing the place of spirits in the lives of mediums over time; with the ways in which spirits are entwined with the biographies of people and families (and sometimes whole communities); with the ways they figure in informal autobiography and memory as people construct and reflect on their lives in narrative and practice, in retrospection and in prospect; and thus with the art of living with spirits, or rather, with spirit possession *as* an art of living.[1]

Here I do not wish to individualize my subjects too strongly both because spirits can be shared among people and form a vehicle of connection between them and because possession cannot help but draw attention to itself, becoming a display that draws, engages, and provokes an audience, much as Socrates did (Nehamas 1998), much as a written text does. Insofar as the events of lives lived with possession become public, so they become objects of contemplation, interrogation, identification, and edification for those around them. Possession thus becomes a vehicle with respect to which the non-possessed or soon-to-be-possessed also reflect on and live their lives, if only by resisting its form, messages, or imprecations.[2] The salience of other lives is heightened through spirit possession, not only because possession is simply noisy and disruptive but because virtually everything about possession calls attention to itself as an artifact.

I see the accomplished spirit medium somewhat like a Western artist or craftsman. An acclaimed violinist needs her instrument in order to create beautiful music; a great philosopher needs the texts of his predecessors. The analogy is rough, but in the Malagasy world the spirits are likewise vehicles, instruments in a technology for creative expression and building, for that dimension of human activity Aristotle referred to as poiesis. But much more clearly than the violin, spirit possession is also a vehicle or instrument for a second dimension of human activity, what Aristotle called phronesis, practical wisdom, that is, the exercise of situated moral judgment, being a decent, dignified, virtuous person, acting on behalf of what is considered right and good. Here there appears a stubborn paradox, or at least a place of resistance, with respect to dominant contemporary Western notions of personhood and of direct, unmediated consciousness in moral judgment. How can the evidently impassioned spirit medium be simultaneously a moral agent? How can she be acting virtuously when she is evidently temporarily displaced by another voice, another person? And in speaking about her agency, do I thereby risk importing an ethnocentric Western concept into a situation of non-Western personhood? Or conversely, by declining to speak of agency in this context, would I collude in a picture of disempowered, less than fully realized moral selves?

I would rather turn the question around and ask what an account of spirit possession can contribute to revising dominant Western views of autonomous selfhood and agency. To speak convincingly, such an account must engage with Western theory, especially by drawing upon those streams of thought that have challenged extreme individualism. I begin with brief reference to one of the strongest of these, the object-relational—or now simply relational—school of psychoanalysis, which recognizes, as Joan Rivière put it, that "Each personality is … a company of many … We are members of one another" (as cited by Chodorow 1989: 158). Such mutual membership is the product of a dialectic of introjection and projection that begins in infancy. Our psychic reality is thus relational as well as individuated. An excessive weighting or overreliance on either pole creates a problematic personality, and each pole may be seen as a kind of defense against the other.[3]

For Stephen Mitchell, who was a major spokesman for relational psychoanalysis, "Being a self with others entails a constant dialectic between attachment and self-definition, between connection and differentiation, a continual negotiation between one's wishes and will and the wishes and will of others, between one's own subjective reality and a consensual reality of others with whom one lives" (1988: 149). Likewise, Nancy Chodorow states: "If a person is to develop at all, the self must come to include what were originally aspects of the other and the relation to the other … We become a person, then, in internal relation with the social world … People inevitably incorporate one another; our sociality is built into our psychic structure and there is no easy separation of individual and society or possibility of the individual apart from society" (1989: 149). It may be, then, that Marilyn Strathern's Melanesian 'dividual' (1988), or something quite like it, is universal at the level of psychic structure. The question is whether cultural idioms and social practices recognize, articulate, and enable—or disclaim, constrain, and mystify—these processes and where, in a given social world, and with respect to given social statuses, the balance between autonomy and connection lies or is expected to lie. The following discussion of spirit possession will demonstrate the point.

Among Malagasy speakers, to gain (most kinds of) spirits is also to become increasingly connected to others. While relative to their hosts spirits are in one sense originally alien beings, non-selves, they are also social persons, and as such they carry with them the prior histories of their relations with humans. To become impassioned by a spirit is to introject aspects of this history. A woman who becomes possessed by a spirit who previously possessed and spoke through her mother or grandmother is identifying deeply with them, not only acknowledging her prior identification but introjecting another aspect of their persons (Lambek 1993). A break in the unity of the conscious self is thus at the same time a bridge to the identities of others. In this respect, I think, spirit possession is radically different from multiple personality disorder, in which dissociation is generally private, alienating, disruptive, fragmenting, and socially distancing.

Spirit possession is thus not entirely beyond the range of at least one Western conception of selfhood. Concomitantly, possession is markedly resilient in the face of social change, accommodating itself to Western contexts and accommodating those contexts to itself. The story I now tell will exemplify these points while raising the question of how a relational perspective can address agency and accountability. The central figure, both narrator and character, is not a spirit medium. He is, nevertheless, someone in whose life a spirit has intervened, sharply and strikingly, and in a manner relevant to and for others, at least for the kind of moral tale anthropologists like me like to tell.

Ali's Brief Military Career

This is a story about a friend of mine, a young man of the very first cohort in the once remote village in Mayotte, which I have studied since 1975, to receive a full French education and subsequently to become a member of what his cousin referred to as the small set of village intellectuals. "We were the ones," said Ali, "who discovered school."[4]

Ali is a very sweet guy and someone who is attempting to make a difference in his community. In August 2000 he was the director of the new elementary school and was very concerned to keep it running well. He was proud that unlike a cousin who directed the school in a neighboring village, he did not allow his relatives to deplete his supplies. He showed me a cupboard filled with notebooks, pens, and other implements ready for the new school year. He had plans to seek subsidies in order to start a school snack program of bread and cheese that would minimize the hardship of poorer families. Ali was also very involved in music, not only as the conductor of a local young people's choir. As a board member of the island-wide Association des Jeunes, he tried to enable participation for talented youngsters in music competitions in the metropole. However, he said he preferred teaching to administration and was hoping to return to school for a specialist degree in music education.

Ali thus took his civic responsibilities very seriously. We could, if we wanted to use the term, consider Ali one of the most 'modern' people in the village. While his wife is away working on a higher degree in La Réunion, Ali, unlike almost everyone else in his community, eats dinner alone and late. He explains he is usually too busy to eat with his in-laws and children. For similar reasons, he rarely gets to the mosque. Time has become a scarce resource and more precious than informal sociality or religious practice.[5]

In the last decade an ever increasing number of people, most of them youths, have begun to move from Mayotte to La Réunion and metropolitan France. In many instances these moves are temporary, but they can last several years. One of the first people from the village to do so was Ali. After completing his *3ième*,[6] Ali first went to continue his studies in La Réunion. But his older sister, who was married to a navigator in the French navy, asked him to join her in France to keep her company during her husband's long absences. So Ali moved to Nantes in 1987, when he was around twenty years old. He finished *2ième* in France and then began to work as an electrician. From photos I could see that his sister's family lived in a tall apartment building. They were dressed in French clothing, and in one picture there is an elaborate Christmas tree set up for the children.

In retrospect, Ali says he prefers life in Mayotte to that in France, especially now that he has a family. The only way France would be better than Mayotte would be if he had a really good job. In Mayotte, the vast majority of people older than Ali had been subsistence cultivators who supplemented cash-cropping when the market made it worthwhile and who are now largely unemployed. In contrast, Ali earned a salary of over 10,000 FF per month when living in Nantes. As he says, money counts.

In fact, Ali was able to save a good deal of money in France. He returned home in 1992 with a car, a lot of luggage, and the cash for a splashy wedding. The wedding, which cost several thousand francs and which he paid for himself, included what he called a *sirop d'honneur* and a *dîner-dansant*, in conscious and expensive mimesis of French affairs. The bride wore a white dress. Before this, while he was in France, his mother had been busy setting up the engagement. On a visit to France, Ali's mother had found him in a relationship with a Malagasy woman. She wanted him to marry in Mayotte and preferably within the village. She brought videos of eligible girls from which he made a selection agreeable to his mother, began correspondence, received a photo with the reply, and knew it was on. Ali's fiancée was in any case a close cousin (*mushemwananya*) through both her parents, and her father was a good friend, though with nowhere near the education of Ali. She was nine years Ali's junior, and he wanted to wait until she had finished high school and was "up to his intellectual level" before marrying. But the wedding was held in 1995 after his fiancée found him with another woman. She said if he was going to sleep with someone, it should be her. It was still important for a bride to be a virgin at marriage, and Ali and his wife ensured this was the case. During the dance celebrating her virginity, his mother's (male) *trumba* spirit rose briefly to express his joy.[7]

Ali's wife soon surpassed him in education by earning her *bac* and equaled him in modern outlook. In a community where most people have between eight and a dozen children, they planned to have three because, as his wife put it to Ali, "If we have four we won't be able to rent a car on family vacations!" (The French have strongly enforced their driving code, including seat belt regulations.) In sum, then, we can say that Ali appears successfully and self-consciously 'modern' (bourgeois?) in outlook and practice.

Although physically and mentally very active, Ali's life has not been free of illness. He says he was a victim of sorcery from his father's other wife, with whom he was sent to live as a child because at the time his home village was without a school. He had a short acute illness and something remained, bothering his stomach for years so that he became very thin. When his mother visited him in France, her trumba spirit rose and said he would need to have sorcery removed when he returned to Mayotte. This eventually took place, and he has felt better since though he has never regained his weight. In secondary school he suffered from headaches, and he gave this as a reason he withdrew before achieving the *bac*.

Ali's life might have turned out very differently were it not for another experience of ill health. During his stay in France, Ali eagerly embarked on a military career. He enrolled in the army and was happily in training at the base in Nantes when his mother arrived on a visit in order to help his sister, who had just given birth. She was not happy with Ali's new direction, and, more to the point, neither was the trumba spirit that had long inhabited her and recently become quite active. To begin with, the trumba made her stay in the apartment difficult. Being very sensitive to bad smells, it took offense at the indoor toilet, and at first Ali's mother refused to use it. They placed her bed as far from the lavatory as they could, but the trumba would rise crying "*Mantsing! Mantsing!* [Stinky]." In fact, said Ali, it rose much more often in France than since her return home.

But the worst thing was that Ali began to feel sick every time he put on his uniform or set foot on the military base. He suffered terribly. He couldn't bend his legs and could barely walk. "It was rheumatism," said Ali. "It took me five minutes to pull on my socks." And it took him some 30 minutes just to get over to the canteen for meals.

To add insult to injury, he was persecuted by his commanding officer, who accused him of malingering and deception. This was not altogether an unreasonable deduction because on weekend leaves Ali felt fine. The moment he reached the bus stop he was well; he walked normally. As he said, "As soon as I left the base, my symptoms disappeared." But each time he returned to base, he was sick and could barely move.

Ali's condition lasted for some three months. Finally, he requested a medical discharge because he was suffering from both the illness and the anger of his commanding officer. He was placed in the hospital for three days and given x-rays over his whole body, but they showed nothing.

So, much to his disappointment, Ali was forced to quit the army. Ali's mother, who, remember, was visiting at the time, had explained to him that it was the family spirit, the *trumba ny razaña*, who sent the symptoms. It was said (*ary*) that the spirit didn't like him in the army. "Military clothes are dirty; spirits don't like them [*tsy tian' trumba*]." His mother said she too was upset and couldn't accept his career decision; she was afraid for him.

I was not able to put two and two together when Ali spoke to me in 1995, but the second time Ali told me the story (in 2000), he made the point explicit. His mother's visit to France had coincided with the beginning of the Gulf War. She confirmed this. Not only was she frightened he would be sent to the Gulf, she said, but from watching the televised reportage, she realized that he would be placed at high risk: "And I could see they were putting black people [*ulu mainting*] in the front lines."

At the time, Ali got angry with the trumba (not with his mother). He said he was a man and wanted to take risks. He was even hoping to train as a submarine diver. On base it was part of Ali's duties to call the ambulance whenever a recruit was injured during training exercises. The trumba said to him, "So can't you see that people in the military get hurt?"

Ali's Agency

Ali's story provides the gist of the issue that anyone interested in understanding personhood across cultures must face. If our own concepts and idioms of personhood come with moral entailments, as they must, how are we to evaluate the conduct of persons whose identity is construed somewhat differently? How are we to understand agency, avowal, and accountability in a universe in which the relational quality of personhood is granted value alongside individual autonomy?

There is perhaps not much in the actions of Ali's mother or the trumba that needs direct explanation. Their interests and arguments are perfectly rational, their agency and observations only too clear, and their fears realistic. Whereas many of my previous analyses of instances of spirit possession entail interpreting the double and ostensibly conflicting voices (messages and desires) of spirit and host, this is a case in which not only their underlying interests but also their stated motives coincide. But the case is more complex with respect to Ali who, several years later, still felt regret that he was coerced by the spirit into giving up something dear to him.

Although Ali is adamant that he himself has never been possessed by the trumba spirit, and never will be, when Ali was on the base, his actions were formally like those of possession. He acted, or rather his body acted, contrary to his conscious intentions. It was as though his body spoke with one voice and Ali with another. His body, if not his mind, was evidently in the grip of the spirit.

Ali's situation thus nicely illustrates a point I have long made, namely, that in thinking about the incidence of possession (at least, in Mayotte), one cannot take account of only the mediums themselves (Lambek 1981, 1989). While it is true that the majority of mediums in Mayotte are women, the spirits nevertheless interact with men as well. Spirits engage with those around them, and neither their presence nor their significance can be explained reductively in terms of trance or the intentions and personalities of the mediums alone.

Ali's mother is, of course, an interesting and powerful woman in her own right. She had the courage and foresight to send away her children for the sake of their education and later followed them intrepidly to France. I remember her pride and her enthusiasm for what she had seen after one of her returns to Mayotte. She has handled the experience of rapid social change with grace, her first encounter with indoor plumbing notwithstanding, but she also sees herself as representative of an older way of life. She has appointed herself my primary raconteur of folk-tales. She is what I would describe as a classy lady in terms of comportment and self-esteem, but also because of an implicit elitism, the assurance of coming from one of the 'best' local families.

Yet this is not simply a kind of mother-son story either. As a trumba, the spirit has a personal identity as an individual member of the Sakalava royal descent line. Moreover, the spirit is identified not specifically with the mother but as a *trumba ny razaña*, a trumba of Ali's family, ancestry, or descent line. It is a trumba which has long possessed members of this family that has a sense of its own importance. For many years the trumba was particularly associated with Ali's mother's mother's brother (the same man who happens to be the grandfather of Ali's wife), who himself spent part of World War II in the French army, but stationed in Madagascar.[8] Before any important event, such as a circumcision or a journey, the spirit would be informed and its assistance requested. It has since gone on to inhabit several younger members of the family—including not only Ali's mother and his wife's father's older brother, but several of Ali's older sisters—and it thus serves, in part, as a sign of the unity, distinctiveness, and continuity of the family (Lambek 1988a). It speaks with the voice of someone who has an enduring association with the family and has long been concerned with its welfare. What Ali hears, therefore, is not simply a transformation of his mother's voice, but a voice that condenses the weight of several generations of ancestors and collateral kin. The spirit acts with the authority of a Sakalava king, but equally with the force of ancestrality and the established commitment to intergenerational continuity and reproduction.[9]

The distinction, then, between the voice of Ali's mother (the host) and the voice of the spirit here lies less in the content of what each is saying in this instance than in the rhetorical force of their respective presence. As the mother tells the story, she and the spirit were in complete agreement. But where her remonstrances might have been ineffective, the trumba's intentions were realized in their effects. In the face of the urgency of the spirit's concern, Ali could scarcely remain impassive. And he did not. He acquired the symptoms of acute rheumatism.

The next question is whether Ali's mother and the trumba were able to enunciate a wish that Ali is unable to acknowledge is also his own. Did he want, on his own account, to retract his decision to enter the army, and should we therefore see Ali's action (or inaction) as a product of his own fear or instinct for self-preservation? Is it a kind of *pre*-traumatic stress disorder? Or should we take a different approach and see it, in Mitchell's terms, as part of the "constant dialectic between attachment and self-definition" (1988: 149), or as representative of the psychic internalization of sociality described by Chodorow (1989: 149)? Did Ali come, to a degree, to internalize the family's wishes as his own? Did he come to take their part? We could let the psychoanalysts fight this out among themselves,[10] but I think that I have already given enough evidence to make the relational argument highly plausible. At least I have shown how spirit possession as a practical idiom exemplifies, articulates, and enables the processes of which the relational theorists speak. But let us move from the murky realm of the psyche to the more sociological concept of agency. In what sense is Ali responsible for his rheumatism?

Here we have something of a double task: how to understand spirit possession as a form of human agency and how, in turn, to rethink agency so that it can take account of possession. In what follows I omit from discussion Marxist conceptions of agency with their emphasis on grasping hegemonic social relations so as to gain a purchase on radical change. I am concerned with action on a less grand scale, as it functions in the day-to-day tasks of taking control of events concerning work, family, and the living of one's life in some meaningful, dignified, and authentic fashion.

In the general social sciences literature, 'agency' is sometimes applied in a rather idealized fashion, ignoring much of what philosophers, psychoanalysts, and anthropologists have taught us about human intentionality and mind. Agency is a naive or romanticized concept insofar as it implies: (a) that acts are transparent to their agents, that they are always the product of deliberate plans with specific ends in mind or of calculation among means and ends in a rational choice model; (b) that agents fully understand the consequences of their acts or the relationships between acts and consequences; (c) that agents' intentions are not often dense, complex, and possibly even contradictory; that agents do not routinely suffer from ambivalence and possibly from self-deception; (d) that agents—or we as observers—can fully and objectively recognize what constitutes their interests; (e) that agency is a capacity of fully autonomous individuals rather than relationally constituted social persons; and (f) that action occurs without respect to convention and commitment, that is, as if agents were not specifically located social persons operating within moral universes, with respect to prior and binding commitments both to specific liturgical orders (Rappaport 1999) and to specific other persons. For example, a person's sexual agency may be informed by prior commitment both to a certain form of marriage that he or she has undergone and to a specific partner.

While all these points are relevant for interpreting Ali's situation, I will focus in particular on the issue of deception. Is his rheumatism a case of simple, outright, knowing deception? If we disagree with his commanding officer on this question, which I think we must, we are faced with a second question: Is it a case of self-deception? If so, how are we to understand and evaluate such self-deception?

I want to argue that although Ali does not avow his agency in the immediate acts of getting sick or choosing to get discharged, in fact he acts responsibly and in terms of an acceptance of responsibility within a wider frame of reference—as a son, as a member of an ancestry, and as a member of a community. His withdrawal from the military is ultimately not very different from his acquiescence to marrying in the direction and manner that his parents wish. In both cases his agency is evident; in neither case is it autonomous. In getting sick he accedes to the will of the trumba. The difference is that in this case he does so apparently self-deceptively, that is, without acknowledging to himself that this is what he has done.

Self-deception often implies denying what is authentic and thus in some sense harming oneself or living a less than fully realized life. But arguably in this case, the consequences for Ali have been a more fully realized life than he could have held in the military, and probably a longer one. Moreover, at exactly which phase can we assert that Ali was more fully self-deceived? Perhaps the brunt of Ali's self-deception lay in his idealization of a military career with dreams of heroic underwater feats rather than the brute realities of the battle-field. As the trumba spirit said to Ali, "Can't you see that soldiers get hurt?"

In an insightful discussion, Fingarette analyzes self-deception as "the dis-avowal of a continuing engagement" (2000: 137). He distinguishes avowal of personal agency (identity) from acceptance of moral agency (responsibility). A sociopath can acknowledge his act (avowing that it was he who committed it) while refusing to take responsibility for it, that is, without any moral concern about it. The self-deceiver, however, does not avow his act, and this may be precisely because,

> What is threatened is some aspect of integrity rooted in moral concern. The less integrity, the less is there motive to enter into self-deception. The greater the integrity of the person, and the more powerful the contrary individual inclinations, the greater is the temptation to self-deception ... It is because the movement into self-deception is rooted in a concern for integrity of spirit that we temper our con-demnation of the self-deceiver. We feel he is not a mere cheat. We are moved to a certain compassion in which there is awareness of the self-deceiver's authentic inner dignity as the motive of his self-betrayal. (Fingarette 2000: 139)

Ali's case is virtually the complete inverse of the sociopathic personality. He does not avow his agency, but he does accept responsibility insofar as he is the victim. He is very concerned about the illness and its implications, and he real-izes that as a result he must request a discharge. He understands that his responsibility is inevitably bound up in his relationship to his mother and to the family trumba.[11]

Another strand of Fingarette's approach is the argument that self-deception occurs all the time, that it is "as ordinary and familiar a kind of mental activity as one can imagine" (2000: 162), if only because our attention cannot be focused everywhere at once. In this view, self-deception is frequently morally neutral, such as when we walk home without being able to recall the route we took, but even in stronger cases Fingarette's inclination is to follow Freud and be nonjudgmental. This is obviously not the case for Sartre's analysis of the specific form of self-deception he termed 'bad faith'. Can Ali be said to have acted in bad faith?

Bad faith can be described as follows:

> Inauthentic and self-deceptive refusal to admit to ourselves and others our full freedom, thereby avoiding anxiety in making decisions and evading responsibil-ity for actions and attitudes. (Sartre, 1956 [1943]) ... One self-deceiving strategy

identified by Sartre is to embrace other people's views in order to avoid having
to form one's own; another is to disregard options so that one's life appears pre-
determined to move in a fixed direction. (Audi 1999: 70)

In sum, bad faith is the dishonest and cowardly refusal to take responsibility for
one's choices and actions. Is Ali's disavowal a matter of cowardice or dishon-
esty? It may be true that Ali has refused to accept his full freedom. But this is
not necessarily out of a refusal to confront an unpleasant truth that he cannot
admit to himself. What is difficult for him to reconcile is the discrepancy
between his courage, enthusiasm, and skill as a man, an adventurer, and a soldier (as far as he understands what being a soldier entails) and his obligations
to his family and to himself as a family man. Choice in favor of the latter is seen
by the military as cowardice, laziness, or retreat, attributions that are simply
not acceptable to Ali. Indeed, there is no reason to assume that he is either
cowardly or lazy, and much evidence to the contrary. However, Ali is left with
the dilemma of finding a face-saving way of making his choice, of withdrawing
from the military, one in which, for reasons of moral integrity as described by
Fingarette, he will not reveal to himself his abrogation of the commitment he
engaged in by signing up.

It seems apparent that the existential emphasis on the freedom of the individual self is very different from the moral questions facing the relationally
embedded person. There is a difference between exercising one's judgment and
claiming absolute freedom of choice.[12] Moreover, Ali's case differs from most
discussions of self-deception precisely because he is not the sole agent of his
deception, and, in a sense, his way out of the dilemma is imposed upon him.
The suggestion of the trumba plays a large role, and the explanation for the illness is reinforced by the family. The means are there at hand for disavowal, for
letting the rheumatism take over. From the standpoint of the family, as opposed
to that of the military, it is the socially correct thing to do.

We could reconstruct the whole story as one of resistance to French hegemony, or we could say that following his mother's intervention, Ali made the
choice to fall under the spirit's influence. Not to have fallen sick would have
been to reject his mother's and the elders' persuasion as well as the force of culture and tradition and the ends to which he had been raised and had already
committed himself.[13] Ali knows that the spirit is tricking the commanding officer; the latter is right, after all, to be suspicious, though what he can never suspect is precisely whom he is dealing with.

Finally, whether we call this self-deception or bad faith or not depends, of
course, on how we understand spirits and spirit possession, how we understand their social reality for people from Mayotte, and how people themselves
attribute agency to spirits. Ali was subject to the spirit's grip, and he suffered
for it. Suffering may be a sign of truth (Lambek 1998). At least it is self-evident;
you cannot argue with it. Thus, an attribution of Sartrean bad faith has to be
relative to how compelling we take the social reality of spirit possession to be
for people of Mayotte in general and here for Ali in particular.[14]

But the fact that Ali's illness is precipitated by the cultural institution of spirit possession enables us to take the analysis to another level.

Rheumatic Irony

So far I have been pushing the case for Ali's sincerity. But Ali's personal sincerity has to be counterposed to the inherently poietic and ironic qualities of spirit possession. Let me begin with irony. In a well-known statement, Becker (1979) argues that spirit possession transforms the ordinary communicative event so that the presupposition of the identity of the speaker is challenged.

> Trance speaking can be defined as communication in which one of the variables of the speech act (I am speaking to you about x at time y in place z with intent a) is denied, most frequently the variable I is paradoxically both speaking and not speaking, or speaking involuntarily or nonintentionally. Trance is a kind of incongruence between statement and intent (I/not I am speaking to you/not you ...), and covers a wide spectrum of linguistic experiences, from the minor trance of singing the national anthem—or any song you *believe*—to the major trance of hypnosis and schizophrenia. (Becker 1979: 232–233)

Disregarding Becker's provocative examples, his analysis clearly holds for the institution of spirit possession as found in Mayotte and many other parts of Africa. What is striking is how close this picture comes to the analysis by certain literary theorists and philosophers of irony.

In a brilliant discussion of Socratic irony, Nehamas quotes Lionel Trilling to the effect that "irony implies 'a disconnection between a speaker and his interlocutor, or between the speaker and that which is spoken about, or even between the speaker and himself'" (Nehamas 1998: 57, citing Trilling 1971: 120). "Irony," Nehamas writes, "is acknowledged concealment" (1998: 67); "irony allows you simply to refuse to let your audience know what you think and to suggest simply that it is not what you say" (ibid.: 55). And so "[i]rony allows us to pretend we are something other than our words suggest. It enables us to play at being someone, without forcing us to decide what we really are or, indeed, whether we really are anyone ... Irony always and necessarily postulates a double speaker and a double audience" (ibid.: 59–60). Finally, to bring home the connection I am making, Nehamas says that "[t]hrough his irony, Socrates *dissociates* himself from his words" (ibid.: 61, my emphasis).

If Ali has not deceived his commanding officer, he suspects that the spirit has. But where does the agency of Ali leave off and that of the spirit begin? Whose agency is at issue? Who is communicating through the signs and symptoms of Ali's body? Ali is ostensibly speaking sincerely, but he is speaking about, with, and through an idiom that is intrinsically ironic. For Nehamas, irony understood as concealment moves interpretation away from the question of truth versus deceit. "Like truthfulness, concealment does not distort the truth; like lying, it

Michael Lambek

does not reveal it" (Nehamas 1998: 62). But in addition, "[i]rony often insinuates that something is taking place inside you that your audience is not allowed to see, but it does not always entail that you see it yourself. Irony often communicates that only part of a picture is visible to an audience, but it does not always entail that the speaker sees the whole. Sometimes, it does not even imply that a whole picture exists. Uncertainty is intrinsic, of the essence" (ibid.: 67).

Once we accept the irony intrinsic to any invocation of spirit possession, the question of self-deception becomes more complex, murkier. There is always in possession a hint that things are not what they seem. Possession is asserted and established as real, but at the same time there is a knowing glint in the spirit's eye (though not in that of the host or, as in Ali's case, in that of the object of the spirit's attention), as though to say, "After all, *I* am not deceived." At some level, Ali, too, is not deceived. His self-deception lies only with the sincerity with which he protects himself from his knowledge. But not deceived about *what*? It is we who deceive ourselves if we mistake the essential uncertainty of human selfhood, or ambivalence, for some substantial core or definitive choice.

Thus, I have been asked how I can call Ali ironic in the absence of conscious intentionality. My response is twofold. First, the irony lies in the recognition of the very ambiguity of intentionality. Second, how can one help being ironic when one takes up, or is taken up by, a discursive form that is itself intrinsically ironic?

I hope you will now not find me unduly ironic if I refer to Ali's condition as one of an *ironic illness*. I do not mean that it is ironic that Ali fell sick, or ironic that his illness was rheumatism, but rather that the very illness is constituted through irony. Ali was sick in an ironic mode. Much better to speak of rheumatic irony than of rheumatic hysteria.

Indeed, embodied irony might prove a fruitful redescription of the condition suffered by the women recorded by Freud and Breuer (1955 [1893–1895]). The tension between Freud's diagnoses and his consistently positive descriptions of his patients' high moral character and lively intelligence could be reread in this light. This would also fit Susan Bordo's (1989) interpretation and comparison of hysteria with agoraphobia and anorexia as caricatures of dominant modes of femininity. In referring to the illness or mode of illness as irony, I am suggesting that the irony is embodied and intrinsic and precisely *not* that it is conscious or reflective. I am not denying the authenticity of the suffering. Rather, I am suggesting that however real the symptoms, they cannot be reduced to a single, clear-cut cause or that, if there were such a cause, we could never know it with complete certainty. The irony of the illness is precisely an expression of its evasion at being pinned down by sufferer, observer, or therapist.

Self-textualizing Acts

The final part of my argument concerns acknowledging spirit possession not only as something done, but as something made—that is, not only as a practice or as an idiom of practice, but as poiesis, as artful creation, and specifically attending to the way in which such creation draws attention to itself. What I am suggesting is that if Ali's condition is one of self-deception, insofar as it involves a spirit, it is self-deception that subtly but inevitably draws attention to itself as concealing something. And insofar as it does this, can it be self-deception after all?

That spirit possession is an aesthetic artifact to be engaged with should come as no surprise; it is the point at which analysis of possession rituals could start (Boddy 1989; Kapferer 1983; Lambek 1981). Spirit possession is simultaneously a part of life, something that really happens, that hurts, harms, or heals and establishes relationships, and an artistic production and performance, a lens or drama through which life is inspected, highlighted, reshaped, reflected upon, and responded to (often with explicit, theatrical irony or satire, as with the spirit's complaints about the smell of the toilet). It is serious business and aesthetic commentary, simultaneously part of the texture of life, the portrait of that life, and the gazing over the shoulder at the portrait. This kind of space for spectatorship, for theorizing (to draw on the original meaning of the word) is available not only for us or for Ali's friends and family, but for Ali himself (cf. Boddy 1988). This is true not only of full-blown possession ceremonies with their costumes and music, but of every appearance of possession in daily life.

What happened to Ali was not something that simply happened and was over, but action that contained the seeds of its own textualization (cf. Barber 1999; Ricoeur 1971; Silverstein and Urban 1996). Indeed, perhaps possession can be described more broadly as composed of *self-textualizing acts*. I cannot pursue this here except to suggest that through the framing and marking qualities of possession, ordinary people simultaneously become *characters* in dramas that are immediate and social but are also at arm's length from their immediate context, having historical associations or allegorical qualities, and that always contain the leavening of irony.[15]

Although Ali is never directly possessed by a spirit, both what happened to him and his narrative of the events have a heightened, created quality. Ali tells a good story. His symptoms have a kind of extravagance, and he describes his condition with verve. There is a dramatic tension as he doggedly hangs in at the military base, suffering and yet trying to convince his superiors of his will to work and stay on, determined to have his condition medically diagnosed and treated. When the x-rays came back negative, he says he was "disappointed" (*déçu*). He wanted his condition medicalized, even though presumably that would have been harder to cure than the effects of the spirit. And yet there are signs—the way the illness started and stopped each time he entered or left the precinct—that he knew all along this was no ordinary illness.

Ali's self-narrative is itself ironic. At one level the story is about whether Ali suffered from ordinary rheumatism or was in the hands of the spirit. But there are multiple levels of ambiguity. One suggests that Ali was self-deceived to hope he could be free of the spirit. Another asks if he was not after all in some agreement with the spirit. Was not his ostensible resistance the space of his self-deception? Can we not hear Ali saying: "If I had only had sufficient critical distance, I might have recognized my own collusion." Or is he saying: "What difference would it have made? The ending was inevitable from the start."

Ali tells a story in which he appears doubly self-deceived. Relatively explicit is his deception in thinking his condition might be ordinary rheumatism. Relatively implicit is his deception in attempting to resist the spirit and his illness. But in thinking he is self-deceived, he may be deceiving himself, and we, too, may be deceiving ourselves. Would we have remained healthy in Ali's situation? Would we have asked for an immediate discharge? Would we have gone to the front? Could we have exercised some Sartrean existential ideal of freedom? Would to claim that we (or Ali) could have done so not be evidence of our own bad faith?

Whatever we would have done in his place, the point is that Ali's story is there before his eyes, but also before ours—to enable us to be presumptuous about our own ostensibly more sovereign agency, to ask the question of ourselves, and, very possibly, to recognize the limits of autonomy in the face of an exigent mother, a determined spirit, and a relationally constituted self. Those people in or from Mayotte who hear about what happened to Ali must reflect on their own knowledge of the force of other persons in their lives—and of course on the delicious fact that their spirits are able to overcome the lure of French military heroism and even the power of military discipline.

The textualization of acts of possession also enables us to expand our appreciation of irony from the playful, rhetorical, and dialogical Socratic version to the tragic Sophoclean one. Ali and others can observe the effects of human agency against or with the tide that fate (structure, determinism) plays in their lives.[16]

My account owes not a little to Nehamas's reflections on *The Magic Mountain*, in which Thomas Mann "shows that the attribution of self-deception to others is one of the surest paths to the deception of oneself" (Nehamas 1998: 32). In a fashion similar to Mann, possession "relentlessly undermines our ability to make unconditional judgments in the same process that it tempts us to keep doing so" (ibid.: 30).[17]

As they become textualized, the events in which spirits intervene in people's lives become objects of contemplation, much as literature can move in the opposite direction to intervene in people's lives. We can read *The Magic Mountain* and be deceived by Mann, much as the hero of the novel deceives himself; so, too, with possession. I am all too well aware that to posit the intrinsic irony of possession and its textualization makes it an object of interpretation and moral pleasure for *me* (I have made my living from it) and that literary theory offers familiar instruction in the appreciation of texts. I have also begun to wonder whether the relationship of anthropologists to their subjects is not intrinsically ironic in much the same way that I have described spirit possession.[18] In sum, if irony is to be attributed like illness, it may be contagious! But I think that through irony and textualization, spirit possession also becomes an object of edification and pleasure for those who engage with it on a more intimate and regular basis. Ali's encounter with the spirit was immediate, painful, and deeply embodied. But it was also distanced and objectified sufficiently to be available to Ali and others in the form of a narrative. The nature of his illness, as artfully enshrouded in ambiguity as that of the hero of *The Magic Mountain*, invites all who encounter it to contemplate agency and its limits, dignity and its vicissitudes, individuality and its relational entailments, hope and contingency, the essential uncertainty of life.

Earlier in the essay I asked what spirit possession might teach us about agency. The answer I propose is akin to Mann's depiction of the ironic saturation of his characters' situation. Any invocation of 'agency' must itself be tinged with irony. Agency is to be taken seriously, but not always literally.

Looking Forward

Let us remember the relational quality of personhood in Mayotte exemplified by spirit possession. We have seen how Ali's agency is harnessed to realize the intentions of another. That other, as his mother, is also a part of himself. And his mother's own other, her self-object, the spirit, is in part a refraction of her parents in turn, and beyond them, of a deeper ancestry for which she is just a contemporary vehicle or trustee.

Earlier I mentioned Ali's comfortable assertion that he would never become host to the spirit himself. I do not know whether to interpret this as a refusal to extend the relational boundaries of the self, as a limit on his ironic self-recognition, or whether to interpret it as a sign of strength or realism, or as undecidable.

Near the end of my stay in Mayotte in 2000, Ali and I were talking about the return of his wife from her year at university and her choice of a career; she had chosen education over medicine. He mentioned that while they were enjoying a drive in the countryside, his wife became rigid in the seat beside him, her arms and legs outstretched so that he had to lift her out of the car. In some concern, I asked whether she had seen a doctor. I should have known better. "Oh," he laughed, "It's not worth going to a doctor. We know already that it is trumbas." He added, "And that's why she didn't want to study medicine. The trumbas can't stand dirty things like blood."

Of course, one of the trumbas who has entered his wife and wants to establish a permanent relationship with her is the very spirit who is to be found in Ali's mother and who accompanied her on her fateful visit to France. As his cross-cousin, Ali's wife, too, is in line to succeed to the spirit, and in her case the marital and affinal connections are probably equally compelling. As for Ali, he will find that the spirit is never too far away.

ACKNOWLEDGMENTS

This essay was inspired by an invitation to speak at the seminar on "Person-hood and Agency in African Studies," at the African Studies Center, Leiden, and was duly delivered 27 September 2000. I am grateful to Rijk van Dijk, Peter Geschiere, Peter Pels, and Robert Ross for the invitation, to the audience for their responses, and to Paul Antze, Janice Boddy, Peter Geschiere, Carol Green-house, and Andrew Walsh for insightful comments on the written text, not all of which I have followed. A revised version has benefited from the scrutiny of departmental seminars at McGill, University of California San Diego, Yale, Oxford, and Wilfrid Laurier Universities. As usual, I am indebted to the Social Science and Humanities Research Council of Canada for supporting my research and writing, and of course to the people in Mayotte who have shared their lives, especially 'Ali'.

NOTES

1. See Lambek (1988b, 1996, 2000, 2002, and 2003).
2. It is true, in any case, that the lives of our friends and contemporaries, insofar as we know them, become the objects of our contemplation—John falling sick when and as he did, Mary having a child, John and Mary raising their children as they do. The ways in which the lives of our friends, colleagues, and consociates become available to us as objects of moral contemplation, and the questions they raise for us, are intensified in 'life term' communities (Moore 1978).
3. Unlike ego psychology, the focus of object-relations is not primarily on individual auton-omy so much as on growth through relationships and on the necessary permeability of selves. I believe this psychic basis to be universal—and to be universally recognized—insofar as I can easily empathize with Malagasy friends and they with me, and we can agree about our descriptions and our likes and dislikes of other persons or our interpre-tations of motivation (even when we are mistaken). I assume this to be true, with a lit-tle mutual effort and good will, anywhere in the world. With sufficient acquaintance of cultural frames and forms of personal expression, one can discriminate among people who appear overly dependent, assertive, aggressive, and so forth—and people whose quiet autonomy is impressive.
4. His name and some of the incidental details have been changed. Since my original field-work, Mayotte has been increasing integrated into the French state and has become the object of rapid development. In 2000 a referendum was held to change its status from that of *collectivité territoriale* to that of *collectivité départementale*. An African island in the Comoro Archipelago of the Western Indian Ocean, it is now using the euro. While most citizens of Mayotte speak Shimaore, a Bantu language, the members of Ali's village are Malagasy speakers. Their antecedents arrived before the French conquest in 1841 or during the early colonial period.
5. Ali says that since his stay in France, he no longer has the patience to sit through night-long religious recitations of the kind frequently performed in the village. However, like others of his social status and education, Ali is by no means opposed to Islam. He willingly joined

in rebuilding the village mosque, and he helped pay for his father's participation in a pilgrimage circuit in Madagascar. He assures me he will pray consistently when he gets older.

6. According to the French system of calculating high school education, completion of *3ième* is three years prior to the *bac* degree, which is the prerequisite for university. La Réunion is a French *département d'outre-mer* in the Indian Ocean east of Madagascar and some 1,700 kilometers from Mayotte. The two islands were connected in 2000 by numerous direct flights. Metropolitan France is some 9,000 kilometers from Mayotte and was reached via La Réunion.

7. In fact, not all new brides are virgins (Lambek 1983). Trumbas (*tromba* in Malagasy spelling) are Malagasy spirits, usually members of the royal Sakalava descent group, whose genealogy stretches back to before 1700 and who rise in and speak through specific mediums (Lambek 1981, 1993, 2002; Sharp 1993).

8. The trumba never fully rose in this man (he never went into full trance), but he would shake when the spirit was manifest and had purchased all of its clothing. The military connection may hold significance for the recurrence and knowledge of the individual spirit, but I have not been able to discover it.

9. The situation is a bit more complex than this in that the expensive ceremony in which the spirit announces its name has not yet been held for Ali's mother, nor was it ever held for her mother's brother. The name of the spirit should thus not be uttered (Lambek 1981), and its common identity among family members remains latent. There is also some conflict and competition over the production of the ceremonies. Succession to specific spirits marks segmentation no less than family unity (Lambek 1988a).

10. As Donald Tuzin noted (personal communication), Freudian ego psychologists might speak of the 'secondary gains' of Ali's illness and the way his 'somatic conversion' provided a face-saving way of submitting to his mother's will. Mel Spiro (personal communication) has suggested simply that part of Ali wanted one outcome and part, the other.

11. For Fingarette "avowal is a necessary condition of responsibility" (2000: 147), yet this does not appear to hold for Ali's case. However, Fingarette also acknowledges that "the issue [of acceptance of responsibility] is complicated by the fact that a person is responsible, in spite of unconcern with respect to a specific engagement, if there are other concerns of the person's by virtue of which he has indirectly committed himself to be concerned for the engagement at issue" (146).

12. However, Sartre's argument was an important ethical and political intervention in postwar France.

13. The argument here is essentially the same as that used to describe the role of suggestion and illocutionary acts in therapy.

14. We might also ask whether *spirits* are portrayed as acting individualistically or relationally, exercising free choice or social judgment. One of the themes of *Human Spirits* (Lambek 1981) is that the possession "cure" entails socializing the spirit and thus moving it from the former position to the latter. The drama of the cure, including vociferous interchanges between the spirit and the healers, provides instruction for everyone. But equally, the socialization of the spirits remains inconclusive and ambiguous; spirits can always utilize means, such as sending rheumatism, that would be illegitimate were they applied by humans. This contrast between humans and spirits is itself one of the edifying features of possession.

15. Such textualizing is incomplete insofar as the indexical qualities never completely disappear. Were they to do so, the intrinsically ironic quality of possession would be lost.

16. Marxian structure (via Hegel) and Freudian unconscious both derive from the Sophoclean version of irony. I am indebted to Paul Antze for these points (cf. Fortes 1983 [1959]).

17. I have been criticized for undertaking to judge Ali's motives and for shifting to an experience-distant mode of understanding, but my aim has been neither to judge nor to criticize Ali, but rather to expose, as Nehamas says of Plato's dialogues, "our ignorance of our own ignorance" (1998: 44).

18. I owe this idea to Andrew Walsh's suggestion (personal communication, 1 October 2000) that when Ali was reciting the story to me, he, too, was doing so ironically—not lying, but not revealing everything either. The anthropologist's stance is also at issue. I am ironic insofar as I hold two sets of beliefs or hold one of them back. "Is it possible," asks Walsh, "that any invocation of an ethnographic encounter (like that between you and Ali) is ironic in the way that any invocation of possession is?" Crapanzano (1980) provides sustained reflection on these issues. See also Fernandez and Huber (2001).

REFERENCES

Audi, R., ed. 1999. *The Cambridge Dictionary of Philosophy*. 2nd ed. Cambridge: Cambridge University Press.

Barber, K. 1999. "Quotation in the Constitution of Yorùbá Oral Texts." *Research in African Literatures* 30, no. 2:17–41.

Becker, A. 1979. "Text-Building, Epistemology, and Aesthetics in Javanese Shadow Theatre." Pp. 211–243 in *The Imagination of Reality*, edited by A. Becker and A. Yengoyan. Norwood N.J.: Ablex.

Boddy, J. 1988. "Spirits and Selves in Northern Sudan: The Cultural Therapeutics of Possession and Trance." *American Ethnologist* 15, no. 1:4–27.

———. 1989. *Wombs and Alien Spirits*. Madison: University of Wisconsin Press.

Bordo, S. 1989. "The Body and the Reproduction of Femininity." Pp. 13–33 in *Gender/Body/Knowledge: Feminist Reconstructions of Being and Knowing*, edited by A. Jaggar and S. Bordo. New Brunswick: Rutgers University Press.

Chodorow, N. J. 1989. *Feminism and Psychoanalytic Theory*. New Haven: Yale University Press.

Crapanzano, V. 1980. *Tuhami: Portrait of a Moroccan*. Chicago: University of Chicago Press.

Fernandez, J., and M. T. Huber, eds. 2001. *Irony in Action: Anthropology, Practice, and the Moral Imagination*. Chicago: University of Chicago Press.

Fingarette, H. 2000. *Self-Deception*. 2nd ed. Berkeley: University of California Press.

Fortes, M. 1983 [1959]. *Oedipus and Job in West African Religion*. Cambridge: Cambridge University Press.

Freud, S., and J. Breuer. 1955 [1893–1895]. "Studies on Hysteria." In S. Freud, *Standard Edition of the Collected Works*. Vol. 2. London: Hogarth.

Kapferer, B. 1983. *A Celebration of Demons: Exorcism and the Aesthetics of Healing in Sri Lanka*. Bloomington: Indiana University Press.

Lambek, M. 1981. *Human Spirits: A Cultural Account of Trance in Mayotte*. Cambridge: Cambridge University Press.

———. 1983. "Virgin Marriage and the Autonomy of Women in Mayotte." *Signs: Journal of Women in Culture and Society* 9, no. 2:264–281.

———. 1988a. "Spirit Possession/Spirit Succession: Aspect of Social Continuity among Malagasy Speakers in Mayotte." *American Ethnologist* 15, no. 4:710–731.

———. 1988b. "Graceful Exits: Spirit Possession as Personal Performance." *Culture* 8, no. 1:59–69.

———. 1989. "From Disease to Discourse: Remarks on the Conceptualization of Trance and Spirit Possession." Pp. 36–61 in *Altered States of Consciousness and Mental Health: A Cross-Cultural Perspective*, edited by C. Ward. Thousand Oaks, Cal.: Sage Press.

———. 1993. *Knowledge and Practice in Mayotte: Local Discourses of Islam, Sorcery, and Spirit Possession*. Toronto: University of Toronto Press.

————. 1996. "The Past Imperfect: Remembering as Moral Practice." Pp. 235–254 in *Tense Past: Cultural Essays in Trauma and Memory*, edited by P. Antze and M. Lambek. New York: Routledge.

————. 1998. "The Sakalava Poiesis of History: Realizing the Past through Spirit Possession in Madagascar." *American Ethnologist* 25, no. 2:106–127.

————. 2000. "Nuriaty, the Saint, and the Sultan: Virtuous Subject and Subjective Virtuoso of the Post-Modern Colony." *Anthropology Today* 16, no. 2:7–12.

————. 2002. *The Weight of the Past: Living with History in Mahajanga, Madagascar*. New York: Palgrave-Macmillan.

————. 2003. "Memory in a Maussian Universe." Pp. 202–216 in *Regimes of Memory*, edited by K. Hodgkin and S. Radstone. London: Routledge.

Mann, T. 1995 [1924]. *The Magic Mountain*. Translated by J. E. Woods. New York: Knopf.

Mitchell, S. A. 1988. *Relational Concepts in Psychoanalysis: An Integration*. Cambridge: Harvard University Press.

Moore, S. F. 1978. "Old Age in a Life-Term Social Arena." Pp. 23–76 in *Life's Career—Aging*, edited by B. Myerhoff and A. Simic. Beverly Hills: Sage.

Nehamas, A. 1998. *The Art of Living: Socratic Reflections from Plato to Foucault*. Berkeley: University of California Press.

Rappaport, R. A. 1999. *Ritual and Religion in the Making of Humanity*. Cambridge: Cambridge University Press.

Ricoeur, P. 1971. "The Model of the Text: Meaningful Action Considered as a Text." *Social Research* 38:529–562.

Sartre, J. P. 1956 [1943]. *Being and Nothingness*. Translated by H. Barnes. New York: Philosophical Library.

Sharp, L. 1993. *The Possessed and the Dispossessed*. Berkeley: University of California Press.

Silverstein, M., and G. Urban, eds. 1996. *Natural Histories of Discourse*. Chicago: University of Chicago Press.

Strathern, M. 1988. *The Gender of the Gift: Problems with Women and Problems with Society in Melanesia*. Berkeley: University of California Press.

Trilling, L. 1971. *Sincerity and Authenticity*. Cambridge: Harvard University Press.

Chapter 3

BARBARIC CUSTOM AND
COLONIAL SCIENCE
Teaching the Female Body in the
Anglo-Egyptian Sudan

Janice Boddy

How the Arab women [in Sudan] ever produced any children is difficult for a European to imagine. The universal and barbaric practice of genital mutilation ... would make intercourse painful. There could be no birth without preliminary slashing and subsequent cobbling together by, in the majority of cases, untrained locals using septic tools ... [T]he constant teaching and preaching of the Mid-wives' Training School, did nothing to alter public opinion ... The apparent determination of Arab women, enduring this primitive treatment, to continue to inflict it on the next generation is shocking. (Kenrick 1987: 110)

What is health? What is a normal, healthy female body? These are rhetorical questions, perhaps, readily disposed of by banal replies. But for the anthropologist, self-evident statements are seldom transparent; they are instead clues to the presence of naturalized cultural assumptions that demand to be explored. What constitutes 'soundness of body and mind' (to use an *Oxford English Dictionary* definition) resists unitary description across cultural, political, and historical divides. Health is an illusive ideal we strive toward in keeping entropy at bay; it is the largely unanalyzed ground of illness and, in the passage above, of aberrance. In other words, health is what illness, aberrance, and infirmity are not. Its parameters depend—reciprocally—on those of its counter-conditions, and these are culturally informed. When others with whom one interacts follow a different regime of health, the contrast can reveal the taken-for-grantedness of one's assumptions and perhaps, in an ironic movement, denaturalize them. But not always. In colonial situations in which a dominant group seeks to replace an indigenous regime with its own, the subordinates' contemplative agency is constrained. So, too, is that of the colonizers, whose vision prevails as truth and their subjects' as its foil: 'superstition', 'backwardness', 'barbarity'.

Despite this, for reasons of humanity, expediency, and cost, colonizers often used native practices and terms as vehicles for implanting novel ideas; they also translated local expressions as literally mirroring their own. This is what happened in the case of midwifery training in early-twentieth-century Sudan. For British and Arab Sudanese women, engaging with each others' body images and ideals in the power-laden colonial context left ample space for ironic miscommunication. If neither group recognized it at the time, the Sophoclean upshot of their encounter surely tells the tale.

Battling 'Superstition'

Beginning in the 1920s, British officials in colonial Sudan sought to abolish the pharaonic form of female circumcision, or infibulation, among self-identified 'Arabs' in the northern two-thirds of the country, where the practice was (and is) entrenched, and to prevent its spread to adjacent non-Arab groups where it was not. Efforts to end infibulation—but not all forms of female circumcision—continued in fits and starts into the latter days of Anglo-Egyptian rule, yet were concentrated between 1920 and 1946. The project's path was not smooth: there were significant clashes among expatriate personnel over the pace of change and how best to ensure it; political and commercial exigencies often intervened; medical and political objectives seldom converged; few Sudanese complied. Change did occur, for in some regions the severity of cutting was reduced, but far from being abolished, the practice was as prevalent at the end of the period as it had been at the start. Since independence in 1956, there have been intermittent attempts to revive the campaign, the latest (as of this writing) proclaimed in March 2003.

British motives for trying to reduce the severity of female genital cutting were predictably touted as humanitarian and civilizing, but what, in the colonial context, did that mean? As research progressed, it became clear that the overriding concern was to make the population more productive and tie it firmly to the 'world market' over which Britain was rapidly losing control. The fertile lands of the Gezira, above the junction of the White and Blue Niles, were being converted into a massive cotton plantation backed by Parliament and British entrepreneurs. Britain sought a reliable source of long-staple cotton required for the fine textiles that its Lancashire mills, faced with growing competition, had lately begun to produce. If successful, the scheme would significantly reduce reliance on mercurial suppliers such as Egypt and the United States. Not least it would enable Sudan's administration to pay for itself, as imperial possessions were expected to do. There was, however, an abiding shortage of native labor to cultivate the project (Daly 1986; Sikainga 1996), a situation aggravated by the influenza pandemic of 1918–1919 (Bell 1998: 296).

British officials viewed Sudanese in racial terms and ranked their capacity for work on an evolutionary scale. They considered southerners or 'blacks', whom northerners had enslaved, to be strong, energetic, but innately undisciplined workers, needing close supervision and control. Northerners or 'Arabs' were regarded as habitually (not *naturally*) indolent, possessed of a 'slave-owning mentality', and averse to heavy manual toil (Hargery 1981; Sikainga 1996). Arabs were thus considered reparable—through education, economic pressure, and the encouragement of 'orthodox' Islam over its volatile, charismatic forms.[1]

Officials were also convinced that Sudan had been severely depopulated in the late nineteenth century owing to famine, disease, and internal warfare. They claimed a decline from over eight and a half million people in 1881 to fewer than two million when Britain took control in 1898 (MacMichael 1954: 73). Though the figures were likely distorted to justify intervention, there had still been considerable misery, upheaval, and loss.[2] Yet a diminished peasantry meant there was now ample arable land. To control and resettle the populace, administrators subsidized farming and refused to liberate farmers' existing slaves. Indeed, well into the 1930s they abetted slave-holding, in the belief that without it, Sudan's shattered agrarian economy would not revive (Daly 1986, 1991; Sikainga 1996; Spaulding 1988). 'Free' labor for colonial projects was therefore scarce and expensive. Presumably, only when the limits of cultivation were reached would a reliable source of land-poor, cheap Arab workers arise.

By 1920 the population had not grown sufficiently to fill the demand for workers on colonial projects. Gezira dams, canals, and settlements were being built with costly foreign labor, and cotton production was slated to start in 1925. Yet it was deemed imprudent to coerce Arab men with corvée or the like, lest they rise up in a new jihad. Armed with metropolitan understandings of motherhood, officials turned to Arab women for both explanation and solution. During the 1920s, northern women's domestic practices, childrearing techniques, inadequate hygiene, preferred position for giving birth, and, above all, customary infibulation were blamed for sustained low birthrates, high infant mortality, and all manner of moral deficiency. This, despite advice from British physicians that conquest and colonial rule had altered disease patterns in Sudan, and the consequent spread of malaria and syphilis accounted for the discouraging state of procreative affairs: the landscape of the Gezira had been altered, and troops were moved quickly from place to place (Atkey in Bell 2000: 157). Arab mothers nonetheless bore the onus of the north's apparent 'failure to progress'.

A memo from the British director of intelligence circulated to all senior staff and medical personnel in 1924 states the case:

> Setting aside the ordinary motives of humanity, the Government is deeply interested in the increase of population and I believe it to be within the bounds of accuracy to say that no very great propaganda with the male population of the country can be expected until the female portion of it, which controls the children for all their early and impressionable years, is raised to a higher standard of mental and moral development, which seems impossible as long as the custom of Pharaic circumcision holds.[3]

The medical director agreed, warning that worse than the physical harm from infibulation is its "mental effect on the child ... as the shock is so severe as to be liable to cause serious mental disorder, thus further handicapping a sex that is ... behind the development of the men of the country."[4] Arab Sudanese women were deemed an unhealthy influence on the next generation. Their bodies and bodily practices would have to be 'civilized', so that their offspring might proliferate and learn to work and consume in useful, intelligible ways.

Reforming Women

Such concerns were key factors in the regime's attentions to public education and health. Professionals in these fields were tasked not merely with swelling the workforce, but also with schooling native sensibilities, working subtle transformations at the level of bodies and minds. Because northerners subscribed to a doctrine of gendered spheres more stringent than in Britain, contact with Muslim women was difficult for officials and civil servants, most of whom were men. Yet the transformation to modernity required women's compliance to produce healthy and disciplined workers, shape the sensibilities of Arab youth, and 'improve' the human and natural environments for intensive cotton cultivation by bettering sanitation and controlling the spread of disease. How could they be reached? Sponsoring general education for girls seemed a likely approach, yet here the regime was reluctant and slow, convinced that objections from Muslim fathers would be too great. Though the government founded a teacher training college for northern girls in 1921 and set up girls' schools in the larger towns, by 1932 the education department acknowledged that "no more than 2/3 percent [0.67 percent]" of girls received an elementary education (G. C. Scott in Daly 1986: 386; see also Beshir 1969: 96 ff.). Yet if very few girls went to school, virtually all would soon become mothers. A more direct and less exclusive approach, pedagogical as well as pragmatic, lay within the province of the Sudan Medical Service. The Omdurman Midwives Training School (MTS) was therefore opened, also in 1921.

The 'MTS'

The school's mandate was "to overcome, combat and improve harmful rites and customs" by instilling in native midwives a knowledge of simple hygiene and biomedical birthing techniques.[5] Though officials remained skeptical of the venture's success, the training of midwives—*daya*s in Sudan Arabic—was dual purposed, for it is they who perform pharaonic circumcisions, then cut through the resulting scar tissue to enable delivery and restitch a woman's genital wound after birth. Because of infibulation, no delivery can go unattended in northern Sudan. Calculated or not, the practice ensures that women monitor each others' pregnancies and births. Midwifery was thus a promising entry point for pro-natal colonialists, ideal for preaching the morality of hygienic, 'orderly' living and the merits of medical science.

The 'barbaric custom' played endlessly on the mind of the school's first matron, Mabel Wolff, a nurse-midwife who had formerly taught in Egypt.[6] But in a discerning move, rather than forbid midwives to continue the practice once trained, she taught them a modified operation that was less radical than the 'full pharaonic' type. The technique was called *tahur al-wasit* or *tahur mit-wasat*, literally, 'intermediate purification'. It involved removing parts of the clitoris and inner labia, then stitching together the outer labia leaving a wider opening than was customary for passing urine and menstrual blood. All this was to be performed with scrupulous attention to hygiene and 'patient' after-care. Wolff's plan was to encourage medical midwives to instruct against genital cutting of any sort, while introducing progressively milder operations until the practice died out or was replaced by the religiously permitted form in which only the hood of the clitoris is removed.[7] This harm-reduction approach (*avant la lettre*) was designed to improve both physical and social reproduction—motherhood in its widest political sense. Importantly, if the procedure caught on, the *daya*'s role would be undiminished, and medical midwives would have secured a stable presence in northern domestic life.

The MTS began with four pupils, two of them elderly practicing *daya*s. Wolff, whose unfamiliarity with "the customs and rites of Sudanese women" made communicating difficult at first, also faced suspicion. How could an unmarried childless woman of thirty know anything about childbearing, let alone "Sudany deliveries"?[8]

During my own first visit to Sudan, I was forbidden to witness a birth because I had not yet wed. Women told me that having been married and prepared for pregnancy is what distinguishes those allowed to observe from those who must wait outside. The potent but unactivated 'red' blood of the newly circumcised and youthful unwed must not encounter the 'black' (dirty, exhausted) blood of childbirth, for the unwelcome conjunction can provoke hemorrhage in the mother and attract troublesome spirits who are liable to make her ill.[9] Midwives in Sudan are regarded with ambivalence and a touch of awe (cf. Kenyon 1991b), not least because they withstand exposure to all forms of genital blood—sexually charged and potent, or exhausted and defiled, often both on the same day—and risk falling prey to possessive spirits. Wolff's apparent fearlessness may have won admiration from MTS pupils and clientele, but whether they saw the work of spirits behind her serious illness of 1929, which brought her sister Gertrude to the school, we do not know.

Wolff would have preferred to train younger women who, she thought, were more educable and had not yet formed the 'bad habits' of those who had begun to work. The less than thorough training of traditional *dayas*—"very conservative, completely ignorant and extremely dirty" (Kendall 1952: 42)—could, she thought, bring her methods disrepute.[10] Yet the medical director insisted.[11] While teaching traditional *dayas* was a concession Wolff was required to make, it did nothing to alter her compatriots' view of midwifery as the lowly vocation of Dickensian Mrs. Gamps.

The paucity of formal education in Sudan, especially for girls, meant that the MTS pupil who could read and write was rare. Moreover, existing midwives had learned to deliver by feel, and many, being older and prone to the ophthalmic troubles of desert climes, were blind. Traditional delivery methods made seeing difficult in any case, for it was customary for a midwife to work beneath a cloth that was drawn over the abdomen and legs of the woman in her care. This was intended to meet demands for modesty. In addition, sightlessness afforded defense against the damaging effects of black blood. But it was also consonant with the sensory dispositions of northern Sudanese women, dispositions oriented not solely or primarily by visual reference, but also by texture, smell, the sense of space and one's bearings within it—indeed, by the values, meanings, and ideas embedded in the objects, spaces, and enclosures of everyday Sudanese life (Boddy 1989; cf. Duden 1993).

To enlarge on this point requires a detour from Wolff's pedagogy. Since Wolff sought to substitute biomedical knowledge for her students' understandings, it would help to know how northern women conceptualized pregnancy and birth. Colonial archives offer fractured descriptions of cultural practices but little about the logic on which they were based. For this we need ethnography.

The ethnographic information that follows is spatially and temporally specific, gleaned from women I lived with in the rural north during the 1970s and 1980s. Yet several women who told me about pregnancy and birth, and the meanings of enclosures and blood, had borne children during the 1920s and 1930s after the Wolffs began to teach. While certain expressions may have changed since then, and others may be new, I think it reasonable to believe that the underlying patterns they invoke are similar to those that informed women's lives in the recent past. Reports of 'customs' and 'superstitions' in the 1920s by an anthropologist in the education department (Crowfoot 1922), British teachers (Beasley 1992; Zenkovsky 1950), and the Wolffs themselves[12] lend credence to that view. Still, I am wary of extrapolating to the past from a provisional ethnographic present. My discussion is intended to give a general sense of indigenous images and ideas, in order to suggest how they became entwined with those presented at the school.

Ethnography

In the village where I lived, high-walled domestic enclosures (*hoshs*), the houses they contain, and women's infibulated wombs are deemed analogous in function and form: all three protect and enclose valued kin, thereby ensuring social continuity. Indeed, the formal Arabic word for womb, *rihm*, is seldom heard, and the idiom *bayt al-wilada*, house of childbirth, is commonly used instead. Wombs also share qualities with the jars used for mixing *kisra*, the wafery staple of northern Sudan. *Kisra*, in turn, is analogous in composition to the body of a child: made from male-produced seed/flour combined with female-produced fluid/water. The vessel used for mixing *kisra* (a *gulla*, now an enameled bowl) must be impervious, so that the contents cannot seep out when the batter is left to proof. In these features it resembles an infibulated womb—as do eggs, foods enclosed in tins, and fruits surrounded by rinds or peels. Such foods are prized as 'clean' (*nadif*), for their moisture is conserved by an enveloping cover and their contents are protected from contamination. Consuming clean food is said to 'bring blood', the potent red blood that is the source and strength of a woman's fertility. Hence, the adage 'a Sudanese girl is like a watermelon'—not just 'because there is no way in' as the saying ends, but also because the fruit's protected inner flesh is moist, red, and clean. And once opened, the shapely rounded melon is filled with potent seed.

These associations resonate in practices surrounding reproduction itself. A miscarried first trimester fetus is placed inside a *gulla*, like the unbaked *kisra* it resembles, then buried within the *hosh* near the kitchen, the women's area in the interior 'belly' (*buton*) of the hosh. Customary means of handling other pregnancy outcomes are extensions of this logic. A stillborn is wrapped as a corpse and buried along the outer wall of the *hosh* just to one side of the men's door, the *khashm al-bayt*, or 'mouth of the house'. As the infant's body has emerged from the womb/house fully formed (formed by the womb's internal heat, much as *kisra* is baked by the heat of a woman's griddle), it comes to rest near the wall of the house/maternal body next to the orifice (*khashm al-bayt*/vagina) through which it has passed and by which its father (formally, legitimately) comes and goes. The term *khashm al-bayt* is an idiom, too, for the patriline arising in the house and *hosh*. The path of the stillborn babe is arrested at the door to the womb, literally, the *khashm al-bayt al-wilada*, 'mouth of the house of childbirth'; she does not enter 'society', the world of open expanses and other homes, for that requires breath, the obvious presence of a soul. Infants who die having breathed are buried, like any other person, in the village cemetery on the fringe of the desert beyond cultivated and humanly occupied space.

These features of everyday logic in one part of northern Sudan are echoed in other regions, too.[13] Their outline here is meant to locate infibulation in a historical and cultural order that reveals its possibility, an order whose meanings must be "understood as positional values in the field of their own cultural relationships rather than appreciated by categorical and moral judgments of our making" (Sahlins 1999: 43). The values linked to infibulation intimate a world where meaning resides in attributes that persons and objects share. Images do not here resolve to underlying truths, but refer to other images and other domains of significance. They do not, in other words, represent reality so much as constitute it, weaving experiences together in a recursive, nonreductive way. Within this world, infibulation is deeply naturalized, as it was when Wolff began to teach.

Undergoing infibulation surely affects a child's developing self-perception, though not always, perhaps, in ways the British assumed. Along with other routine procedures, such as smoke-bathing and depilation, that purify women's bodies, cleanse them, and make them smooth by means of heat or pain (Boddy 1989), the experience helps to develop a child's dispositions physically, cognitively, and emotionally, thus orienting her to a specific 'universe of probabilities' (cf. Bourdieu 1990). The trauma of circumcision is not meaningless. Indeed, over time its meaning becomes increasingly clear to those who undergo and reproduce it. For through exposure to the connections immanent in the practical acts and objects of everyday life, meaning is gradually built up and continually reinforced. Routine tasks, such as baking bread or the simple act of opening a tin of tomato purée, are replete with unspoken import. They are media through which subjective reality is subtly orchestrated, planted in bodily memory, and repeatedly renewed. Indeed, the very walls of a local house, its thresholds, rooms, and doors, speak to the infibulated woman of her self (Boddy 1998: 102). While not all domains of northern Sudanese life are as coherently modeled as this, the congruity of ideas that identify infibulation with valued enclosures, womanhood, procreation, and the husbanding of fertility makes them especially powerful, compelling, and politically effective.

Thus, infibulation was not an obsolete or isolable 'trait' that the British could extract from its cultural matrix like a rotten tooth or could expect women to discard on their advice. Yet unlike some of their compatriots, the Wolffs did not seek a peremptory ban on the practice, but favored its gradual abatement, as we've seen. They therefore chose to work *with* rather than *against* local understandings.

Methods and Morals

How, then, and what did the Wolffs teach? Their papers, written for the most part by Mabel, suggest that they paid heed to local sensibilities and taught by invoking students' embodied memories. They did not teach literacy—having neither the mandate nor the expertise—but used images that first summoned and then sought to reposition women's experiential dispositions. They taught in Arabic, wherever possible incorporating 'women's vocabulary',[14] a lexicon replete with homonyms that nonliterate women use as synonyms and similes. They built discursive bridges between local understandings and their own by creating analogies to the objects and acts of Sudanese daily life with which women's bodies are linked—though whether the sisters fully appreciated vernacular logic is not clear from the evidence at hand. By these means, they devised an ingenious and powerful synthesis of biomedical and lay techniques that dovetailed with local concepts, even as they strove to undermine them.

Still, however sensitive, the strategy of linking lessons to women's daily lives may have foiled the Wolffs' wider aims. "I illustrate by local colour all their lectures," Mabel wrote, "as I find they understand and assimilate them better—viz. in giving them an anatomy and physiology lesson I compare the body to a house and the organs [to] the furniture—the functions of the lungs as windows that air the house, etc."[15] She lectured: "[T]he body resembles a furnished house and all the contents have a special use."[16] Did her students experience a shock of recognition? Or were their responses subdued, the wisdom so recognizable, banal, so matter-of-fact? For these were analogies pupils could surely grasp, a native 'house' (*hosh* or *bayt*) being not just homologous with a woman's body in local parlance, but an *infibulated* one at that. Wolff did not invent this association, but surely she invoked it. Students may well have gathered from her homey images that their much maligned 'common sense' was more modern than they had been told. Or perhaps that Wolff understood things as did they. Undoubtedly, students creolized instructional terms (cf. Hunt 1999), creating notional malapropisms—at least, from the sisters' point of view. For to the Wolffs, any resonance between local ideas and biomedical constructs was accidental or heuristic, not sincere. Their mission remained unchanged: to substitute rational science for harmful practices and fallacious beliefs (cf. Bell 1998).

In steps consonant with their nonliteracy and multisensory predilections, MTS students were taught to identify chemicals and drugs not only by sight but also "by touch, smell or taste," container shape and color having wisely been deemed unreliable.[17] They learned to handle scissors, using "pieces of motor tyre ... for practising slitting and suturing the vulval obstructions resulting from ritual circumcision."[18] They practiced delivery with "full antiseptic precautions and prolonged washing"[19] on a realistic, if uninfibulated, papier-mâché model (called 'The Phantom') with movable parts and replaceable fetus, and learned the 'proper' bathing and feeding of infants on articulated Caucasian baby dolls. What could not be taught by practical means, students were required to learn by rote. They learned in an eminently physical, embodied way.

Hygiene was the core of the school's pedagogy. "The first lesson a midwife must learn," wrote Mabel, "is the importance of good manners, morals and cleanliness." Cleanliness was expected of the midwife's person, her hands and nails, and of her children, husband, house, midwifery equipment and work,[20] and students were admonished accordingly. To Wolff, 'cleanliness' meant more than the material absence of dirt and germs. It was, in itself, a moral state (Bell 2000: 308). Here one detects the impress of Christianity, in which cleanliness and godliness are linked, and washing clean is an idiom of social and spiritual 'enlightenment' (cf. McClintock 1995). Thus, Wolff, a practicing Christian, counseled, "You must remember that in midwifery there are two or more lives dependent on your skill and care, each baby you help from darkness to the light of Day, is a gift from God and you should be at all times worthy to receive it."[21] The image was not only Christian but Muslim Sudanese: a child is considered

'Allah's gift' who, in being born, moves from the darkness of the womb (swathed in depleted black blood) into the social world and the prospect of divine light (*Nur*, one of the names of Allah). Thus, Wolff's inaugural lecture, addressed to every freshman class, at once summoned Islamic ideals and undermined them, for to be truly worthy of receiving 'Allah's gifts', a midwife needs the civilizing guidance of the MTS (see Torsvik 1983).

As Wolff mapped British domestic practice onto northern Sudanese ideas, she proposed substitutions that were—perhaps fortuitously—astute. For instance, women in Sudan speak of circumcision (*tahur*) as creating bodies that are ritually pure (*tahir*), physically clean (*nadif*), and smooth (*na'im*). And these states invoke both hygiene and enclosure—smoothness; being covered or 'sealed'—in local thought. As you read the following passage from the sisters' lecture book, think of the logic of enclosure earlier described:

> Most illnesses are caused by the entrance into the body by way of the mouth [*khashm*], the eyes, the nostrils, through the skin or a wound (or ulcer) of minute living things which cannot be seen except under a microscope. Just as there are a great variety of insects and seeds, so there are microbes, each illness being caused by its own particular microbe ...
>
> There are microbes that will turn milk sour and meat putrid and food poisonous, but if food is sterilized and kept in *sealed tins*, the microbes cannot penetrate and the contents such as tomato sauce, milk, sardines and numerous other foodstuffs, will keep good for long periods but as soon as the tin is opened microbes get on the food and it will soon be poisoned and unfit to eat.
>
> *If our bodies are healthy and strong like the sealed tins*, the microbes cannot harm us, but if microbes get a hold of us, they may give us some illness according to what microbe has infected us.[22]

The analogies made perfect, if perverse, colloquial sense.

Wolff intended that MTS graduates become "missionaries ... in the cause of cleanliness and simple hygiene." "Their growing number and increasing influence" would, she believed, help "combat the almost universal custom of complete female circumcision which is so barbarous in execution, and is fraught with danger to both mother and babe." Indeed, MTS pupils were already sowing "the first seeds of a silent revolution to cleanliness and hygiene ... in the homes of the people."[23]

Yet the tactic of drawing links to students' everyday lives was hardly innocuous or one-sided, as the Wolffs may have presumed, for surely their students conceptualized back. Expressing scientific concepts in vernacular terms is no transparent business, as work by Emily Martin (1987, 1991) and others has shown. In Sudan it meant adapting science to existing ideas, here creating ties, there conciliations between local theories of purity and British theories of sanitation. While Wolff's lectures provided the basis for such syncretisms, they were likely more thorough and persuasive when conveyed by Sudanese, the 'silent revolutionaries' charged with working colonial knowledge into the conventions of making women and giving birth.

As may be surmised, this did not always have the desired effect. For given the midwife's pivotal role, the partial medicalization of birth brought with it a partial medicalization of circumcision. Indeed, as the Wolffs' lesson book advised: "Should a midwife do circumcisions ... she must perform the operation with all cleanliness just as she would a labour case, and attend the case daily for seven days, or more if necessary, in order to avoid infection of the wound."[24] Though clearly beneficial, the regular use of local anesthetics, antiseptics, sterile implements, and surgical suture suffused 'tradition' with medical mystique. Biomedicine did not thereby authorize infibulation, which had all the legitimacy required. But it does seem to have lent the practice novel support, which surely facilitated its endurance, however altered in form.

Status and Access

Who were these student midwives? The Wolffs accepted mature, respectable women of sound moral character and nonslave status, hoping thereby to ennoble the profession as well as appeal to cloistered Arab wives. Unsurprisingly, never-married women were precluded from practicing, while young (and to the Wolffs, more suitable) candidates were subject to "strong prejudice." Those selected to train were therefore married or divorced; most were older and respected matrons.[25] Based on information, albeit imperfect, in the MTS register, the average age of student midwives was 51 in 1921, dropping to 39 in 1925, and never falling "much below the high thirties thereafter" (Bell 2000: 305).

Women often came to the school with infants and toddlers in tow, and provision was made to house and feed them all for the three (later six) months' duration of the course (Kendall 1952: 45). The domestic retinues of indigenous women were thus regularly brought within the confines of the MTS, which consisted of several buildings inside a high-walled *hosh* that was also the sisters' home. Students cooked and cared for themselves and their children, providing the Wolffs with intimate knowledge of northern Sudanese family life without them having to venture far. In 1937 Mabel reported that anywhere "from one to two dozen children, ranging as a rule between the ages of six months to twelve years," lived at the school each term.[26] Trainees, a Sudani observer wrote, lived in clean and orderly rooms, with their children "playing in the yard as if they belong to one family under the care and patronage of Miss Wolff and her sister, who kindly take into their charge the food, the cleanliness and bringing up of those children."[27] Behind the modesty walls of the school, far from the prying eyes of officials or husbands and other kin, Sudanese domestic life was being regulated by the Wolffs, even when lessons were not underway.

So long as standards of respectability were met, the tradition whereby the midwife's role passes from mother to daughter was preserved. According to a Sudan Medical Service report from 1932, this guaranteed the acceptance of trained *dayas* in the neighborhoods where they worked. As "the children and grandchildren of the village or tribal midwives," graduates would return "to their own villages" where "they have, by tradition, the right of entry to every hut."[28] The female population, awash "in a sea of conservatism and prejudicial custom," was at last being reached by the boons of civilization, wrote Wolff, "on the surest principles ... entirely through the Sudanese and through their most conservative element, the women." The work was "not attempting rapid ... changes in a small part of the population but a gradual enlightenment and improvement over a large area and it is introducing that enlightenment into the very foundations of the people and their homes."[29]

By laboring to infuse their students with fresh sensibilities, the sisters sought to amend 'bad habits' and 'harmful customs'. But importantly, they saw such practices as ideal ports of entry into the lives of female Sudanese. Wolff felt strongly "that until *only* recognized licensed midwives are allowed to perform the circumcision operations and facial scar marking, our influence over the midwives, as well as amongst the majority of the people, will always remain unsatisfactory."[30] She saw controlling access to all customary surgery as the surest way to eliminate objectionable forms. Facial scarring was a public means to mark tribal or ethnic affiliation; as such, it was useful to 'native administration' and, unlike infibulation, seemed to have eluded colonial condemnation. Ironically, tribal marking has largely ceased in northern Sudan, while female circumcision, a more intimate identifier, has not.

Agency and Birth

The Wolffs were pragmatic and did not oppose customary practice as long as it didn't compromise their work. But in addition to circumcision, there was another tradition that they refused to abide. This was the preferred upright posture for giving birth, which smacked to them of savagery.

> The usual method of delivering ... is to suspend a rope from the ceiling, dig a hole in the ground over which is spread a special round mat plaited with a hole in the centre, the daya squats on the mat with bared legs which she spreads out across the hole and has in readiness by her side a razor with all but the tip of the blade wrapped round with in most cases a very dirty piece of rag, the patient stands over the hole and clings onto the rope and when she gets too tired or exhausted she is supported by various relations.[31]

Traditional *daya*s were known as *dayat al-habl*, 'midwives of the rope'; those trained by the Wolffs were popularly called *dayat al-hakuma*, 'government midwives', or *dayat al-mashamma*, 'midwives of the Macintosh', after the waterproof sheet they used to cover the birthing bed. Wolff's first reclining delivery was hotly contested, but when the "patient ... progressed favourably under [her] *better* and *cleaner* methods," she "found there was a gradual improvement in the attitude of the people."[32] By 1926, Wolff claimed she was making headway against the *habl*:

[A]s the trained women are becoming more popular ... the younger generation of women are themselves foregoing the untrained women and their barbarous methods for the trained midwife. In fact young mothers will proudly say their child is an 'ibn or bint el mashamma' meaning they were delivered lying on a mackintosh sheeting instead of the primitive old method of hanging onto a rope, & even the age of infants is reckoned from the ... advent of the trained midwives with the 'Mashammas'.[33]

The rope was not wholly forbidden by Wolff, for women in the early stages of labor could use it, should they choose. Only when birth was imminent was the recumbent postured required.[34] This meant parturition without the aid of gravity. Yet to be fair, the Wolffs believed an upright posture "invariably" caused the woman to lean forward, making delivery more strenuous, painful, and slow.[35] Chances of the infant being injured when the mother's genital scar was cut were also, perhaps, reduced with the mother lying down.

Unstated but perhaps more important was that the rope interfered with the midwife's reconfigured role. Wolff called their clients 'patients'. By the time the sisters began to practice, birth was seen in Britain less as a woman's natural feat and more as a pathological event demanding biomedical management. Scholars such as Emily Martin (1987) and Barbara Katz Rothman (1982) suggest that Cartesian dualism (resulting in the notion of the human body-as-machine) and androcentric ideology (in which the [young] male body is the *normative* body-as-machine) helped pathologize women's bodies in Western societies. Female reproductive events appeared to be complications of this norm, requiring 'treatment', 'supervision', and 'care'—hence, the notion that a woman in childbirth, like a reluctant machine, requires external guidance and control (see Martin 1987). Given that infibulated women are compelled to seek surgical assistance at birth, the image of them as 'patients' must have seemed self-evident to the Wolffs, a good transcultural fit. Further, in a striking photograph of the MTS schoolroom taken in the early 1930s, several Caucasian training dolls are shown lined up beneath the poster of a profiled human head and large-framed, breastless torso with internal parts rectangularly stylized and exposed. The poster is entitled "The Human Factory."[36] The step from indigenous homologies of the house and female body to a foreign image of a normative and apparently male body as a mechanized factory, may seem slight, but the consequences were potentially profound. For to the extent that the image was taken up, Sudanese women were being distanced from their conventional selves and their agency subtly reassigned.

A telling Wolffian analogy demonstrates the point. In 1932 prenatal care was added to midwives' responsibilities and introduced to the women thus:

[We asked,] when they put a cooking pot (halla) with food on the fire, did they leave it until the food was burnt and spoilt or was it usual to occasionally inspect the contents of the pot? Now amongst the womenfolk, the words 'Kashf el Halla' [pot check] have become a recognized meaning for 'Ante-Natal Examination' and attendances are so far very encouraging.[37]

Again, wittingly or not, in likening gestation to cooking, the Wolffs applied local ideas while fitting them to a biomedical view. Women, recall, tacitly compare pregnancy to making the batter for bread: mixing (female) fluid and (male) seed in an impervious container, something only the infibulated are properly able to do. As depicted by the Wolffs, pregnancy is like making a stew—a mechanical, asexual, curiously disembodied process that needs to be helped along, monitored by continuous visual surveillance. And note that the midwife, instead of the mother-to-be, is now the 'cook' responsible for care of the 'pot' (Boddy 1998: 40).

Medical midwives were expected to reform the Arab Sudan from the domestic inside out. Through scientific hygiene and medically disciplined birth, they were to manage women's bodies on behalf of the colonial state. But the success of MTS reforms was uneven at best. My discussions with rural women suggest that they made selective use of introduced images and techniques (Boddy 1998). When Wolff wrote in 1921, "It is pitiful to see the poor patients' dread of the 'Mousse' [razor, used to open the infibulation for birth] and their useless suffering and yet how they are bound down by the abominable custom,"[38] she could not have anticipated how thoroughly modern anesthetics would be incorporated into the techniques of infibulation and postpartum repair.

However useful medical midwives were to the state, the fact that they received even a modicum of government support was a result of Wolff's incessant efforts to persuade her superiors of the need. Families were expected to pay for deliveries and circumcisions—by custom, in kind and some coin. Some did, but many were too poor. Further, most Muslim Sudanese saw midwifery as charitable work. "The midwife," wrote Wolff, "gains ... sufficient 'Heavenly blessings' to amply compensate her for her trouble ... though it gives her no material benefits in this world."[39] Trained midwives complained of their disadvantage relative to untrained *daya*s, who were not burdened with maintaining scarce, arcane equipment at their own expense and had "none of the difficulties of gradually working up a practice and overcoming people's opposition and prejudices."[40] Small stipends were approved in 1929, though Wolff faced an uphill battle to get midwives' supplies replaced through rural dispensaries free of charge.[41] Stipends, of course, gave medical officers more control over trained *daya*s, a point that may have swung the decision in favor of approval.[42]

Fusions and Distinctions

As the MTS grew, its ablest graduates were enlisted as staff teachers and rural inspectors. To the Wolffs' intense frustration, administrators declared them entitled only to third-class travel accommodations, given their low rates of pay. The women so carefully chosen and groomed as exemplars of propriety were thus forced to journey in cramped, overcrowded conditions on steamers and trains, often overnight or for several days, exposed to unfamiliar men. The sisters endlessly protested the elitism that gave women schoolteachers better wages and second-class travel warrants, though the midwives' work was "just as important as theirs."[43]

One way to emphasize the respectability of medical midwives was to clothe them in uniforms, to set them apart from laywomen and *daya*s of the rope in ways consonant with sartorial canons of the colonial regime. Thus, student midwives wore immaculate white dresses, aprons, and head scarves. Upon graduating, each received a white outfit, which was "greatly valued as the visible sign of their profession."[44] And to ensure that officials recognized them when on call, they wore "a distinguishing blue scarf" over their white robes (Kendall 1952: 50).[45]

Midwives were expected to keep their uniform spotless; if it became stained or worn, they were obliged to replace it from their own limited means. Indeed, so berated were they about the need to keep clean that to Wolff's "horror" she once found a trainee dressed "only" in "a loin cloth ... squatting in front of the patient ... like a monkey... [because] she was afraid of soiling the government uniform."[46]

Graduates also received a certificate and a midwifery box the size of a small tool kit, made of tin, affixed with a wooden handle, and equipped with the requisite supplies of their vocation. The trained *daya* "is intensely proud" of her midwifery box, Wolff claimed, "as it is the visible sign of her superiority over the untrained."[47] So coveted were these signs, by 1932 Wolff was urging medical officials that "untrained midwives should not be allowed to have boxes and drugs and pose as trained midwives" or wear similar uniforms,[48] indicating that emulation of 'Macintosh *daya*s' by '*daya*s of the rope' was becoming rife.

It may not be coincidental that tin boxes ('*ilba*s) filled with medicinal stores play a significant role in spirit therapeutics, too, and the illness (*zar*) caused by spirits known as *zayran* is widely experienced as an assault on a woman's reproductive health. North of Khartoum, a *sitt al-'ilba* or 'lady of the tin box' is a long-term adept of the *zar*[49] gifted with prophetic dreams. Her title refers to the tin that stores the mixtures of incense used to summon various named *zayran*. A woman with possession symptoms—miscarriage, infertility, amenorrhea, or less specific *zihuj*, 'lassitude, depression'—will visit a *sitt al-'ilba* in order to have her suspicions verified or disproved. If confirmed by the seer's dreams, she will undergo a private fumigation with incense appropriate to the troublesome spirit's type. This rite, called 'opening the tin box' (*fatah-t al-'ilba*), is meant to placate an offending *zar* until the afflicted has funds to stage a proper cure (Boddy 1989; Constantinides 1972). 'Opening the tin box' begins the process of restoring a woman's spirit-threatened fertility. The offending *zar* is summoned to materialize in an afflicted body, then asked to depart, to restore the host's integrity. Similarly, when the midwife opens her '*ilba*, she deploys remedies to reverse the physical, spectral, and social vulnerabilities that sexuality, pregnancy, and birth are deemed to entail. She must open the parturient woman's body, release the being within, and close her again after delivery; in circumcising, she defensively 'closes' the vaginal orifice of a premenstrual, unmarried girl.

The parallels between medical midwifery and the *zar* are suggestive. Still, sturdy metal boxes have long been used as storage containers in northern Sudan. Was the midwifery box simply a practical conveyance, or was it also symbolic, designed to elicit more recondite understandings? Did the Wolffs capitalize on the link between tin boxes and techniques to preserve and restore female fertility? Or did the midwives do so themselves? From inquiries in Sennar, south of Khartoum, Susan Kenyon found that as a repository of healing wisdom, the *'ilba* has a lengthy past; it predates Wolff's arrival in Sudan. In Sennar, a *zar* leader's *'ilba* is the means by which her "powers and paraphernalia are handed on from one generation to the next "(Kenyon 1991a: 101; see also 1991b). The leader "derives her powers and knowledge from her *ilba*, which she has either inherited from a relative or acquired by apprenticeship with another leader. Each box has its own history, elaborated contents, and intangible assets, many of which are known only to the leader herself. Both literally and figuratively it encapsulates a set of beliefs" (Kenyon 1991a: 101). Likewise a midwifery box. And like it, a *zar 'ilba* acts "as a mnemonic device which both aids and reinforces other historical sources, primarily oral accounts supplemented by documentary evidence" (ibid.). The *'ilba* not only "contains the means to contact and control *zar* spirits" but also "symbolises the identity, power and knowledge that is associated with a particular leader ... As more knowledge and power are acquired, so the contents and the type of container itself become more elaborate" (ibid.).

Now, in MTS photographs of the 1930s, midwifery boxes are plain and unadorned, as Kenyon reports they are today in Sennar.[50] Yet in the area where I worked, they are decorated elaborately in red and gold. These are the colors of the wedding cloth (*garmosis*) that covers a bride when she is presented to the groom and whenever she gives birth. The red and gold of the bridal veil suggest dynamic gender complementarity and social and physical reproduction—the red of enclosed and fertile female blood, the gold of coins and jewelry that concentrate the value of outside work, brought into the *hosh* by men (Boddy 2002). This imagery is echoed in the *zar*. During a full possession cure, the bridal veil of the ailing woman, who is called the 'bride of the *zar*', is placed over the sheep that will be sacrificed to calm the offending spirit; the sheep substitutes for the woman, who thereby covenants to propitiate her spirit periodically. In return, the spirit should now relent, and restore the woman's reproductive health.

One task of a *zar* ritual is to convince a woman that procreative mischance does not originate in her body but beyond it, in the caprice of an exotic and powerful entity who has seen fit to 'seize' her womb. She is thus confirmed as inherently fertile, and her sense of self, closely linked to her reproductive role, is thereby reinforced (Boddy 1989). In this regard, a successful *zar* rite is the ethereal correlate of a repaired infibulation after birth: both are intended to re-enclose the female body, to protect and renew its productive integrity.

In this sense, *zar* leaders are like medical midwives, helping to channel and assuage external powers that are apt to disrupt fertility by capturing, loosening, or infecting a woman's blood. Possession healing and midwifery are parallel techniques for defending the female self, and practitioners share a general set of aims. They even intersect, for despite their scientific training, medical *dayas* often consult *zar* healers about their own reproductive woes.[51] The larger point is this: women conversant with spirit therapeutics were called on to adapt bio-medical knowledge to Sudanese domestic life and, in doing so, seem to have performed their own vernacular synthesis with the *zar*. Medical midwifery may have become more widely sensible thereby, but its scientific basis was tempered by indigenous ideas of the healthy female self.

Colonial Ironies

By 1928, Wolff had reason for optimism on the population front: "On the whole the health of the mothers in puerperium has enormously improved since … 1921, this is even remarked on by the midwives and older mothers themselves who say that women attended by the trained midwives are more prolific than in former times when sterility following a first and second confinement was very common and still appears to be in the Provinces."[52] This was achieved, however, without a noticeable decline in infibulation. It would seem that population increase could be achieved with little change in cultural logic, that is, the concern for producing children who are morally entangled in locally sanctioned ways.

The Wolffs were agents of the colonial state, recruited to help 'cure' Sudanese society by changing indigenous regimes of practice and thought: how women conceptualized their bodies, experienced pregnancy and birth, raised their children, performed domestic tasks. By instructing native midwives, the sisters strove to reshape sensibilities and instill 'modern' dispositions in northern Sudanese. To no small extent this conflicted with existing moral practice, though the sisters would hardly have described it as such, preferring 'superstition' and 'barbarism' instead. They nonetheless tried to facilitate the transition by couching their wisdom in vernacular terms. They sought to revise indigenous culture from the inside out, using native concepts as vehicles for implanting new ideas. The approach could be considered an exercise in applied ethnography, despite the Wolffs' antipathy to the cultural logic that sustained social life in northern Sudan. But the vehicles they chose for the task were not empty. They were already occupied by meanings that inform and are shaped by women's agentive selfhood. While the sisters' tactics worked to a point, the outcome was not what they had anticipated: female circumcision acquired new layers of sanction and support when modified by biomedical concepts and techniques. Indigenous notions of 'purity', 'cleanliness', and 'enclosure' blended with and were enriched by what the British taught, yet their logic was not appreciably undermined, nor were the social conditions it helped to realize and uphold. The Wolffs' disingenuous use of native ideas and the literalism they attributed to their own—to invoke Lambek's introductory remarks—may have precluded an appreciation of their method's ambiguity, its ironic potential and appeal.

Thus, pharaonic circumcision endured, despite the success of biomedicine in colonial Sudan and the relative ease with which it became a locus of first resort. Everything the Wolffs did was intended to convince Sudanese to abandon the 'barbaric custom'. In their efforts, the sisters became caught in 'webs of meaning' that envelop the practice and may have unwittingly contributed to its persistence.

Under the Wolffs' auspices, Western techniques of hygiene and health were disengaged from their home contexts and selectively absorbed into northern domestic life. In part, this was done with the sisters' blessing, yet much conceptual fusion surely took place without their realization and beyond their control. Their most enduring contribution, perhaps, was to gather local midwives under the aegis of the state, where they could be monitored and—it was hoped—controlled.

Eventually, however, the sisters seem to have been victims of their own achievements and perhaps, too, of the Gezira scheme's ephemeral success, for an apparent rise in the birthrate during the depression of the early 1930s led officials to sustain austere government funding for the midwives' school. A native revolt in Kenya over missionary attempts to abolish female circumcision sent shivers through Sudan's administrative ranks, while parliamentary investigations embarrassed the regime by exposing the custom's tenacity. These events emboldened officials to approve more drastic steps.

The Wolffs retired in 1937, after several difficult years. Their replacement, Elaine Hills-Young, had been carefully chosen by British political staff as an antidote to their excess. She immediately forbade trained midwives to perform female genital cutting of any sort, even the lesser form permitted—not required—by Islam. It is hardly surprising that few *dayas* complied; most continued working in secret. But Hills-Young brooked no compromise, and those who were caught risked losing their licenses, stipends, and supplies.[53] She and Ina Beasley, who became supervisor of girls' education in 1939, felt Sudanese women required firm guidance to abandon their backward ways. Together, they struggled to implant Western notions of selfhood, denouncing native views as primitive, ignorant, and false (see Beasley 1992: 8). Morality, they argued, is a matter of personal character; virtues are cultivated within the self, not through external constraint, and by individuals who bear sole responsibility for their behavior. The message was captured in posters showing "the shadow of the old hag, Superstition, being driven away from little girls by the lovely maiden, Enlightenment" (Beasley 1992: 405).[54]

The idea that morality was not internalized by Sudanese fails to hold, as we've seen. Nonetheless, a public movement launched in the late 1930s by Beasley, Hills-Young, and other Britons sought to dislodge infibulation from its cultural matrix, to prise it from collective concerns such as family honor and moral procreation. This attempt to unravel local ideas was destined, by and large, to fail.[55] For despite the Wolffs' abhorrence of infibulation, the creolizations that undoubtedly arose from their teachings had already detached science from its conceptual apparatus, enabling biomedicine and custom to coexist.

Janice Boddy

But was this the evil that Hills-Young and her collaborators believed? In the end, their attempt at abolition was no more successful than the Wolffs' had been. It also fed existing political divisions and fomented confrontation between British and Sudanese. So one must wonder, had the Wolffs' pragmatic methods received sufficient support, might they have stood a better chance of success, incremental though it would have been? And would postcolonial Sudanese governments have found it necessary to launch new anti-infibulation campaigns, the latest, as of this writing, announced in the winter of 2003?

ACKNOWLEDGMENTS

I am, as ever, extremely grateful to the women of Kabushiya and Gedo regions of northern Sudan for our continuing conversations. Several individuals and institutions have greatly facilitated the archival portions of this work: El Haj Bilal Omer of the Institute of African and Asian Studies, University of Khartoum; Clare Cowling, archivist, Royal College of Obstetricians and Gynaecologists; S. M. Dixon, Wellcome Trust for the History of Medicine; the staffs of the Public Records Office, London; National Records Office, Khartoum; Rhodes House Library, Oxford; Church Missionary Society Archive, Birmingham University; Rathbone Archive, Liverpool University; SOAS Archives, London University; Middle East Archive, St. Anthony's College, Oxford; and the British Library. Jane Hogan of the Sudan Archive, Durham University, has been an invaluable help and fund of knowledge. Research and writing have been supported by the Social Sciences and Humanities Research Council of Canada, the Connaught Fellowship Fund of the University of Toronto, the Harry Frank Guggenheim Foundation, and a Rockefeller Foundation Residency in Bellagio, Italy. My deepest thanks to them all. Any faults in the essay are mine alone.

NOTES

1. Further, their "styles of moral and political behaviour were more intelligible and predictable" to Europeans than those of southern "pagan" groups (Sanderson and Sanderson 1981: 81).
2. Thesiger (1987: 182) suggests that the population had been reduced by half during the Mahdia.
3. Willis to DCs, 19 February 1924, National Record Office (NRO), Khartoum, Civsec 1/44/2/12: 8.
4. "Medical Department Circular, 17 February 1924," NRO Civsec 1/44/2/12: 4.
5. M. Wolff and G. Wolff, "Draft of a Paper to the British Hygiene Council," February 1933, Sudan Archive Durham University (SAD) 582/10/12.

6. When 'Wolff' appears in the singular, it is Mabel to whom I refer. Both sisters retired in 1937.
7. See SAD 581/5/13.
8. MTS First Annual Report, 20 October 1921, SAD 579/3/15; see also M. Wolff, "Speech to the Committee of Guild of Service," SAD 579/3/24, and Kendall (1952).
9. A woman cannot modestly admit to being possessed by spirits until she is married. See Boddy (1989).
10. See O. Atkey, "Female Circumcision in the Sudan," 7 April 1930, NRO Civsec 1/57/3/121 and 1/44/2/12, 1924–1937.
11. Bousfield (MOH Khartoum) to Wolff, 23 February 1921, SAD 579/3/5. See also Bell (1998).
12. See their photo albums and notebooks on customs in the Sudan archive, for example, SAD 583/5, 583/3, 745/2, 745/3, 580/1.
13. Discussions with Sudanese anthropologists, especially Dr. Rogaia Abusharaf and Dr. Amal Fadlallah, suggest that the symbolic lexicon I describe is widespread; the Wolffs' photographs and ethnographic observations indicate its historical depth. See, for example, SAD 580/1, SAD 745/3.
14. One example of this would be the term *bayt al-wilada*, house of childbirth, which women use more commonly than the standard word for womb, *rihm*, as discussed above.
15. M. Wolff, "Speech," op. cit., n. 8, SAD 579/3/29.
16. "Elementary Practical Lessons for Midwives of the Sudan," n.d., SAD 581/5/8.
17. "From the Sudan," *Nursing Notes* (April 1937: 56), SAD 581/4/4.
18. Eardley Holland, "President's Report on His Visit to the Sudan, December, 1945," Royal College of Obstetricians and Gynaecologists Annual Report (1946: 9).
19. Dr. Fairbairn, "Midwifery Service in the Sudan," Royal College of Obstetricians and Gynaecologists Report (1936). SAD 581/4/1.
20. "Elementary Practical Lessons," op. cit., n. 16, SAD 581/5/7.
21. Ibid., SAD 581/5/7.
22. Ibid., SAD 581/5/16, emphasis mine.
23. "Report by M. Wolff," quoted in Kendall (1952: 47).
24. "Elementary Practical Lessons," op. cit., n. 16, SAD 581/5/13.
25. M. Wolff, "Speech," op. cit., n. 8, SAD 579/3/24; MTS Annual Report, 1925–1926, SAD 581/1/2; Wolff to Medical Inspector, Blue Nile Province, 14 November 1928, SAD 582/1/40; Kendall (1952).
26. M. Wolff, "Re. Dr. Fairbairn's letter of 21st May, 1937." SAD 581/4/6.
27. "A Visit to the Midwifery Institution Omdurman by Magboul El Sayed Al Awad, Omda of Omdurman, 6 July 1937." SAD 581/4/10.
28. Sudan Medical Service Report, 1932, quoted in ms. "The Sudan: A Medical History," A. Cruickshank and J. F. E. Bloss, SAD 704/4/69.
29. "Report by M. Wolff," quoted in Kendall (1952: 48).
30. "List of Trained Midwives Struck Off or Suspended to 1931," SAD 582/2/51.
31. M. Wolff, "Speech," op. cit., n. 8, SAD 579/3/25.
32. Ibid., SAD 579/3/24-25, original emphasis.
33. MTS Annual Report, 1925–1926, SAD 581/1/2. Initial resistance to the *mashamma* was tied to the fear that it was made of pigskin, anathema to Muslims, of course (Kendall 1952: 44).
34. Wolff to Director, SMS, 8 April 1934, SAD 582/4/26.
35. M. Wolff and G. Wolff, "Draft," op. cit., n. 5, SAD 582/10/12.
36. Photograph, "Learning to Scrub Up," SAD 583/5/38. The poster appears to depict organic processes as an assembly line producing material goods.
37. MTS Annual Report, 1932, SAD 581/1/46.
38. MTS Annual Report, 1921, SAD 579/3/15.
39. Wolff to Director, SMS, 17 January 1929, SAD 581/1/11, following up Wolff to MOH, Khartoum, 7 January 1929, SAD 582/1/55.
40. Ibid.

41. Rugman to Director, SMS, 3 March 1929, SAD 582/1/58; see also MTS Annual Report, 1929, SAD 581/1/8-11; Wolff to Governor, Dongola Province, 22 February 1930, SAD 582/2/19; Midwives Inspection, 1931, SAD 582/2/73.
42. Wolff to Director, SMS, 17 January, 1929, SAD 581/1/11.
43. Wolff to Director, SMS, 16 June, 1932, SAD 582/3/4. See also MTS Annual Report, 1933, SAD 581/11/60; and M. Wolff to G. Wolff, 30 November 1935, SAD 582/7/106.
44. MTS Second Report, 1921, 29 January 1922, SAD 579/3/20.
45. Unlike Islamic and Egyptian green, blue was the imperial color, worn around the helmets of officers in the Sudan Political Service (Kenrick 1987), popularly known as 'Blues' (for their success in Oxbridge sports competitions), who ruled the 'Land of the Blacks' (the meaning of 'Sudan').
46. M. Wolff, "Speech," op. cit., n. 8, SAD 579/3/28.
47. Ibid., SAD 579/3/29.
48. "Midwives Inspection, 1931," SAD 582/2/73.
49. The term *zar* refers to a type of spirit that can possess humans, the illness such spirits cause, and the therapeutic measures taken to relieve them. See Boddy (1989).
50. S. Kenyon (personal communication, November 2000); see also Kenyon (1991b: plate 12).
51. Several *zar* healers I spoke to said that spirits are averse to Western medicine, or rather deny its claim to superiority. Spirits, I was told, are powerful enough to foil even the surest biomedical remedies. Yet healers call on trained *dayas* to help them deliver, and trained *dayas* consult *zar* healers to help them manage their spirits.
52. MTS Annual Report, 1928, SAD 581/1/5. Spelling standardized and punctuation added.
53. British medics, along with political personnel, voiced little or no concern over male genital cutting performed in unsanitary conditions. This was, in part, because male circumcision is decreed by Islam, and the colonial regime was loath to antagonize Muslim subjects. Moreover, male circumcision was considered far less threatening to population levels than infibulation. Indeed, the lesser form of female circumcision, called *sunna* or 'religiously approved', was not discouraged in the least.
54. In this and other ways, the government campaign against pharaonic circumcision in Sudan bears resemblance to missionary medical efforts in Africa aimed at reforming personhood through conversion, as well as those of a colonial power seeking to control populations. This distinction has been elaborated by Vaughn (1991).
55. The issue is addressed in my book manuscript, *Civilizing Women: British Crusades in Colonial Sudan*.

REFERENCES

Beasley, I. 1992. *Before the Wind Changed*. Edited by J. Starkey. Oxford: Oxford University Press.
Bell, H. 1998. "Midwifery Training and Female Circumcision in the Inter-War Anglo-Egyptian Sudan." *Journal of African History* 39:293–312.
———. 2000. *Frontiers of Medicine in the Anglo-Egyptian Sudan, 1899–1940*. Oxford: Clarendon.
Beshir, M. O. 1969. *Educational Development in the Sudan, 1898–1956*. Oxford: Clarendon.
Boddy, J. 1989. *Wombs and Alien Spirits: Women, Men an the Zar Cult in Northern Sudan*. Madison: University of Wisconsin Press.
———. 1998. "Remembering Amal: On Birth and the British in Northern Sudan." Pp. 28–57 in *Pragmatic Women and Body Politics*, edited by M. Lock and P. Kaufert. Cambridge: Cambridge University Press.

———. 2002. "Tacit Containment: Social Value, Embodiment, and Gender Practice in Northern Sudan." Pp. 187–221 in *Religion and Sexuality in Cross-Cultural Perspective*, edited by S. J. Ellingston and M. C. Green. New York: Routledge.

Bourdieu, P. 1990. *The Logic of Practice*. Cambridge: Polity.

Constantinides, P. 1972. "Sickness and the Spirits: A Study of the 'Zar' Spirit Possession Cult in the Northern Sudan." Unpublished Ph.D. dissertation, University of London.

Crowfoot, J. W. 1922. "Wedding Customs in the Northern Sudan." *Sudan Notes and Records* 5, no. 1:1–28.

Daly, M. W. 1986. *Empire on the Nile: The Anglo-Egyptian Sudan 1898–1934*. Cambridge: Cambridge University Press.

———. 1991. *Imperial Sudan: The Anglo-Egyptian Condominium, 1934–1956*. Cambridge: Cambridge University Press.

Duden, B. 1993. *Disembodying Women: Perspectives on Pregnancy and the Unborn*. Cambridge: Harvard University Press.

Hargery, T. M. 1981. "The Suppression of Slavery in the Sudan, 1898–1939." D. Phil. dissertation, Oxford University.

Hunt, N. R. 1999. *A Colonial Lexicon: Of Birth Ritual, Medicalization and Mobility in the Congo*. Durham: Duke University Press.

Kendall, E. 1952. "A Short History of the Training of Midwives in the Sudan." *Sudan Notes and Records* 33, no. 1:42–53.

Kenrick, R. 1987. *Sudan Tales: Recollections of Some Sudan Political Service Wives, 1926–56*. Cambridge: Oleander.

Kenyon, S. M. 1991a. "The Story of a Tin Box: *Zar* in the Sudanese Town of Sennar." Pp. 99–117 in *Women's Medicine: The Zar-Bori Cult in Africa and Beyond*, edited by I. M. Lewis et al. Edinburgh: Edinburgh University Press.

———. 1991b. *Five Women of Sennar: Culture and Change in Central Sudan*. Oxford: Clarendon.

MacMichael, H. A. 1954. *The Sudan*. London: Ernest Benn.

Martin, E. 1987. *The Woman in the Body*. Boston: Beacon.

———. 1991. "The Egg and the Sperm: How Science Has Constructed a Romance Based on Stereotypical Male-Female Roles." *Signs* 16, no. 3:485–501.

McClintock, A. 1995. *Imperial Leather: Race, Gender and Sexuality in the Colonial Contest*. New York: Routledge.

Rothman, B. K. 1982. *In Labor: Women and Power in the Birthplace*. New York: W.W. Norton.

Sahlins, M. 1999. *Waiting for Foucault and Other Aphorisms*. 3rd ed. Cambridge: Prickly Pear Press.

Sanderson, L. P., and G. M. Sanderson. 1981. *Education, Religion and Politics in the Southern Sudan 1899–1964*. London: Ithaca.

Sikainga, A. A. 1996. *Slaves into Workers: Emancipation and Labor in Colonial Sudan*. Austin: University of Texas Press.

Spaulding, J. 1988. "The Business of Slavery in the Central Anglo-Egyptian Sudan, 1910–1930." *African Economic History* 17, no. 1:23–44.

Thesiger, W. 1987. *The Life of My Choice*. London: Collins.

Torsvik, B. 1983. "Receiving the Gifts of Allah: The Establishment of a Modern Midwifery Service in the Sudan, 1920–1937." Unpublished M.A. thesis, University of Bergen.

Vaughn, M. 1991. *Curing Their Ills: Colonial Power and African Illness*. Stanford: Stanford University Press.

Zenkovsky, S. 1950. "Zar and Tambura as Practised by the Women of Omdurman." *Sudan Notes and Records* 31, no. 1:65–81.

Chapter 4

THE LACAN WARD
Pharmacology and Subjectivity in Buenos Aires

Andrew Lakoff

This essay examines some of the possible effects of psychotropic medication. The biomedical model of such effects is that they restore reason and agency to the subject by treating the chemical pathology that has disrupted normal mood or thought. We can term this a 'literal' understanding of behavioral medication—as that which acts directly on disorder. But this is not the only way for experts to understand—indeed, to use—such medication. In what follows, I contrast the literal reading of the effects of such drugs with an 'ironic' one, in which the medication acts as much on expertise as on the disorder of the patient. The essay describes how a distinctive form of psychoanalytic knowledge maintained its presence in an unexpected place: an acute psychiatric ward in a public hospital in Buenos Aires. It did so not despite but rather through the use of medication. Medication did not do precisely what it was meant to do—act on the chemical site of disorder. Instead, it helped to sustain what was simultaneously the source of analytic authority and the object of its knowledge—patient subjectivity. In this setting, the production of subjectivity practically depended on, but remained conceptually autonomous from, the effects of medication.

This understanding of medication depended upon the uncertainties inherent to the pathologies these drugs are designed to treat—around the source, site, and proper treatment of mental disorder. Doctors' responses to these uncertainties, in turn, combined a specific model of the human with a sense of the ethical task of expertise. In this case, the ethical task was to nourish human subjectivity in the face of threats from bureaucracy, capitalism, and scientific reductionism. A number of related techniques were used to protect against such threats: the bureaucratic function of the hospital was kept separate from analytic practice, patient narratives were gathered and transformed into texts that became the objects of psychoanalytic work, and medication was used to enable patients to speak.

Psychic Energy

What became clear in this setting was that the effects that psychotropic drugs are understood to produce depend, at least in part, upon the milieu of expertise into which they enter. In this sense, these drugs are instruments whose function is shaped by the form of rationality in which they are deployed; they are the means to various possible ends. As it turns out, this has been apparent since the earliest expert discussions of the possible uses of these drugs. Soon after the introduction of antipsychotic medication in the early 1950s, the new drugs began to provoke reflection on the relation between chemical intervention and human subjectivity. The predominance of psychoanalysis in cosmopolitan psychiatry at the time sparked an initial attempt to integrate these substances with dynamic models of the self. The key question was whether such medications could affect psychic structure in a way that would render even the most intractable of patients amenable to psychoanalysis.

In a 1957 conference Zurich, innovators in the emerging field of psychopharmacology met to compare notes on their results with the new drugs. The organizer of the conference, Nathan Kline, was a psychodynamic psychiatrist, director of research at Rockland State Hospital in New York, and a professor of clinical psychiatry at Columbia University. "Are pharmacologic theories in contradiction to everything we have learned about psychodynamics?" asked Kline (1959: 18) in his introduction to the conference volume. "All the evidence is in the opposite direction," he emphatically answered. "What is needed," he continued, "is integrating concepts that might provide possible pathways of linkage between the two sets of facts."

The diverse set of contributions to the volume illustrated the broad-minded attempt of Kline and his colleagues to integrate the psychodynamic with the pharmacological. For instance, in "A Psychoanalytic Study of Phenothiazine

Action," William Winkelman (1959: 309) wrote: "It is time for us to treat [the patient's] personality and character structure with knowledge of the effects of drugs on the structures to be treated." Drugs, wrote Winkelman, did not have direct effects on the ego, but affected the energy available for the psychic structure. In an anecdote (ibid.: 312), he described how a patient, feeling better, wanted to discontinue psychotherapy: "It was explained to him that the relief was in symptoms only, and would not and could not eliminate the cause." Drugs operated on the surface, not on the depths of the condition—but work on the depths, which depended on the transference relation, might be facilitated by the medication. Under the influence of these new drugs, Winkelman argued, the relationship between the ego, the superego, and the id had to be reevaluated. One immediate result, he reported, was that the administration of tablets, whether drugs or placebos, fostered stronger transference.

In his own contribution, Kline (1959: 484) wrote of the varying psychodynamic effects of the new psychoactive medications: while reserpine allowed for the breakthrough of fairly deep material, chlorpromazine strengthened repressive mechanisms. However, both drugs were useful as disciplinary tools in the effort to do psychoanalysis with psychotic patients: "[C]hlorpromazine and reserpine make it possible to quiet the schizophrenic sufficiently so that he can enter into psychoanalysis and tolerate the temporary threats of id interpretations." As for the relation of surface to depth, "the drugs do not qualitatively alter the dynamic structure nor do they interfere with the analytic process." But this did not mean that the operations of the two domains were completely separate: the specific effect of the drugs was to reduce the *quantity* of instinctive drive, or psychic energy, and thus lessen the necessity of defense against unacceptable impulses. Thus, drug dosage could be manipulated in order to further the analytic process: "When the analysis loses its momentum, the dosage can be reduced until sufficient psychic pressure once again builds up. In this way the rate of analytic progress can be regulated by the analyst."

This moment of conceptual transaction between psychopharmacology and psychoanalysis proved short-lived, as the two disciplines diverged in the ensuing years. However, the use of the new drugs in clinical contexts continued to affect the direction of psychoanalytic theory, if in unstated ways. As the psychiatrist and historian Gladys Swain (1994) has pointed out, while the discovery of antipsychotic drugs in 1952 was the condition of possibility for the growth of psychoanalytic theory and practice with psychosis, medication is almost never mentioned in this work.

Kline's volume points to the underdetermined character of these medications' effects, from the vantage of expertise. As these early speculations indicate, the ideal of the contemporary biomedical paradigm in which pharmaceutical interventions match specific mental disorders was only one way the understanding of these drugs could unfold. Investigation of how these drugs operate in diverse clinical situations illuminates the relation between knowledge and technique in the practice of healing—and especially, the resilience and adaptability of epistemic forms.

El Mundo-Psi de Buenos Aires

While in the 1990s—the "Decade of the Brain" in the United States—neuro-science became the guiding ideal of North American psychiatry, Argentina presented a very different epistemic milieu. Perhaps the most striking feature of the Buenos Aires *mundo-psi* in the late 1990s was the prominence within it of Lacanian psychoanalysis, especially in the city's public hospitals and counseling centers. There were a number of explanations for the phenomenon. Some observers suggested that *lacanismo* was simply the latest fad in a long-running Argentinean fascination with psychoanalysis. Others, however, argued that the turn in the mental health community toward Lacan's hermetic philosophical system had been complicit with the military dictatorship's efforts to depoliticize the mental health field—that Lacanianism's detachment from social problems allowed it to survive the 'dirty war' period, while more engaged movements were brutally repressed by the dictatorship following the 1976 coup.

Historians have pointed to the structure of the city's mental health system and the politics of the professions over the previous half-century as an explanation for the rise of Lacan in Buenos Aires (see Plotkin 2001; Vezzetti 1996). Beginning in the 1950s, the orthodox Argentinean Psychoanalytic Association (APA) limited analytic practice to medical doctors. In turn, many clinical psychology graduates embraced Lacanian theory as a way to rebel against the strictures of the APA and to authorize themselves as analysts without medical training (Balan 1991). During the dictatorship period, Lacanians formed private study groups and were able to maintain their community outside of established institutions, so that when the Faculty of Psychology reopened in 1983 after the fall of the dictatorship, they were well placed to lead the institution. In the fluorescence of psychoanalysis that accompanied the democratic transition, these instructors trained literally thousands of psychology students. Meanwhile, prominent Lacanian physician-analysts entered the city's public hospital psychopathology services, which became important sites for postgraduate clinical training and for the production of psychoanalytic knowledge.

By the late 1990s, critics began to question the appropriateness of this institutionalized form of *lacanismo* as a public health practice in the city's hospitals. Soon after I arrived in Buenos Aires in 1998, the physicist and science warrior Alan Sokal came to the city to promote his new book, *Intellectual Imposters*, and delivered a lecture to a large audience at the University of Buenos Aires. As expected, Sokal decried the influence of postmodern cultural relativism and antiscientific thinking on progressive political thought. Moreover, he said, while this was merely an academic debate in the United States, in Buenos Aires, where Lacanian psychoanalysis dominated the mental health sector, it was a problem of public health. There were loud cheers from the audience.

Whatever its motivations, such criticism suggested a potential disjuncture between the resolutely pragmatic needs of the public hospital and the ethereal realm in which Buenos Aires *lacanismo* traveled. Sokal's accusation was echoed by several of the doctors at the hospital where I was doing ethnographic research on the collection of samples for a genetic study of bipolar disorder. Patients were often misdiagnosed and given the wrong medications, these doctors complained. More generally, they argued, an antiscientific ethos reigned among analytically oriented mental health professionals, such that it was impossible to adequately measure and efficiently approach the city's mental health needs. The problem was especially acute given the effects of structural adjustment policies and economic crisis on the public sector. They pointed across the entry corridor to the women's ward—the "Lacan ward," as one derisively called it—as an exemplary site for such malpractice. I began to do fieldwork in the women's ward, posing a question: How could this hermetic knowledge system be put to work in the context of the public hospital, whose infrastructure was crumbling and which took in patients from the most marginalized social classes?

The Medical Order

Located in a general hospital, Hospital Romero's psychopathology service was an outgrowth of postwar psychiatric reform in Argentina, whose aim was to shift patients from overcrowded asylums back into the community by replacing lifelong institutionalization with brief hospital stays and a decentralized network of care. The function of the in-patient ward at Romero was one of risk prevention: in making decisions as to whether to intern or to release patients, doctors had to balance the threat of suicide or violence—which was the justification for hospitalization—against the institutional logic of limited hospitalization times. While doctors were instructed to move patients through—in Lorna Rhodes's (1991) phrase, to produce "empty beds"—and there were attempts by the municipal government to audit the length of patient stays, these remained considerably longer than in comparable institutions in the United States.[1] In the women's ward, patients were sometimes hospitalized for as long as four or five months at public expense. If a case seemed to be intractable, the patient might then be transferred to the city's main psychiatric hospital for women, Moyano, labeled a *manicomio*, insane asylum, by the doctors at Romero.

Such requirements formed part of what physician-analysts called "the medical order"—the set of bureaucratic demands regulating institutional action.[2] As Alicia Fiorentino, one of the physician-analysts, put it: "In the hospital, we have to operate within a specific juridical discourse in which we diagnose and medicate the crisis, and then control it." Physician-analysts occupied an ambiguous position: on the one hand, they were authorized to direct the institution because of their official certification as medical doctors within the order of a public hospital. But their formal status as physicians often came into tension with their professional identity as psychoanalysts: the filling out of forms, medication decisions, and patients' somatic complaints interfered with what seemed to be more crucial work on patient subjectivities. At a more superficial level, the urbane, professorial habitus of the analysts contrasted sharply with the harried disrepair of the doctors in the men's ward.

Public hospitals in Argentina provided both steady (if very modest) incomes and a source of prestige for physician-analysts,since they remained central sites of medical training and knowledge production. On the other hand, employment in a psychopathology ward carried certain dangers. While membership in the analytic community connoted cosmopolitan sophistication and political progressivism, biomedical psychiatry was associated with the medical-penal order, with violent techniques such as shock treatment and lobotomy, and with the fearful space of the asylum. For this reason, physician-analysts tended to resist any ties to biomedical psychiatry. If one was both employed in a psychopathology ward and politically progressive, to insist on being an analyst—and *not* a psychiatrist—was a way to avoid the stigma associated with the asylum.

There were twenty beds in the women's ward, and patients slept in parallel rows of wooden cubicles that led toward a meeting room in the back. The open-door policy of the ward meant that patients could move about the hospital grounds during the day but had to have permission to go beyond, into the city. Doctors came in only during the morning, while nurses, residents and voluntary interns managed the patients the rest of the time. In the afternoon, the doctors typically returned to offices in more prosperous Barrio Norte or Palermo where they saw private clients, often working twelve to fourteen hours per day. The staff gathered at least once a week to discuss the progress of the patients. In the meeting room, the orientation of the staff was clear: framed photos of Freud and Lacan stared down from the back wall. A computer was used, sometimes to track patients, but also to look up references from a complete index to Lacan's seminars.

Meetings, workshops, classes, and patient presentations provided some solace from the din of the ward itself. One psychology resident called it "the trenches," a term that called attention to the difficulties of defending a sheltered space of thought from the disorder of the ward. In these gatherings, however, the medical order would often impinge from outside: insistent banging on the door by patients, babies' cries, visits from hospital administrators or pharmaceutical company representatives. And it was also within: the patients under discussion had typically been hospitalized either by judicial order, because of suicide risk, or due to questions about the source of somatic syndromes. On particularly chaotic mornings, the head of the ward, Jorge Gitel, would do his best Robin Williams imitation, calling out "Good morning, Vietnam!" in English. Dark humor was one way to deal with the ironies of the situation. "Another success for psychoanalysis!" he would exclaim when patients failed to improve.

In this context, with neither contract nor couch, there was no question of actually doing psychoanalysis with patients. Nonetheless, the hospital was a space, if not for training analysts, then at least for maintaining analytic identity. This was a challenge, given that patients in the hospital were far from ideal analysands. It was accomplished through a strict distinction between the work of the doctor and that of the analyst, which mapped onto a separation between the body and the subjectivity of the patient. Medication, as the means for managing symptoms so that subjectivity could be investigated, played a crucial but unspoken part in sustaining this distinction.

Structuralist Dualism

"What I can't explain is how one could have a theoretical construct like *lacan-ismo* and medicate heavily without having your head explode." Alejandro Noailles, the director of the psychopathology department, was describing the seemingly contradictory practices of his colleagues in the women's ward. The issue in the ward was not whether or not to use medication. Patients who are hospitalized in a psychiatric ward are not those who raise the question of 'cosmetic psychopharmacology', because their suffering is quite obvious and severe.[3] But the everyday use of medication was not much discussed in staff meetings, perhaps because it was not especially interesting: transformations effected by medication did not provide material for analytic conversation.

Psychopharmacology was considered to be part of 'psychiatric' discourse, an element of the normalizing medical order. This did not mean that physician-analysts were opposed to medication, but rather that psychoanalysis and pharmacology could not be in dialogue. They might coexist, each in its proper sphere. "Medication works on the symptom, but not the subject—the neuron is the medium of subjectivity, but they are not the same," explained Gabriel, a psychologist. It was not that he was against psychiatry, said Norberto Gomez, one of the staff doctors. He was interested in psychiatry and psychopharmacology, but did not agree with the erasure of subjectivity: "They are different realms. To medicate a symptom does not require one to stop investigating subjectivity."

Medication took form in the ward as an element of an individualizing technology: it worked on the body, in order to help produce the subject as a speaking being. As Fiorentino told me, whereas "neuroscientists give medication so that patients don't speak, I give it to help them speak." Liliana Hirsch echoed this. Medication "can allow the patient to speak," she said. "It helps when it accompanies speech." "When a psychosis is unraveling," a psychology resident told me, "medication is a necessary intervention—in order to be able to work by using speech." Patients were medicated in order to be calm and manageable enough to engage in some form of talk therapy.

Gitel explained the division of labor between pharmacology and speech in the following way: "I think that psychopharmaceuticals operate to lower the threshold of sensitivity of the stimulus response, but do not operate on the reader. So I can medicate and change the hormonal or neural equilibrium of the apparatus, but the reader, who is the producer of the delusion, is an effect that I don't think is regulated by the neurochemical but is this subject. The delusion comes from here"—from the subject. For Gitel, medication treated only the symptoms, not the structure of the illness. To do work on the psychotic structure, it was necessary to distinguish problems of the organism from questions of subjectivity.

He described the relation between the biological organism and the subject in Lacanian psychoanalysis as "a dualism, not idealist but structuralist, in which there is no suture between the apparatus of the central nervous system and the reader." The physician treated the brain with molecules, while the analyst dealt with the patient's psyche. I asked Gitel, who is a jazz musician, if it was difficult to reconcile the two roles of physician and analyst. He replied: "It is like listening to a concert in two or three planes: on the one hand you listen to the harmony, and on the other you listen to the melody and on the other, you also listen to the texture. But yes, you have to be a good musician to hear so many planes."

"Psychoanalysis listens for the particularities of the patient," said Cecilia, a psychology resident, "while the pill is for everything. In this point the two discourses are incompatible: in how to understand the subject. Psychiatry thinks it knows and the patient doesn't, whereas psychoanalysis says the patient is the one who knows." But what if the patient claimed to have a certain disorder? I asked. She replied that this was a knowledge that was difficult to access: "Unconscious knowledge is a knowledge that is unrecognized [*desconocido*] by the patient." It was difficult for patients to act as experts about their own condition, as unconscious structure could emerge only in the therapeutic encounter. Patients who claimed such authority were often considered 'contaminated' either by analytic categories or by biological ones.[4]

I was especially interested in moments when the models of the patients came into conflict with those of the analysts. In one case, a woman with obsessive rituals seemed to be more interested in talking with the psychologist about her current symptoms than about her past. There was a specific sequence of rituals the patient had to perform in order to avoid contamination. She washed her hands repeatedly, for hours at a time, including at the hospital. Fiorentino thought that it was a very grave case: "There is no subjective commitment," and so no possibility of transference. While the attending therapist tried to work on the rituals, the doctors were more interested in the problem of contamination, in the idea underlying these symptoms. What kinds of objects were contaminated? What was the significance of the number of stages of contamination?

"Putting oneself in the symptoms won't do anything," advised Gomez. In doing so, "one is sustaining the pleasure of the symptoms." The psychologist should work instead on questions of subjectivity: "What is the structure?" "We could 'arm' the rituals," someone suggested. That is, if it was a psychosis, the intervention might use the rituals to reinforce the patient's delicate defenses.[5] "The rituals take five or six hours," noted Cecilia. "Maybe we can arm something else?" "The only observation, in the psychoanalytic sense, would be not the rituals but the obsessions," said Gitel. "She doesn't talk about her history," Cecilia explained. "For her, what's going on is genetic, organic." The patient was, it seemed, something of an expert in psychiatric semiology. She claimed to have obsessive-compulsive disorder, and said that it was an organic condition. "She speaks of Henri Ey and manic-depression, about the genetic sources of her illness," Cecilia reported. "If we go that way," warned Gitel, "we won't get anywhere. We need to look at the life of the signifier. She cannot reside in speech if she thinks it's genetic. She is not going to talk to you if she doesn't know that it is overdetermined by speech." "She says that it's a chronic illness, that it needs to be medicated," said Cecilia. "This is a match," Gitel responded.

"She is a calculating subject: she is the genetic, and you are the psychologist. Unless she is neurotic, the match is equal—genetics versus speech."

The Specificity of the Case

Biomedical psychiatry posed the threat that human subjectivity, in its particularity and individuality, would be ignored by the homogenizing techniques of science. As Gomez put it: "Without any doubt, methodologically, science necessarily tries to exclude subjectivity. In the scientific method, subjectivity cannot be implicit, which doesn't mean that science is not useful. But in the field of psychoanalysis, this logic doesn't have any space." The objection of psychoanalysts in Romero to neuroscience and genetics as sources of knowledge in treating psychopathology was to their refusal to admit that humans are distinctive.

Fiorentino explained why psychoanalytic knowledge was incommensurable with that of biomedicine: "The subject of desire is what is left out of psychiatry, and is what psychoanalysis concerns itself with." The patient's language was the site for finding this subject: "In medicine they look at the sign and are not interested in hearing the patient speak," said Fiorentino. "Psychoanalytic symptoms," on the other hand, "are read through words." The human transcended the organism, and language was what was universal within the human individual. Because people speak, they could never be studied in the same way as animals.[6]

The crucial distinction to be made from biomedical psychiatry was the analyst's orientation to the specificity and uniqueness of each patient. As Fiorentino told me, "Psychoanalysis differs from psychiatry because it is interested in the individual case as its clinical object, not in generalized diagnostic categories. Each madness has its own logic."

Philosopher John Forrester (1996) describes psychoanalysis as an example of "thinking in cases." This way of thinking forms a distinctive "style of reasoning," as opposed to deductive logic or probabilistic analysis. Rather than seeking to apply general principles to a given situation, case reasoning uses exemplars as models for approaching an otherwise uncertain object. Importantly, Forrester points out, sciences of the case not only study individuals, but also participate in their production. In hospital psychiatry, he notes, the patient's file is not just a source for understanding the patient's past, but in fact produces that past in concrete form, in the written traces left by consecutive doctors and therapists.[7]

A set of paradigmatic cases described by Freud served as exemplars for analysts' encounters with their patients in the women's ward. Cases were produced around practices of writing and metaphors of reading. The thick folders of repeatedly admitted patients contained psychiatrists' changing diagnoses, the notes of various analysts, and medication histories. The process of formulating an understanding of the patient's subjective structure was spoken of as a 'reading'. However, in the hospital one did not encounter texts but rather patients, and they were generally in bad shape, not immediately willing to provide adequate narratives. They were often silent or crying, sometimes heavily sedated. These were not the Viennese bourgeoisie of Freud's divan. Typically, they were not emotionally, intellectually, or economically equipped to be psychoanalytic patients in the classical sense.

In order to take part in something like psychoanalytic work, patients had to be assimilated to discursive needs. This meant soliciting analyzable stories from patients, stories that were structurally analogous to the texts. 'Interesting' patients were those whose stories were available, and who made an analytic reading possible. Producing such narratives was a complex labor, involving hours of listening to patients' speech. Most of this listening was done not by the physician-analysts but by voluntary interns and psychology residents, who compiled patient narratives and abstracted them in files, reports, and patient presentations. An oversupply of psychoanalytically trained clinical psychologists in the labor market made it possible to do such time-intensive work, given the limited resources of the public health system.[8]

What the case eventually revealed were the patients' specific 'routes of subjectivity'. Independent of the physical body, subjectivity was common to all persons but always distinctively individual. "Psychoanalysis points at something irreducible in a human being—subjectivity. Subjectivity is of each one; it is the most personal of each one," said Gomez. "What one tries to read in the discourse of the patient is not the history of the patient, but the impressions of subjectivity in the history of the patient—these points of rupture in the story [*historia*], the posture of each one in front of his own story." The temporal frame of the life history directed the analyst back to past events that underlay the patient's current predicament.

Authorization and Experience

What authorized analysts to perform this special form of listening? How did they gain access to patients' 'routes of subjectivity'—an access denied to the patients themselves? In psychoanalysis, subjectivity (of the analyst) and truth are linked in a way that is quite distinct from the ideal of the natural sciences, in which the world itself is supposed to testify to the validity of a truth-claim. Here one finds a complex relationship between the ongoing authority of the founding texts of the discipline and the process of discovery, within the self of the analyst, of the truth of the founders' claims. And while Lacan proclaimed that "the psychoanalyst is authorized only by himself," this work can be accomplished only in relation to a master, and the passage has a pregiven structure and set of institutional preconditions (Roudinesco 1997: 338). In Romero, analysts' explanation of the grounds for their interpretations and interventions relied upon their experience of the training analysis. One physician-analyst at Romero described the process of self-authorization: "It does not have to do with what he has read or with what another tells him or with what a title authorizes him to do, but with his own experience of analysis, of having located in his analysis the routes of his own subjectivity. This brings him to position himself as an analyst for another."

According to philosopher Isabelle Stengers (1997: 90–91), by making access to knowledge dependent on the experience of the analytic scene, psychoanalysis claims the privilege of not needing to give an explanation. "At the heart of the analytic scene there appears to function a very curious 'black box': the analytic scene itself," she writes. "The analytic scene appears to create those who will have the right to speak about it, and therefore operates in itself as the foundation of right." Psychoanalytic authorization thus has characteristics of both *ascesis* and revelation: it requires a specific kind of work on the self to discover within oneself the truth of Freud's discovery (Freud 1973: 326) that the ego "is not even master in its own house, but must content itself with scanty information of what is going on unconsciously in its mind." This ambivalence between discovered and revealed truth has rendered psychoanalysis susceptible to both proclamations of scientific status and accusations of religiosity.

Classification and Intervention

In order to decide what sort of intervention to make, analysts had to know what they had before them. The psychic structure indicated the position of the subject, which in turn directed the strategy of the analyst. The initial task, then, was to classify the patient according to one of the basic psychic structures outlined by Freud. This was quite different, analysts emphasized, from making a 'psychiatric' diagnosis, which was done only for bureaucratic purposes.

The most important structural distinction to make was between neurosis and psychosis. Whereas with neurotic patients one could work with the tool of transference, there was, according to Freud, no possibility of achieving transference in psychosis.[9] Freud (1961 [1924]: 149) explained the difference between the two structures in terms of the site of psychic conflict: "Neurosis is the result of a conflict between the ego and the id," he wrote—that is, an internal psychic conflict—whereas "psychosis is the outcome of a disturbance in the relations between the ego and the external world." The split between the ego and the outside world accounted for the separation from reality that marked psychosis. The resulting delusion "is the patch that covers this breach in the relation between the ego and the external world." At a basic level, then, the presence of delusion was an indication of psychosis. Moreover, the implication was that such delusion performed an important role in allowing the psychotic patient to function despite his or her "loss of reality." This made it a delicate problem to work with psychotic patients: one did not want to strip patients of their defenses.

For Lacan (1981), translating Freud's spatial scheme into linguistic terms, psychosis was characterized by a failure to enter the symbolic order. He described a process of "foreclosure" in which an unwanted thought or image was expelled rather than repressed, a refusal of symbolization that had catastrophic effects. Lacan located the emergence of the psychotic delusion in this inability to internalize the superego, or "Name-of-the-Father" function, through repression (cited in Bowie 1991: 108–109): "It is the lack of the Name-of-the-Father in that place which, by the hole that it opens up in the signified, sets off the cascade of reshapings of the signifier from which the increasing disaster of the imaginary proceeds, until the level is reached at which signifier and signified are stabilized in the delusional metaphor." Cast outside of the symbolic order, the psychotic remained in a condition of ontological otherness, unable to enter into intersubjective relations.

In a lecture to a group of medical students, Gitel outlined his approach to psychosis. Psychosis is not an illness, he said, but is, rather, the patient's position in front of reality: "Hallucination is the lived language of the subject." The patient's delusion is an attempt to restore lost ties with reality, a "restitution." And since there is no transference in psychosis, one cannot work with the tools of traditional psychoanalysis. In fact, Gitel warned against treating psychotic patients as one might treat neurotics, by trying to use transference; in doing this, one might unleash the psychosis further, destabilize it. It was thus important to identify the structure early on. Neither medication nor psychoanalytic treatment could cure the psychotic. "Delusion is not medicable," said Gitel, "because, fortunately, there is no idea that can be changed by a pharmaceutical. What lowers is the level of anxiety, of anguish, and the productivity that this generates."

Gitel described the temporality of psychosis, based on a moment of rupture. He drew a schema of the history of a psychosis, in which there is a 'before' and 'after' the unraveling: "This episode represents a break with reality." It could take several months of hospitalization for the patient to take on this history, a process that included sessions with the patient at which notes were taken, weekly meetings, perhaps a workshop, and the therapists' external supervisions. Gradually, a collaborative interpretation emerged.

How did this theoretical understanding of psychosis—and the seeming impossibility of its treatment—relate to the pragmatic task of dealing with psychotic patients in the hospital? What did a psychoanalytic approach look like in a situation in which the technology of psychoanalytic cure—the transference relation—was explicitly inoperative?

"Psychosis is a limitation of psychoanalysis," admitted Liliana Hirsch, another physician-analyst in Romero. "It is a tool that helps me to think the subjective position of the psychotic. You cannot apply the same thing to a neurosis as to a psychosis. One does a 'deconstruction' with psychoanalysis. People criticize the use of psychoanalysis in psychosis with the idea of using a couch—this is not done, it would be a barbarity."

"In psychosis, a cure through therapy is not possible," said Gabriel, "but one can stabilize it." As opposed to neurosis, the treatment for psychosis was not based in interpretation. The object was not to expand the delusion further by talking about it, but rather to deflate it. In fact, the act of therapeutic intervention could have a dangerous effect on the patient. "Speech can perform an unraveling," explained Gabriel. "One has to be careful with psychotics," said

Rosana, a psychology resident, "it doesn't help to listen to them." As an alternative, the idea of 'arming' the psychotic patient emerged as a kind of adaptive therapeutic form for treating psychotic patients in the hospital. Analysts in the women's ward tried to help these patients 'construct a fiction' that would enable them to manage in the outside world.

At one meeting, Gitel presented a patient who was hospitalized after a walk-in consultation. The woman said that she had bipolar disorder and needed to be on the *plan de bipolars* (i.e., mood-stabilizing medication). She lived with her parents and child, and had suspended use of her medication during a sexual relationship with her neighbor. The incident with the neighbor apparently unleashed her psychosis. She had delusions of persecution—fantasies of pregnancy and AIDS. The delusions had to do with the neighbor's look: she felt watched and couldn't leave her house at night. After the relationship, she felt dirty, undignified. The patient thought that it was a matter of medication, but Gitel argued that there were questions about the structure of persecution, concerning her relationship with the neighbor. "It is endogamous," said Gitel, referring to the father and the neighbor, "let's try to move it to a more exogamous logic."

The woman asked for antidepressants: she is very "psychiatried"—"a good student of bipolar discourse," said Fiorentino. Though she was being medicated with mood stabilizers and antidepressants, the doctors agreed that it was a 'structural question': she was neither manic nor melancholic. Over the next weeks, the psychologist uncovered a conflictive situation with the father: when she was an adolescent, the father had looked at her "not with a father's eyes." She felt fat, ugly: the problem related to food—there was a scene in the kitchen with the father. "There is this desire, this imperious necessity to be with a man," said the psychologist. A month after her arrival, the delusions continued. She was convinced that she was pregnant and that the neighbor was the father. Gitel decided to add an antipsychotic to her mood stabilizer. He said that it was an interesting case, diagnostically. She had come in with a diagnosis of bipolar disorder, but there were other phenomena, delusions having to do with electricity. She was disaggregated, with persecutory thoughts about her father. She spoke of being controlled. After the separation, there was the signifier of the look, a sense of persecution. The psychologist located the unleashing of the psychosis in terms of the father's control of meals. By late April, it became clear to her that the patient did not metaphorize: it was a case of psychosis.

Bipolarity

The status of bipolar disorder was a source of controversy among doctors with differing theoretical orientations at Romero. In the men's ward, the condition was widely diagnosed, and was the subject of the transnational genetic study that had initially led me to the hospital. Within a biomedical framework, bipolar disorder is seen as a problem of mood regulation, in which the patient moves between states of intense agitation and heightened sensibility to periods of serious depression and withdrawal. Unlike schizophrenia, bipolar disorder does not necessarily have a dire prognosis. It is potentially treatable—though not curable—with mood stabilizers, and there is speculation that the disorder is linked to particularly creative personalities, to well-known artists and writers such as Van Gogh and Edgar Allan Poe.[10] For the patient, it is thus a preferable diagnosis to receive than schizophrenia.

But what is its relation to the structural categories of psychoanalysis? While Freud wrote of mania and melancholia, these cannot easily be assimilated to the DSM definition of bipolar disorder. In fact, the latter has the potential to disrupt the strict differentiation made in psychoanalysis between neurotic and psychotic structure. This is because in the manic phase of bipolar disorder, the patient may suffer delusions and hallucinations that recede when the patient is stabilized with medication. The *content* of delusion is not important to the diagnosis or treatment of bipolar disorder; since it is a question of mood, rather than thought, it is the patient's bodily chemistry rather than the subject and its history that is the source of pathology.

According to the doctors in the men's ward, the diagnosis of bipolar disorder implied a different relationship between psychiatrist and patient than did schizophrenia—or for that matter, psychosis. Since bipolar patients functioned well on mood stabilizers, they could potentially manage their own medication. They might then take on a certain role of authority in treating their own condition. The patient, these doctors thought, should be seen as a health consumer, and doctors as service providers.

These doctors encouraged the formation of patient groups and the active production of 'biosocial' identity with respect to bipolar disorder. According to this model, a potential effect of medication was to help shape patient self-identity: those whose condition was improved by a specific drug began to understand themselves in its terms. Medication, rather than the investigation of unconscious conflict, seemed for such patients a more likely path to health.[11]

In contrast, bipolar disorder was something of a dubious category for the analysts across the hall in the women's ward. Liliana Hirsch implied that the diagnosis had been invented to help sell psychopharmaceuticals. "The fashion of bipolarity is winning because it is something so objectifiable," she said. "The politics of psychiatry is correlated to the consumption of psychopharmaceuticals: 'bipolarity' justifies an exaggerated quantity of pharmaceutical consumption."

Gitel had a more ambivalent view. He accepted the existence of bipolar disorder but did not see it as commensurable with the analysis of patients in terms of their subjective structures. He considered bipolar disorder to be a physical condition that could exist parallel to either of the Freudian structures of neurosis and psychosis. He could thus speak of mania in the psychoanalytic sense and bipolar disorder as two distinct aspects of a patient. For instance, Gitel and Rosana discussed a patient who had stopped eating, who became obsessed with death following a car accident. "She doesn't think she's ill," explained Rosana. The patient was insomniac, disturbing other patients at night. "It is a mania, in the more Lacanian sense," explained Gitel. "The accident produced a question in the Real. And she's also bipolar."

Noailles attacked the notion that one could separate medication issues from structural diagnosis. One contaminated the other, he said. Diagnosis in analytic terms was often used to make medication decisions. Physician-analysts diagnosed psychosis in structural terms, then prescribed antipsychotic medication to alleviate the symptoms. This meant that delusional symptoms in bipolar disorder led inexorably to the use of antipsychotics—and in Argentina, this usually meant the cheaper, older-generation drugs whose side effects, such as Parkinsonism, could be devastating. He thought there was a public health disaster in Argentina, in which large numbers of patients were kept sedated and unnecessarily institutionalized through misdiagnosis and the wrong medication. This, for Noailles, was the scandal of treating hospitalized patients psychoanalytically. "If you're Lacanian, you always diagnose psychosis," he said. "There's no choice, because the texture of the theory brings you to it. It is inevitable—'the elemental phenomenon, non-dialectizable'—and then you go and give halpidol or olanzapine."

What happened when these different positions encountered one another? It is illustrative to look at the case of a member of the Argentinean bipolar patient support group (FUBIPA) who was hospitalized in the women's ward in a manic state. The young woman, Marta, initially tried to educate her doctors about bipolar disorder, giving them literature from the support group and asking for lithium treatment. She was a particularly difficult patient, with many outbursts requiring attendance by the residents and tranquilizing medication. And although she was given mood stabilizers and other drugs, her condition seemed to worsen during her stay at the hospital.

Marta's disturbances could be read in various ways. Sebastian, the medical resident who was treating her, described her as a "resistant bipolar," that is, a bipolar patient for whom the standard medication indications did not work. For him, this implied that one should experiment with other drug combinations— perhaps an atypical antipsychotic combined with a mood stabilizer. "Nothing can be accomplished here through chemicals," responded Fiorentino. "One can medicate for bipolarity," she said early on, "but not for hysteria." For her, to call the patient a "resistant bipolar" was to ignore the singularity of the case. "This is the thing about human beings," she told me, "they talk. And they thus become unique—you cannot place them in clear categories."

Marta's symptoms had different possible meanings. If she spent too much money, this might be a characteristic of bipolar disorder, or it could be that she was 'performing' its symptoms, since she knew the disorder's characteristics so well. Alcohol abuse? Again, it could be part of the bipolar symptomatology or else an identification with her deceased father, who had been an alcoholic. The questions that were posed among the staff had to do not with medication, but with her personal life: Why did she identify with men? What had happened in her love relations? Why did she think the hospital staff was uninterested in her? Because she reported hearing her dead father's voice, the possibility was raised of a psychosis. The psychologist noted that the first episode of her illness had come not long after her father's death, and so the problem of unfinished mourning became an axis of reflection in the case (Freud 1957 [1917]).

Gitel distinguished Marta's bipolar disorder from the "structural" issues involved in the case: there was perhaps a problem with her central nervous system, but the real question had to do with the subject. "It is a problem with love," he said. "She is bipolar, but what is the structure here?" he asked. "There is something more than being bipolar. It is a Freudian mania." As for medication, he wanted to be "empirical." "Let's go with a classic," he proposed—an anxiolytic and an antipsychotic.

Like her father, Marta was a poet, and her writings were seen as a possible place for "building a sustainable fiction" in order to construct a workable subjectivity and come to terms with her ambiguous sexuality. But the case became less hopeful as time passed, and her actions grew more extreme: she attempted suicide twice within the hospital grounds, once by cutting her wrists with sharp rocks, and later with an overdose of medication. She routinely created scenes in the ward by throwing herself against the walls and furniture, and residents were instructed not to speak with her, but to directly inject tranquilizing medication.

"She doesn't have anguish in a Lacanian sense, something one could work with," Fiorentino worried. "This delusion, this mania, what can we do with it?" In time, the staff agreed to describe her as having a "borderline personality"—a structure between neurosis and psychosis.[12] A psychology resident told me: "The bipolar disorder is child's play compared to the personality disorder she has."

Eventually, a bureaucratic problem arose: Marta had been interned more than sixty-nine days, and special paperwork was required to keep her longer. In the space of the clinic, such demands came from the administrative rationality of the medical order, oriented toward reintegrating patients into society. As Fiorentino told me, "They think that by limiting internment times they can make psychotics into normal people." But it was impossible: "There is no social space for the psychotic."

"Maybe she needs a change," someone suggested. As the crises continued, the staff prepared to give up and began the process of transferring her to the infamous women's asylum, Moyano. "But what can they do for her in Moyano?" someone asked. There was no answer. "There just are patients like this," said Fiorentino to console Marta's psychologist.

Then, quite suddenly, Marta improved and was released by the end of the month. Sebastian attributed the change to the correct medication formulation—valproate and clozapine—while Paula, the psychologist, thought it had to do with a change in the therapeutic strategy, which had enabled her to face the problem of mourning in a new way. Marta left as she had arrived, without a definitive diagnosis or course of treatment. It was not clear whether her improvement was due to the medication, to the psychologist's approach, or to the threat of a transfer to Moyano.

Conclusion

In the hospital, the distinction between neurosis and psychosis worked to differentiate normal from pathological, as Gitel noted in his lecture: "Eighty to 90 percent of us have neurotic structures. The rest are psychotic or perverse." Bipolar disorder and its treatment raised the question of whether a patient could move, via pharmaceutical intervention, from one state to the other, from psychotic to neurotic. Whether or not medication—in this case, a mood stabilizer—transformed the person, or rather what kind of transformation it effected, depended upon what stance the expert held vis-à-vis the configuration of the human person.

Given structuralist dualism, the pharmaceutical altered neither the delusion of the patient nor the knowledge system of the doctor. As Gitel said, "There is no idea that can be changed by a pharmaceutical." Bipolarity and psychosis could exist, side by side, in the organism and the subject respectively. The pharmaceutical worked on the organism so that humanness, as language—that which is impervious to chemical intervention—could emerge. It enabled the subject to speak. But then when the patient spoke, it was often in the language of neuroscience and genetics. The 'match' between genetics and speech was a contest not only over how to name the disorder, but also over who would be in charge of applying the medication and to what end.

Structuralist dualism was a solution to the difficulty, in the public hospital, of being both a physician and an analyst. It allowed the realm of subjectivity to be bracketed off from the medical order, and medication mediated this function. The danger, as Noailles warned, was that in devoting themselves to the task of being analysts rather than physicians, the experts might produce more harm than good.

Referring to the Sokal debate, one psychiatrist from the men's ward told me: "We shouldn't be worrying about postmodernism here in Argentina—we need to meet basic health needs." He was pointing to the country's ambiguous status between developed and underdeveloped, and arguing that certain kinds of questions were not relevant in the space of the Buenos Aires public hospital—given the very palpable differences between health infrastructures in Argentina and in the North.[13] This issue was palpable when the doctors in the women's ward shut the door to the clinic and began to talk—not only about Freud and Lacan, but also about Spinoza, Hegel, Derrida. You could almost forget that you were in a crumbling hospital in a marginal sector of the city, with patients who were often illiterate. What did it mean, then, to turn this ward into a space for practicing philosophy? The ironic use of medication—to sustain subjectivity rather than to transform pathology—made the hospital a place where one could remain an analyst, despite the exigencies of the medical order.

The question of the task of the healer and the role of the drug hinged on where to locate disorder. Was it in the organism or in language? If it was in language, treatment demanded an art that could never be encompassed by neuroscience. The attempt to make psychiatry a science was doomed, for Lacanians in Romero, because humans are a particular kind of being, "differentiated from animals by their use of speech," as Gitel put it. Or as Fiorentino said, "A mouse can have heart disease but it cannot be hysteric."

ACKNOWLEDGMENTS

I would like to thank Paul Antze and Michael Lambek for the invitation to participate in the panel "Illness and Irony," at the 2001 meetings of the Canadian Anthropology Society in Montreal. This work is based on field research conducted in Buenos Aires in 1998 and 1999. The names are pseudonyms. The research and writing of this material was supported by grants from the National Science Foundation and the Townsend Humanities Center at University of California, Berkeley.

NOTES

1. See also Luhrmann (2000) for a description of pressures toward increasingly short inpatient stays in U.S. hospitals.
2. The oft-mentioned reference for this term was the book by French critic Jean Clavreul (1978).
3. See Peter Kramer's (1993) classic discussion of the use of antidepressants to make people feel "better than well" in *Listening to Prozac*.
4. Lacan (1981: 48) was explicit that the analyst should not take seriously the patient's self-description. Understanding was not the point of the analytic relation: "If I understand I continue, I don't dwell on it, since I've already understood," he wrote in his seminar on the psychoses. "This brings out what it is to enter the patient's game—it is to collaborate in his resistance. The patient's resistance is always your own, and when a resistance succeeds it is because you are in it up to your neck, because you understand. You understand, you are wrong." See also Roustang (1990).
5. I describe the difference between psychosis and neurosis below.
6. As Lacan put it (1977: 264), humans are "an animal at the mercy of language."
7. Here Forrester cites Foucault's (1977) work on writing practices and the entrance of individuals into the field of knowledge in nineteenth-century clinical medicine. In a similar vein, Ian Hacking (1995), writing of the dissemination of psychoanalysis, analyzes the way in which life histories entered governmental administration as part of the emergence of "memoro-politics" in the nineteenth and twentieth centuries.
8. Given the lack of employment opportunities for psychology graduates, entrance to the city's clinical psychology residency program was highly competitive. Of twelve hundred applicants each year, twenty-five received posts. Most residents told me that they chose to come to Romero because of its reputation: it was known in psychoanalytic circles for its Lacanian orientation.
9. Some post-Freudians such as Wilfred Bion claimed that transference in psychosis was possible.
10. And in the United States, as Emily Martin (1999) has noted, to CEOs.

11. The patient's assertion of a biological identity that is potentially manipulable through self-alteration differs from sociobiological determinisms, as Paul Rabinow (1996) has indicated.
12. The validity of this category was also subject to debate. Some Argentinean psychiatrists dismissed it as a *bolso de gatos*, a grab bag. One widely read North American bipolar disorder expert recommended treating such cases as bipolar patients. See Akiskal (1996).
13. The argument could also have been applied to the seemingly placeless discourse on 'postmodernity' being produced among some Argentinean intellectuals. See, for example, Sarlo (2001).

REFERENCES

Akiskal, H. S. 1996. "The Prevalent Clinical Spectrum of Bipolar Disorders: Beyond DSM-IV. *Journal of Clinical Psychopharmacology* 16, no. 2: suppl. 1, 4S-14S.

Balan, J. 1991. *Cuentame tu vida: Una biografia colectiva del psicoanalisis argentino*. Buenos Aires: Planeta.

Bowie, M. 1991. *Lacan*. Cambridge: Harvard University Press.

Clavreul, J. 1978. *L'ordre médical*. Paris: Seuil.

Forrester, J. 1996. "If *p*, Then What? Thinking in Cases." *History of the Human Sciences* 9:3.

Foucault, M. 1977. *Discipline and Punish: The Birth of the Prison*. Translated by A. Sheridan. New York: Pantheon.

Freud, S. 1957 [1917]. "Mourning and Melancholia." In *The Standard Edition of the Complete Psychological Works of Sigmund Freud*, vol. 14, edited by J. Strachey. London: Hogarth Press.

———. 1961 [1924]. "Neurosis and Psychosis." In *The Standard Edition of the Complete Psychological Works of Sigmund Freud*, vol. 19, edited by J. Strachey. London: Hogarth Press.

———. 1973. *Introductory Lectures on Psychoanalysis*. Harmondsworth: Pelican.

Hacking, I. 1995. *Rewriting the Soul: Multiple Personality and the Sciences of Memory*. Princeton: Princeton University Press.

Kline, N. S., ed. 1959. *Psychopharmacology Frontiers*. Boston and Toronto: Little, Brown and Company.

Kramer, P. 1993. *Listening to Prozac*. New York: Penguin.

Lacan, J. 1977. *Écrits: a selection*. Translated by Alan Sheridan. New York: Norton.

———. 1981. *Seminar, Book III: The Psychoses*. Edited by J.-A. Miller. Translated by R. Grigg. New York: Norton.

Luhrmann, T. M. 2000. *Of Two Minds: The Growing Disorder in American Psychiatry*. New York: Knopf.

Martin, E. 1999. "Flexible Survivors." *Anthropology News* (September): 5–7.

Plotkin, M. B. 2001. *Freud in the Pampas: The Emergence and Development of a Psychoanalytic Culture in Argentina*. Stanford: Stanford University Press.

Rabinow, P. 1996. *Essays on the Anthropology of Reason*. Princeton: Princeton University Press.

Rhodes, L. A. 1991. *Emptying Beds: The Work of an Emergency Psychiatric Unit*. Berkeley: University of California Press.

Roudinesco, E. 1997. *Jacques Lacan*. Translated by B. Bray. New York: Columbia University Press.

Roustang, F. 1990. *The Lacanian Delusion*. Translated by G. Sims. New York: Oxford University Press.

Sarlo, B. 2001. *Scenes from Postmodern Life*. Translated by J. Beasley-Murray. Minneapolis: University of Minnesota Press.

Stengers, I. 1997. *Power and Invention: Situating Science*. Minneapolis: University of Minnesota Press.

Swain, G. 1994. *Dialogue avec l'insense: Essais d'histoire de la psychiatrie*. Paris: Gallimard.

Vezzetti, H. 1996. *Aventuras de Freud en el Pais de los Argentinos: De Jose Ingenieros a Enrique Pichon-Riviere*. Buenos Aires: Paidos.

Winkelman, W. 1959. "A Psychoanalytic Study of Phenothiazine Action." In *Psychopharmacology Frontiers*, edited by N. Kline. Boston and Toronto: Little, Brown and Company.

Chapter 5

ILLNESS AS IRONY IN PSYCHOANALYSIS

Paul Antze

If psychoanalysis can be said to yield knowledge, then it is certainly a knowledge laced with irony. At the most obvious level, this is the irony of contrast and incongruity, an irony that seems to revel in showing up the low origins of high things, the identity of opposites, and the sway of deep and disconcerting forces over the most trivial events of daily life. This is the irony that, notoriously, sees religion as obsessional neurosis, children as sexual perverts, civilization as disease, and the claims of conscience as inverted wishes for incest and parricide. It is an irony with a sharp edge and a clearly subversive impulse—an impulse closely akin to the one that Freud inscribed as the epigraph to his *Interpretation of Dreams*: "Flectere si nequeo superos, Acheronta movebo" (If I cannot bend the heavens above, I will move the infernal regions) (Freud 1976 [1900]: 31).

Notes for this chapter begin on page 120.

Historians such as Carl Schorske (1979) and John Cuddihy (1974) throw an interesting light on this impulse. For Schorske, it belongs to a larger cultural movement that arose in response to the crisis of bourgeois values in fin-de-siècle Vienna—a movement embodied in writers such as Arthur Schnitzler and Hugo Hoffmansthal who concerned themselves with the darker currents flowing just below the placid surface of respectable society. Cuddihy gives Freud's version of this critical project an even sharper edge. In proposing that all humans share a common (and equally scandalous) underlife, he says, Freud found a way to universalize (and thus dissolve) the 'uncivilized' aspersions cast upon Jews to justify their exclusion from the upper reaches of Viennese society. Taken together, these two accounts provide an illuminating sociological perspective on the broadly ironic impulse that drives much of Freud's thinking, especially about culture.

However, psychoanalysis entails another, more specialized form of irony that may hold even greater interest. I am thinking here of what might be called the ironic structure of the analytic situation. The classic analytic hour consists largely in a rambling monologue, an effort by the analysand to 'say whatever comes to mind'. The analyst learns to listen to this in a special way, however, attending to salient motifs and patterns, but also to gaps and absences. From an analytic standpoint, the real interest of the monologue lies less in what it shows than in what it betrays in spite of itself, in what it works to conceal. The assumption, in effect, is that the patient's manifest speech hides other voices bearing the secret of his illness. Guided by psychoanalytic theory and an array of specific interpretive tools, the analyst tries to make out these voices and bring them into the conversation, so that the monologue eventually becomes a dialogue or even a polylogue—and the patient can begin to hear them as his own. Structurally speaking, this process embodies the classic trajectory that Kenneth Burke (1945) ascribes to dramatic irony, in which a single voice or perspective gives way to a series of voices, each questioning, qualifying, and thus 'ironizing' the others.

At the same time, a sharper and more troubling irony appears in what the voices say. The new meanings that psychoanalysis finds or reads into the lives of its patients do not simply enhance or supplement those the patient brings to the encounter; they seem to arrive by way of *reversals*. Such reversals appear at all levels of the interpretive process. Even at the most basic level of free association, for example, Freud counsels analysts not to accept an absence of thoughts at face value, but as a sign that the patient is "possessed by a thought which concerns the person of the physician ..." (1984 [1912–1913]: 107). Similarly, when a patient reports a dream, the parts described as vaguest or most doubtful are to be taken as the most important, since the dreamwork imposes "a complete transvaluation of all psychical values" and these parts betray the highest degree of repression (1976 [1900]: 661).[1] The same principle applies when the patient rejects an interpretation: the more vehement the denial, the more accurate the interpretation is likely to be.[2]

At a higher level of abstraction, reversals of this kind play a central part in all of Freud's case histories. When his patient Dora reports "a violent feeling of disgust" in response to an amorous advance by Herr K., Freud interprets it as a sexual response that has been displaced from genitals to mouth and subjected to the *"reversal of affect"* one typically finds in hysteria (1977 [1905]: 59). Or again, interpreting the Wolf Man's childhood nightmare of white wolves sitting in a tree, Freud reads the stillness of the wolves as symbols of violent action and their bushy tails as marking fear of castration, with the entire dream pointing back to a scene of parental coitus witnessed in early infancy (1979 [1918]: 265–270). In the Schreber case, he interprets Schreber's delusions of persecution by the psychiatrist Flechsig as arising from "an outburst of homosexual libido," with Flechsig as its focus of erotic interest (1979 [1911]: 177).

If there is a pattern here, it would seem to be exactly the one that Burke (1948: 517) proposes as an "overall formula" for the reversals of dramatic irony: "[W]hat goes forth as A returns as non-A." What are we to make of this? From the standpoint of psychoanalytic theory, the answer is simple. These reversals are not accidents but direct reflections of a fundamental assumption (perhaps *the* fundamental assumption) behind its 'dynamic' view of the psyche. In Freud's words: "The emotional life of man is in general made up of pairs of contraries ... Indeed, if it were not so, repressions and neuroses would perhaps never come about. In the adult these pairs of contrary emotions do not as a rule become simultaneously conscious except at the climaxes of passionate love; at other times they usually go on suppressing each other until one of them succeeds in keeping the other altogether out of sight" (1977 [1909]: 271).

Taken by themselves, however, oppositions do not create irony. Irony can arise only when one side of this doubleness is hidden from an actor but evident to others or the actor himself at a later time. It depends, in other words, on a difference in *knowledge*. In psychoanalysis, this difference hinges on the concept of the unconscious, which serves to articulate a whole array of tensions and contradictions between the known and unknown in the lives of patients and, by implication, the rest of us. And it is here that the irony built into the clinical structure of psychoanalysis raises its troubling questions. If it is true, as Freud says, that much of our life is driven by impulses lying outside of consciousness, and that the unconscious consists precisely in what is *opposed* or *contrary*, what is "incompatible with the ego," then it becomes much harder to be sure what our actions mean or even who is acting. To what extent are we the authors of anything we do? Can we ever know our own intentions? Does knowing make a difference?

These are old questions. Although they sound straightforward, clear answers have been elusive. Freud's own responses appear equivocal at best. His writings are full of suggestions that neurotics are somehow complicit in their illness, or that they have fallen ill through a kind of "moral cowardice" (Freud and Breuer 1974 [1895]: 188) and that they have something to gain by staying that way. He observed that most of us revise our memories of early childhood to suit our adult convenience (1985 [1910]: 174), and that even when supposedly repressed memories become conscious, patients describe them as something they "had always known" (1963 [1914]: 158). At the same time, he insisted on the "law of complete psychic determinism," which dictates that every mental event is the result of "an unbroken chain of prior mental events," making freedom of choice an illusion (1965:[1901]: 240). He likened the power of the unconscious to that of posthypnotic suggestion, which can cause subjects do the oddest things without knowing why. And, most notoriously, he claimed that psychoanalytic research had shown that "the ego is not master even in its own house." (1973 [1915–1917]: 326).

One way of coming to terms with this ambiguity is to recognize that psychoanalysis has always relied on two distinct but complementary models of unconscious motivation, each with its own narrative structure and thus its own way of reading symptoms. Freudian case histories draw some of their richness and complexity from the mixing of these two interpretive strategies. The difference here corresponds roughly to the one that Freud drew between "primary" and "secondary" gain in illness. In the first case, neurotic symptoms are shown to be meaningful as expressions or displacements of repressed infantile sexual fixations; the "gain" is an indirect libidinal satisfaction, albeit one that comes at a high price. Interpreting symptoms from this standpoint means looking back to childhood and weaving some version of the classic Freudian tale involving primal scenes, erogenous zones, and an ill-starred family romance. In the second case, the gain is of a more immediate kind. Here the interpretation looks to the current context of the patient's illness, asking what advantages it might bring—for example, as a way of avoiding a decision or winning attention from an unsympathetic mate. Again roughly speaking, we could say that the first line of interpretation draws on 'id psychology' (or the psychology of id-superego relations), while the second looks more to the ego's investment in the illness. While for obvious reasons Freud found the first motive for illness more theoretically interesting, he also warned practitioners that the second could be a formidable clinical adversary.

In what follows, I want to look more closely at these two models. The aim, however, will not be to illuminate their theoretical or clinical importance for psychoanalysis, but to consider their relation to the history of irony. My argument is that both approaches to symptoms are ways of reading irony into illness, but that the ironies at stake are of two very different kinds. Freud often said that his ideas were not new, that they had been anticipated by poets and artists over the centuries, and that psychoanalysis merely gave them scientific form. In keeping with this claim, I think it can be shown that both forms of unconscious motivation embody structures laid down by the two oldest and most influential forms of irony in Western literature. As I shall try to show, even in their earliest versions, both kinds of irony hinge on a basic contrast between knowledge and ignorance, which then serves to articulate differences between action and passion, doing and suffering. However, they do so in different, even diametrically opposite, ways. My hope is that connecting these with Freud's thinking about unconscious motivation will offer a new perspective on the relation between knowledge and agency in psychoanalysis.

Rhetorical Irony: From *Eirôn* to *Eirôneia*

The modern reader attuned to irony will find it almost everywhere in Western literature, not least at its very beginnings. Paul Friedrich, for example, argues that irony is "the dominant and organizing trope" of Homer's *Odyssey* (2001: 226). However, the ancient Greeks themselves would not have recognized the reversals propelling Homer's story as instances of irony. Their term *eirôneia* derives from the noun *eirôn* (a deceiver or dissembler), which in turn stems from the verb *eirein* (to speak the opposite of what one means). According to G. G. Sedgwick (quoted in Muecke 1969: 47), the Periclean Greeks used the term to denote "a general form of behavior connoting slyness." There is a clear ambivalence about this. Demosthenes, for example, spoke of the *eirôn* as someone who evaded his responsibilities as a citizen by pretending unfitness; for Theophrastus an *eirôn* was "evasive and non-committal, concealing his enmities, pretending friendship, misrepresenting his acts and never giving a straight answer" (Muecke 1982: 15). On the other hand, in Plato's *Republic*, *eirôneia* becomes a term of exasperated, if grudging, admiration for Socrates and his "smooth, low-down way of taking people in" (ibid.). If there is a prototype for irony in this narrower sense, it can also be found in the *Odyssey*—not in its narrative structure, but in the wily ways of its protagonist, who chooses, for example, to show up in Ithaca disguised as a humble oarsman, the better to size things up. While his aims are clearly strategic, his exchanges with the suitors and Penelope herself are full of what we today would call irony—words that mean one thing to his benighted listeners and something quite different to those in the know.

It was Aristotle who raised this somewhat devious technique to the level of a rhetorical figure. In his *Rhetoric* and again in the *Ethics*, *eirôneia* stands for something like 'self-deprecative dissimulation'. He describes the ironical speaker as someone who "professes that he does not have, or has in less measure than the world supposes, the good qualities that he does in fact possess" (1953: 70). While for Aristotle this is still an instance of using words deceptively, it is one that creates "an impression of superior refinement" and is thus better suited to the gentleman than its opposite, boastfulness. But even here we find traces of ambivalence, since Aristotle is quick to warn against the "pretentious humbugs" who take the pose too far (ibid.: 133).

This Greek view of irony as involving a strategically motivated (but morally ambiguous) pose of innocence or incapacity underpins one whole understanding of the term that is still very much with us today. I am thinking of the abundant literature that treats irony as a 'verbal' or 'communicative' phenomenon. However, while the Greeks concerned themselves mainly with the question of when and whether anyone should 'say the opposite of what he means', modern writing about this kind of irony has been much more interested in how it is done. After all, even for the Athenians, the *eirôn* was no mere liar, but someone who used language in a special way. What is it that sets apart this way of speaking, or indeed acting? How does it work?

It is clear enough, first of all, that rhetorical irony involves a specific kind of semantic ambiguity, one that lends itself to mutually opposed interpretations. This can be achieved in a variety of ways—for example, by using words that are themselves ambiguous, by overstating a point so that it verges on sarcasm, or by employing metalinguistic qualifiers (tone of voice, facial expression) that throw doubt on the overt meaning of one's words. But there is more than ambiguity at stake here. Rhetorical irony takes place in a social context. It is an intentional act—the work of an 'ironist'—and understanding the act usually means understanding the intention. It also involves an audience and, in many cases, a victim. Summarizing a widely held view, D. C. Muecke proposes that this kind of irony is "a double-layered or two-storied phenomenon with victim (if there is one) at the bottom and ironist at the top." There is always an opposition between the two levels—"contradiction, incongruity or incompatibility"—and "an element of innocence (real in the victim, pretended in the ironist)" (1969: 19). Alexander Nehamas puts the same point a little differently: "Irony always and necessarily postulates a double speaker and a double audience. One speaker does and one does not mean what is said; one audience does and one does not understand what is said" (1998: 45). For these reasons, rhetorical irony lends itself well to political invective ("and Brutus is an honest man"), since it provides a way of insinuating something without stating it directly. In this way, as James Fernandez suggests, ironists can "point to an alternative reading of a situation, while evading the challenge of direct dissent and protecting themselves from censorious response" (Fernandez and Huber 2001: 5).

From the standpoint of our concerns here, it is interesting that the double meaning central to rhetorical irony generates not only a double audience but two different situations, two versions of what has happened. In the first version, the ironist appears as a hapless innocent facing a savvy opponent, while in the second, the tables are turned: the ironist is the one who knows and is pulling the strings, usually at someone's expense. Thus, rhetorical irony generates two different configurations of knowledge and agency, although they are scarcely on an equal footing. To those who understand what is going on and thus 'get' the irony, the first version is a deceiving appearance, while the second is the reality.

Dramatic Irony: From Theatre to Life

What we call dramatic irony today was already well developed in the tragedies of ancient Athens, even if the Greeks did not connect it with *eirôneia*. Aristotle, in setting out the ingredients for a successful tragedy, spoke rather of *anagnorisis* (discovery) and *peripeteia* (reversal of intention). Working from the premise that every tragedy, by definition, depicted a catastrophic change of fortune, Aristotle maintained that in the best tragedies, the change came not as "one continuous whole," but through a sudden shift arising out of "the structure of the Plot itself, so as to be the consequence, necessary or probable, of the antecedents" (1947: 637). *Anagnorisis* and *peripeteia* were the keys to this shift. For Aristotle, the *peripeteia,* or reversal, was "a change ... from one state of things in the play to its opposite," occurring "in the probable or necessary sequence of events." His exemplary case was the scene in *Oedipus Rex* where "the opposite state of things is produced by the Messenger, who, coming to gladden Oedipus and remove his fears as to his mother, reveals the secret of his birth" (ibid.: 637–638). *Anagnorisis* was "a change from ignorance to knowledge and thus to either love or hate, in the personages marked for good or evil fortune." Aristotle thought *anagnorisis* achieved its most impressive effect (that is, most conducive to pity and terror) when it actually caused the *peripeteia*; here, again, his example was *Oedipus Rex* (ibid.: 638).

In putting "reversal of intention" together with "a change from ignorance to knowledge," Aristotle clearly identified the structural core of dramatic irony. However, his brief and schematic discussion did not begin to capture the richness and complexity of this element in Greek drama, much less to examine its possibilities as an attitude toward life in general. Those developments came much later. According to Muecke (1982), the word 'irony' itself began to acquire its present range of meanings only in the closing years of the eighteenth century. While until this time, he says, "irony had been thought of as essentially intentional and instrumental, someone realizing a purpose by using language ironically ..., it now became possible to think of irony as something that could instead be unintentional ..., something that happened" (ibid.: 19).

Muecke points out that the first stage of this new development "was to think of irony in terms not of someone being ironical, but of someone being the victim of irony, attention thus shifting from the active to the passive" (1982: 19). It was then just a small step from being the victim of an ironical remark to being the victim of ironic events or circumstances. In Germany, where much of the new thinking took place, this shift then paved the way for a series of grander and more metaphysical ironies, including the 'irony of fate' and Hegel's "irony of history." These eventually culminated in the view that Muecke calls "General Dramatic Irony": "We think we are free agents, but what we are, all that we are, all that we think and all that we 'choose' to do has been determined by an unbroken chain of cause and effect" (1969: 137).

The final step in this process came not in Germany but in England, with the publication of Connop Thirlwall's highly influential essay "On the Irony of Sophocles" (1833). Thirlwall was the first to see the tragedies of Sophocles, with their "contrast between man with his hopes, fears and wishes and undertakings, and a dark, inflexible fate," as instances of irony in its new expanded sense. According to Muecke, however, Thirwall's key contribution was to connect this global irony with the smaller ironies of speech in Sophoclean tragedy, especially "the irony of a character's utterance having unawares a double reference: to the situation as it appears to him, and, no less aptly, to the [very different] situation as it really is" (Muecke 1982: 29). It was also Thirlwall who established the term 'dramatic irony' as a name for narratives employing such double meanings together with the peculiar mixture of fatefulness and striving, discovery and reversal seen in the tragedies of Sophocles.

The Two Ironies as Interpretive Strategies

The foregoing discussion puts us in a better position to address our central concern here, which is with irony not as a rhetorical or literary achievement but as a way of understanding the world. What happens when we move from looking at how these two ironies are made to asking how they are imputed or found? How do they differ as ways of reading events?

Clearly, they are alike in certain respects. Both depend on a contrast between appearance and reality; seeing irony of either kind means looking beyond the obvious or given to something else that it conceals, to a second, hidden meaning that subverts or overturns the first. Likewise, ironic situations of either kind derive their structure from what might be called a knowledge differential—between those who 'get' the irony and those who don't (in dramatic irony, this may be the same person at different times). This means that reading any situation ironically entails some implicit claims about what people know and when they know it.

At the same time, there are obvious differences. Rhetorical irony requires an ironist who in turn commits the irony for reasons. This means that wherever this kind of irony is suspected or imputed, the interpretive work draws us quickly into thinking about the ironist's motives (Was she really that naive, or was she making fun of me?). Dramatic irony, on the other hand, arises from circumstances that are typically complex and embedded in a larger story. Seeing the irony requires a more global kind of understanding, one that embraces the whole sequence of events. Here, the interpretive task is less a matter of grasping a single actor's motives than of seeing a larger controlling pattern, one that might involve a long historical conflict, or an ineluctable chain of events, or an underlying mythic form—or all of these at once.

As interpretive templates, rhetorical and dramatic irony diverge in a final way that is even more striking. As we have seen, both ironies set up double situations (one overt but 'illusory', the other hidden but 'real') in which actors are positioned by differences in what they know or understand. These differences have a direct bearing on another difference, this one involving *agency*—the difference between action and passion, doing and suffering. Here I would argue that rhetorical and dramatic irony prove to be mirror opposites.

As we have seen, rhetorical irony typically involves a deceptive pose of innocence or incapacity, which the ironist assumes for his own strategic reasons. This is especially clear in its early Greek versions: think of Odysseus in disguise, or the *eirôn* pretending to be less than he is, or even the strategic ignorance of Socrates. In all these cases, the ironist appears to be at a loss but actually knows what he is doing. In dramatic irony, the opposite is true. Think of *Oedipus Rex*. Here, too, there is deception, but it is Oedipus who is deceived. He thinks himself a great hero, a canny solver of riddles, a man of action who has overcome his fate; as it turns out, he is "the most wretched of men," and his own misguided actions have brought him to ruin. To put it briefly, then, we might say that in rhetorical irony, action wears the mask of passion, whereas in dramatic irony (at least in its Sophoclean form), it is passion or suffering that cloaks itself in the deceptive garb of action.

Illness and Agency: Freud on Hysteria

Psychoanalysis, as Mark Micale points out, began as a theory of hysteria. It arrived on the scene, moreover, at a time when "medical thinking about hysteria had reached an intellectual impasse" (1995: 25). One the one side, there were the physicalists who regarded hysteria as a true neurological disease, traceable to degenerative heredity or environmental shock. For them, the treatments of choice were equally physical: cold baths, rest cures, dietary regimes, electrical shocks. On the other side were those who blamed the "hysterical temperament," with its supposed "eccentricity, impulsiveness, emotionality, coquettishness, deceitfulness and hypersexuality" (ibid.: 24). As far as they were concerned, hysteria was not a disease at all, but a form of malingering, and so they put their faith in bracing lectures and calls for stricter discipline. By the time of Charcot's death in 1893, neither account seemed wholly persuasive.

Both of these alternatives could be described as reflecting a simplistic opposition between illness and agency. If an illness was real, it was involuntary and thus devoid of intention or meaning. On the other hand, if symptoms betrayed even a hint of the intentional, then something else was afoot, and the patient simply needed to 'pull herself together'. I would argue that Freud's originality lay at least partly in finding a way beyond this sharp divide to a more complex understanding of the whole relationship between agency and illness. His concept of the unconscious opened the way to a profound rethinking not only of illness and its hidden meanings, but of agency and its limits as well. As I suggested at the start of this essay, there is something basically ironic in the very structure of the Freudian unconscious. What I want to argue now is that in elaborating this idea, Freud followed a path laid down by the two central forms of irony discussed above.

Studies on Hysteria, which Freud published with his mentor, Josef Breuer (Freud and Breuer 1974 [1895]), begins with the famous proposition that "hysterics suffer mainly from reminiscences." What Freud and Breuer meant by this was that all hysterias have their origins in "psychical traumas," events that, because of their intensity or emotional valence, become disconnected from the rest of mental life and thus acquire the power to generate symptoms. They also made the claim that "each individual hysterical symptom disappeared when we had succeeded in bringing clearly to light the memory of the event by which it was provoked and in arousing its accompanying affect" (ibid.: 57). However, in their separate chapters the two authors came to develop two very different conceptions of these pathogenic events. For Breuer, psychical traumas were shocking or frightening events that took place during quasi-hypnotic states of consciousness ("hypnoid states"), found on the edges of sleep or at moments of nervous excitement. An initial trauma would make the patient susceptible to other, similar events and thus could eventually snowball into a complex array of hysterical symptoms. Curing the patient was more or less a matter of reversing the process, using hypnosis to summon up vivid memories of recent traumas and then working backward to the initial event.

For Freud, by contrast, the "traumas" behind hysterical symptoms were to be found not in special mental states or even specific events, but rather in the relationship between such events and other mental processes. More specifically, Freud argued that all hysterias—and indeed all neuroses in general—could be traced to "an incompatibility ... between the ego and some idea presented to it" (ibid.: 187). The "actual traumatic moment" was the one at which "the incompatibility forces itself upon the ego and at which the latter decides on the repudiation of the incompatible idea" (ibid.: 188). The conclusion was clear: since hysterias originated in emotional conflicts, treating them required a careful inquiry into the patient's personal life. In contrast to Breuer's account of "Freulein Anna O.," Freud's cases in the *Studies* did exactly this. As Freud himself saw (ibid.: 231), this step entailed a radically new way of looking at illness:

> I have not always been a psychotherapist. Like other neuropathologists, I was trained to employ local diagnoses and electro-prognosis, and it still strikes me ... as strange that the case histories I write should read like short stories and that, as one might say, they lack the serious stamp of science. I must console myself with the reflection that the nature of the subject is evidently responsible for this ... The fact is that local diagnosis and electrical reactions lead nowhere in the study of hysteria, whereas a detailed description of mental processes such as we are accustomed to find in the work of imaginative writers enables me, with the use of a few psychological formulas, to obtain at least some insight into the course of that affection.

These early case histories are often likened to detective stories in the sense that they involve puzzles, clues, and, in each case, a solution. However, they might also be compared to the plays of Ibsen or the stories of Arthur Schniztler, at least in their portrayal of the secret yearnings, betrayals, and frustrations of domestic life. Compared to Freud's later cases, they are mere vignettes. However, they are full of small dramatic ironies, at least in the limited sense that they involve discoveries that bring reversals. The typical pattern, in fact, is a double reversal, in which a piece of unwelcome knowledge is repressed, causing illness, and then 'recognized' in the course of therapy to bring about a cure. In the case of Lucy R., for example, the patient is a governess who was secretly in love with her employer. She falls ill at the moment she is presented with clear evidence that he does not return her love. However, the reader, like the analyst, discovers this only toward the end of the story, which deals mainly with the mysterious symptoms that the patient has thrown up to defend herself from this news. When, with Freud's help, she finally sees the truth about her symptoms and her situation, her symptoms vanish. The case of Katharina offers an interesting variation on this theme. Here, the patient suffers from panic attacks that have their origin (as we eventually learn) in an attempted seduction by her father when she was still a child. But the panic attacks begin only in late adolescence when another event opens her eyes to the meaning of this early experience. This is what Freud came to call *nachträglichkeit* (deferred action)—his word for those recognition/reversals in which a later discovery confers traumatic force on an earlier experience,.

As attempts to reframe the relation between illness and agency, these stories convey a strangely mixed picture. On the one hand, they follow the classic pattern for dramatic irony, in which the protagonist is shown to suffer from a kind of ignorance, a failure to see her real situation. And yet, as Freud repeatedly observes, there is something willful about this ignorance: "The hysterical patient's 'not knowing' was in fact a 'not wanting to know'—a not wanting which might be to a greater or lesser extent conscious" (ibid.: 353). The initial splitting that gives rise to symptoms is, he insists, "a deliberate and intentional one," usually driven by the wish to avoid a harsh truth or a difficult decision. "Thus, the mechanism which produces hysteria represents on the one hand an act of moral cowardice and on the other a defensive measure which is at the disposal of the ego" (ibid.: 188).[3]

Seen from the standpoint of Freud's mature theory, *Studies on Hysteria* scarcely qualifies as psychoanalysis. Nonetheless, it is a first groping attempt in that direction and reveals a good deal about his general style of thinking. Less than a year after its publication in 1895, Freud became convinced that a different approach was needed, one that would look beyond the patient's immediate life to deeper and earlier causes. After a brief flirtation with the 'childhood seduction theory', he began to develop the theory of infantile sexuality that became the cornerstone of all his later work. This new way of understanding illness and its origins required, in turn, a new and more complex way of telling patients' stories, one that would reflect the interplay between meanings arising from two completely different contexts: one rooted in infancy and the other in the patient's current circumstances. In grappling with this problem, Freud arrived at the two distinct lines of interpretation mentioned earlier. We must now consider each of these separately.

Rhetorical Illness and the Irony of Symptoms

Over the course of his career, Freud devoted far more attention to the infantile sources of neurosis than to those lying immediately at hand. However, his views on the latter came into sharp focus at a time when he had barely begun to think about psychosexual development, so I shall take them up first. These ideas are associated with several different terms: initially, "motives for illness" but later "advantage through illness" and "secondary gain." Freud considered them most explicitly in his case history of "Dora" (1977 [1905]), but they retained an important, if distinctly secondary, role in all his later work.

As a piece of psychoanalytic writing, "Dora" lies midway between Freud's earlier vignettes on hysteria and his later, more elaborate case histories. As the formal title indicates, it is a mere "fragment of an analysis." The patient, Dora, suffers from a variety of symptoms, the most prominent being *tussis nervosa*, a nervous cough, and *aphonia*, a periodic loss of speech. Freud does take some trouble to connect these symptoms with her childhood psychosexual development, especially her "sensual sucking" as an infant, her precocious masturbation, and her still excessive attachment to her father. He makes a detailed attempt to link the irritation in her throat to repressed fantasies of oral intercourse. And yet in comparison to his later case histories, this discussion is cursory. He is much more interested in the current context of the illness.

There are good reasons for this, since Dora's family situation is more than a bit peculiar. Her mother, whom she detests, is a remote figure obsessed with domestic cleanliness. Her beloved father is carrying on an affair with the wife of his best friend, Herr K. Herr K., in turn, has a romantic interest in Dora herself, whom he showers with small presents and attempts to seduce at one point. Dora's feelings toward Herr K. (at least by Freud's account) are ambivalent in the strongest sense of the word: she is erotically attracted to him and yet repelled by his advances—to Freud, a clear sign of hysteria.

Freud attempts to situate Dora's fluctuating symptoms within this complex picture. In doing so, he draws a distinction between the processes that originally give rise to symptoms and the "motives for illness" that cause the symptoms to persist. These latter always come down to "some advantage" that the illness brings the patient. In a brief excursus he explains that such motives often begin in childhood, as, for example, when a little girl notices that her parents are more affectionate when she is ill, and so learns to use illness as " a means of enticing out her parents' love." "When such a child has grown up to be a woman," he says,

> she may find all the demands she used to make in her childhood countered owing to her marriage with an inconsiderate husband, who may subjugate her will, mercilessly exploit her capacity for work, and lavish neither his affection nor his money upon her. In that case ill-health will be her one weapon for maintaining her position. It will procure her the care she longs for; it will force her husband to make pecuniary sacrifices for her and to show her consideration ...; and it will compel him to treat her with solicitude if she recovers, for otherwise a relapse will threaten. Her illness will have every appearance of being objective and involuntary ...
>
> And yet illnesses of this kind *are* the result of intention. They are as a rule leveled at a particular person, and consequently vanish with that person's departure. The crudest and most commonplace views on the character of hysterical disorders are in a certain sense right ... except on a single point: they overlook the psychological distinction between what is conscious and what is unconscious. (ibid.: 77–78)

Freud tries to persuade Dora that her entire illness has just such an unconscious aim, which "could be none other than to detach her father from Frau K." He tells her he is convinced "she would recover at once" if her father were to tell her that he had broken off with Frau K. for the sake of her health. But he adds that he hopes this will not happen, "for then she would have learned what a powerful weapon she had in her hands and she would certainly not hesitate on every future occasion to make use once more of her potentialities for illness" (ibid.: 74–75).

Freud goes on to interpret Dora's actual symptoms in a similar, if less strategic, way as providing her with a covert means of expressing her feelings for Herr K. When Dora points out that Frau K. always seems to be indisposed when her husband returns from his travels, Freud suspects that something similar may be afoot in her own case. He quickly establishes that Dora's periodic attacks of coughing and aphonia also correlate with Herr K.'s comings and goings, but in the opposite way: she coughs and loses her voice when he is away but recovers when he returns. Her illness, he concludes,

> was therefore a demonstration of her love for K., just as his wife's was a demonstration of her *dislike*. It was only necessary to suppose that her behavior had been the opposite of Frau K.'s … And this really seemed to have been so, at least during the first period of the attacks. Later on it no doubt became necessary to obscure the coincidence between her attacks of illness and the absence of the man she secretly loved, lest its regularity should betray her secret. (ibid.: 71)

The kinds of connections that Freud makes between Dora's symptoms and her circumstances all bear a striking resemblance to those that define rhetorical irony. Neurotic symptoms, such as ironic words or deeds, have a double meaning, one overt, the other hidden. The neurotic, like the ironist, pretends innocence and incapacity: she says she is ill and can't help what she is doing. And yet she is using her symptoms strategically—for example, to control an abusive husband or, in Dora's case, to pressure her father into ending his affair. Because of their ambiguity, neurotic symptoms also lend themselves to the kind of covert commentary we associate with irony—allowing the sufferer to express feelings in a way that escapes repercussions. Finally, at least as far as present circumstances are concerned, the work of understanding a symptom is very much a matter of grasping the intention behind it. The one difference, albeit a crucial one, is that the neurotic doesn't 'know' what she is doing. The gap between knowledge and ignorance that makes irony possible appears here as a gap between conscious and unconscious knowledge. Freud's task, in his own view, was to find a way of closing the gap. If the hysteric is to be helped at all, he says, "[a]n attempt must be made by the roundabout methods of analysis to convince the patient herself of the existence in her of an intention to be ill" (ibid.: 78).

Freud's treatment of Dora was an unrelenting application of this program. As critics have often pointed out, his manner with her was often less that of therapist to patient than of a lawyer to a hostile witness. His penchant for badgering and lecturing the young girl no doubt had its own unconscious determinants, but it also reflected his belief that her main problem was a certain deviousness by which she kept herself and everyone else in the dark. The cure, then, was to replace the indirect (and ironic) language of her illness with straightforward talk, on the assumption that once the game is known, it can no longer be played.[4]

While this approach did not succeed with Dora (who broke off treatment after less than three months), Freud continued to champion its importance for at least another decade. In an address given to the Second International Psychoanalytic Congress in Nuremberg in 1910 (1963 [1910]), he went so far as to suggest that as psychoanalysis succeeded in decoding neurotic symptoms and making their hidden meanings generally known, it was bound to have a profound impact not only on individuals but on society at large. His discussion of this point is remarkable for its depiction of neurotic symptoms as a kind of secret language and even more for the potency he accords to psychoanalytic knowledge in its simple declarative form. Since it is clear, he says, that neuroses depend for their existence on "distortion and disguise," it also follows that "[w]hen the riddle they hold is solved and the solution accepted by the sufferers, these diseases will no longer be able to exist" (ibid.: 84). Once this knowledge becomes general, "[d]isclosure of the secret will have attacked, on its most sensitive point, the 'aetiological equation' from which the neuroses descend, will have made the 'advantage through illness' illusory, and consequently in the end nothing can come of the changed situation ... but an end of producing these illnesses" (ibid.).[5] If it is true, as I have been suggesting, that Freud's understanding of "advantage through illness" draws its pattern from rhetorical irony, then it makes sense for him to insist that neurosis depends on a difference in knowledge—in this case, between the (unconscious) author of the symptoms and everyone else. The implications for treatment are equally clear: do away with the difference (so that everyone 'gets' it), and you do away with the irony, making the symptoms pointless.

Dramatic Illness and the Irony of Life

In contrast to Freud's relatively brief attention to the strategic use of illness in the present, his concern with its infantile origins was a lifelong project. It began in 1897 when, in the course of his self-analysis, he found evidence of his own repressed incestuous and patricidal wishes. These led to his theory of the Oedipus complex and then to the bolder hypothesis that children are sexual beings who pass through a series of developmental stages focused on different erogenous zones. As Freud elaborated this theory of infantile sexuality, he became convinced that it held the missing key to understanding neurosis and character structure in adults—and perhaps other matters as well.

Freud's theory is not easily encapsulated, but it hinges on the assumption that the child's sexual activities in infancy become prototypes for everything that follows. He came to believe that the simple and undeniable pleasures of sucking, defecation, and genital stimulation shared by all children are far from simple in their effects. They are often the site of intense conflicts and vivid fantasies that bring fear, longing, frustration, anger, or guilt. Their ultimate outcome depends on the interplay of many different factors, some "phylogenetic" or universal, others instinctual or constitutional, others cultural or moral—or purely accidental. Nonetheless, Freud held that childhood sexual experience could give rise to neurotic illness only under certain conditions: first, circumstances must conspire to produce a *fixation* of interest on a particular sexual stage, zone, or activity; and, secondly, the fixation must arouse such intense conflict that it is eventually repressed. Neurotic symptoms arise as displaced substitutes for these repressed infantile pleasures. In a sense, to use Freud's own phrase, they *are* the neurotic's sexual life. However, as he recognized, this way of understanding neurosis has the effect of blurring the difference between neurotics and the rest of us, since we all repress infantile sexual wishes to a greater or lesser degree (Freud 1973 [1917–1918]: 404). Thus, as he argued later (1962 [1930]), we might all be said to suffer and to produce symptoms, even if they are not seen as such.

Even this brief summary points up an obvious difference between interpretations that seek the infantile meanings of illness and those associated with "secondary gain." Here, there is no question of looking for a specific aim or intention. Making sense of the illness requires a more global kind of understanding, one that works through a series of developments in search of a larger pattern—exactly as in dramatic irony. This is certainly the ethos informing all of Freud's major case histories (1977 [1909], 1979 [1909], 1979 [1911], 1979 [1918]), which spend a great deal of time tracing out the vicissitudes of different fantasies and libidinal impulses—their waxing and waning, collision, convergence, or compromise—and are very long stories indeed. The point of these narratives is not to locate a specific cause for each symptom, but rather to arrive at a general picture in which all of the symptoms—and much else about the patient's life—can be seen to make sense.

The patterns that emerge in dramatic irony can take many forms, but in Greek tragedy they are typically shaped by forces beyond human control—fate, prophecy, or the will of the gods. Freud's own quest for the origins of neurosis led in a similar direction. While his case histories dwell at length on the minutiae of patients' lives, their real point always lies elsewhere, in what they reveal about a set of larger controlling influences—the Oedipus complex, the psychosexual stages, the life and death instincts, the primal crime, primal scenes, primal repression. Freud didn't view any of these influences as belonging exclusively to neurosis; on the contrary, he argued that neurosis merely disrupted their smooth functioning and thus made them accessible to study. However, he came to see the patterns as something like a set of keys that could unlock almost any clinical or cultural puzzle; the interpretive task came down to finding a way of reading them into the details of a particular life or a situation. Thus, for example, in his account of the "Little Hans" case (1977 [1909]), it is the theory of the Oedipus complex that enables Freud to penetrate a daunting wealth of clinical detail and make sense of Hans's fear of horses.[6] In the "Wolf Man" case (1979 [1918]), on the other hand, the controlling pattern originates in a hypothesized "primal scene" of parental intercourse whose remnants Freud detects in almost every facet of the patient's subsequent life.

At a more intimate and practical level, however, dramatic irony appears chiefly in the *repetitions* that Freud regarded as central to every neurosis. These could take a wide array of forms, some of them positively uncanny. In some cases, "[t]he impression they give is of being pursued by a malignant fate or possessed by some demonic power ... Thus we have come across people all of whose human relationships have the same outcome: such as the benefactor who is abandoned in anger after a time by each of his *protégés* ...; or the man whose friendships all end in betrayal by his friend;... or again the lover each of whose love affairs with a woman passes through the same phases and reaches the same conclusion" (1984 [1920]: 292).

The repetitions seen in clinical situations are usually more pedestrian, but they have a similar origin in the infantile fixations at the base of every neurosis. Unknown to himself, the neurotic is caught up in an endless attempt to reproduce certain highly charged relations and situations from childhood, even in the midst of adult life. Like Oedipus in the Sophoclean tragedy, he is someone who thinks he is willing, acting, and choosing, but in fact he does not know who he is or where he is going. He is repeating a pattern decreed in advance and shaped by powers he does not understand.

The analogy to Oedipus can be taken further when we look at Freud's account of what happens as the neurotic enters treatment. At first, like the Theban king confronted with the plague, he is full of earnest resolve to find the source of his illness, which he thinks of as something outside of himself. Faced with questions or interpretations that suggest otherwise, he becomes defensive, displays resistance. In doing so, however, he also begins to reenact the very patterns from infancy that define his illness, applying them now to the analytic situation and his relation to the analyst; this, of course, is the transference. While the patient may feel his responses are perfectly rational, the analyst learns to hear them differently, as echoing other scenes in other places. From the analyst's perspective, in fact, the patient's behavior begins to take on the kind of ironic doubleness found in *Oedipus Rex*, in which the protagonist's very denials somehow affirm what he denies. As Freud puts it (1963 [1914]: 60):

[T]he patient *remembers* nothing of what is forgotten and repressed, but he expresses it in action ... For instance, the patient does not say that he remembers how defiant he used to be in regard to the authority of his parents, but he behaves in that way toward the physician ... He does not remember that he was intensely ashamed of certain sexual activities, but he makes it clear that he is ashamed of the treatment to which he has submitted himself, and does his utmost to keep it a secret; and so on.

Because it is a gradual process, psychoanalysis has no equivalent to the sudden moment of discovery and reversal at the climax of *Oedipus Rex*. What we do find, however, is a series of small moments of this kind in which the patient manages to move from repeating to recalling and thus to catch a glimpse of an alien part of herself. These moments can be difficult, since formally speaking they have the same structure as the terrible discovery that befell the Theban king: "I am the abomination I was seeking." And yet clearly the parallels end here. For Oedipus, after all, the discovery is a catastrophe, while for the analytic patient it is a therapeutic breakthrough. What are we to make of this? The question takes us quickly to a larger set of issues about the role of irony in psychoanalysis, both as a practical technique and as a way of engaging the world. In concluding, I address them only briefly.

Conclusion: Ironic Knowledge, Ironic Agency

As I have tried to show, the interpretive method developed by Freud appears to move in two opposed but complementary directions. The first one, modeled on rhetorical irony, looks to ways in which the patient uses her symptoms for strategic ends. Its premise is that her suffering (or some of it, anyway) is really a kind of acting that serves readily understandable motives. The second line of interpretation, modeled on dramatic irony, leads in the opposite direction. Its premise is that the patient's symptoms are merely the tip of the iceberg, that her problem is her whole stance in life, and that the only way forward is to come to terms with wishes she has rejected.

Even if we don't accept their premises, it is easy to see that these two lines of interpretation offer the analyst a powerful rhetorical resource. Whatever its merits as a theory or a source of personal insight, psychoanalysis is undeniably also a practical art that seeks to change the way patients understand themselves. Indeed, over the past two decades some influential analysts (Hillman 1983; Schafer 1992; Spence 1982) have come to see the clinician's task as essentially one of narrative reconstruction, the aim being not so much to capture an elusive truth as to find a story that 'works' for the patient. As interpretive strategies, the two kinds of irony discussed here can be seen as opposed but complementary ways of advancing this process by subverting the comfortable stories that patients typically bring into treatment. For those patients who resist change with pleas of illness or incapacity, there is the medicine of rhetorical irony, which exposes the active part that they play in their own suffering. For those who minimize their difficulties, insisting that they have no real problem, there is the more unsettling medicine of dramatic irony, which reveals that they are living under the sway of childish impulses they do not understand.

At the same time, a purely rhetorical view of irony in psychoanalysis appears to beg all the important questions. As Freud himself pointed out (1979 [1918]: 284), patients will take the hard work of analysis seriously only if they believe they are dealing with something real. What is more to the point, the very possibility of irony in psychoanalysis seems to require its access to realities that others cannot see. If it is true that irony always depends on a knowledge differential, then analytic irony would appear to hinge on the privileged status of analytic knowledge—its access to hidden things. What is more, since where irony is concerned knowledge is the mark of agency, each of the ironies exposed by psychoanalysis is also an implicit claim to analytic mastery. And since Freud's ironic aperçus extended beyond his patients to include religion, art, literature, and even civilization itself, those claims grow very large indeed.

This is where the questions arise. What warrant is there for this claim to a special knowledge? Doesn't it belie a certain hubris? And what, if anything, insulates the analyst or psychoanalysis itself from the dramatic ironies of the unconscious? These are precisely the questions that have animated a whole series of critical rejoinders to Freud over the past twenty years. While some of this work challenges the value of psychoanalysis on scientific grounds (Grunbaum 1984; MacMillan 1991), a larger and more intriguing group of studies accepts the subversive methods of analysis only to turn them on the founder himself.[7] The collective result of this work has been a compelling demonstration of the part played by Freud's own hidden desires—and those of his transferentially committed followers—in shaping the analytic edifice.

If there is a lesson here, it may be in J. Hillis Miller's observation that "irony … cannot be used as an instrument of mastery. It always masters the one who tries to master or take power with it" (1982: 108). Interestingly enough, some analysts draw a similar lesson from Freud's own thought. In his book *Terrors and Experts* (1995), Adam Phillips imagines a psychoanalysis that has learned to take its own precepts to heart. He notes that "Freud, after all, had done a very paradoxical thing: he had invented a form of authority, the science of psychoanalysis, as a treatment that depended on demolishing forms of authority" (ibid.: 30). As a way out of this paradox, Phillips suggests a distinction between the "Enlightenment Freud," an expert on human needs, and a "Post-Freudian Freud," who understands that "to be an expert on the unconscious is a contradiction in terms" (ibid.: 6). To follow this latter Freud, he says is to "become a new kind of expert, an expert on the truths of uncertainty." As for psychoanalysis itself, it "becomes an ironic critique … a primer of necessary ignorance, a reminder of the ironies of knowledge" (ibid.: 8).

Situated within this new and humbler version of psychoanalysis, the two interpretive lines considered here take on a more modest and reflexive quality. Beyond applying equally to everyone—analysts, patients, and the rest of us as well—they begin to offer something resembling a moral lesson. Following the pattern of rhetorical irony, they remind us that we often have more to gain from our troubles than we will admit and that becoming a victim or patient is always—among other things—a way of acting on the world. Following the pattern of dramatic irony, they remind us that we will always be somewhat obscure to ourselves, that we can never be entirely sure of who we are or why we act as we do. Taken together, these two attitudes seem to call for a sense of agency inflected not by confident knowledge but by a lively sense of the unknown and a certain permeability to the world and its accidents—a sense of agency, in other words, that is always tempered by irony.

NOTES

1. "Doubt whether a dream or certain of its details have been correctly reported is once more a derivative of the dream censorship, of resistance to the penetration of the dream-thoughts into consciousness ... If then, an indistinct element of a dream's content is in addition attacked by doubt, we have a sure indication that we are dealing with a comparatively direct derivative of one of the proscribed dream-thoughts" (Freud 1976 [1900]: 660–661).

2. This point is not quite as scandalous as it sounds. In his essay "Constructions in Analysis" (1963 [1937]), Freud notes that the patient's vehement denial may well mean that an interpretation is correct, but only in the presence of other corroborating evidence.

3. Passages such as this bring to mind the ancient Greek *eirôn*, who dissembles to avoid responsibility. In this case, of course, the patient is also the victim of the dissembling, which was perhaps, as Freud says, "the most expedient thing to do ... [although] a greater amount of moral courage would have been of advantage to the person concerned" (Freud and Breuer 1974 [1895]: 188).

4. As Freud said of his method: "The best way to speak about such things is to be dry and direct ... I call bodily organs and processes by their technical names ... *J'appelle un chat un chat*" (1977 [1905]: 82).

5. As for the would-be neurotics themselves, Freud states: "They would have to be honest, own up to the instincts that are at work in them, face the conflict, fight for what they want or go without, and the tolerance from the community which is bound to ensue as a result of psychoanalytical knowledge would help them in their task" (1963 [1910]: 85).

6. It is interesting that Freud cannot resist striking a prophetic pose at the moment of imparting this explanation to the boy (1977 [1909]: 204): "Long before he was in the world, I went on, I had known that a little Hans would come who would be so fond of his mother that he would be bound to feel afraid of his father because of it; and I had told his father this." Freud reports with amused satisfaction that on the way home afterwards, Hans asked: "Does the Professor talk to God, as he can tell all that beforehand?"

7. See, for example, Bass (1985), Bernheimer and Kahane (1990), Mahony (1984, 1996), and Rudnytsky (1987).

REFERENCES

Aristotle. 1947. "Poetics." In *Introduction to Aristotle*, edited by R. McKeon. New York: Modern Library.

———. 1953. *The Ethics of Aristotle*. Translated by J. A. K. Thomson. Harmondsworth: Penguin.

Bass, A. 1985. "On the History of a Mistranslation and the Psychoanalytic Movement." Pp. 102–141 in *Differences in Translation*, edited by J. F. Graham. Ithaca: Cornell University Press.

Bernheimer, C., and C. Kahane, eds. 1990. *In Dora's Case: Freud—Hysteria—Feminism*. 2nd ed. *Gender and Culture*. New York: Columbia University Press.

Burke, K. 1945. "Four Master Tropes." Pp. 503–517 in K. Burke, *A Grammar of Motives*. New York: Prentice-Hall.

Cuddihy, J. M. 1974. *The Ordeal of Civility: Freud, Marx, Levi-Strauss, and the Jewish Struggle with Modernity*. New York: Basic Books.

Fernandez, J., and M. T. Huber, eds. 2001. *Irony in Action: Anthropology, Practice, and the Moral Imagination*. Chicago: University of Chicago Press.

Freud, S. 1962 [1930]. *Civilization and Its Discontents*. New York: W.W. Norton & Co.

———. 1963 [1910]. "The Future Prospects of Psychoanalytic Therapy." Pp. 77–88 in *Therapy and Technique*, edited by P. Reiff. New York: Collier Books.

————. 1963 [1914]. "Recollection, Repetition and Working Through." In *Freud: Therapy and Technique*, edited by P. Reiff. New York: Collier Books.

————. 1963 [1937]. "Constructions in Analysis." Pp. 273–286 in *Freud: Character and Culture*, edited by P. Reiff. New York: Collier Books.

————. 1965 [1901]. *The Psychopathology of Everyday Life*. New York: Norton.

————. 1973 [1915–1917]. *Introductory Lectures on Psychoanalysis*. New York: Penguin Books.

————. 1976 [1900]. *The Interpretation of Dreams*. London: Penguin Books.

————. 1977 [1905]. "Fragment of an Analysis of a Case of Hysteria ('Dora')." Pp. 31–166 in *Sigmund Freud Case Histories I: "Dora" and "Little Hans,"* edited by A. Richards. London: Penguin Books.

————. 1977 [1909]. "Analysis of a Phobia in a Five-Year-Old Boy ("Little Hans")." In *Sigmund Freud: Case Histories I: "Dora" and "Little Hans,"* edited by A. Richards. London: Penguin.

————. 1979 [1909]. "Notes upon a Case of Obsessional Neurosis." Pp. 33–100 in *Sigmund Freud: Case Histories II*, edited by A. Richards. London: Penguin.

————. 1979 [1911]. "Psychoanalytic Notes on an Autobiographical Account of a Case of Paranoia ("Schreber")." Pp. 131–226 in *Sigmund Freud: Case Histories II*, edited by A. Richards. London: Penguin.

————. 1979 [1918]. "From the History of an Infantile Neurosis ("The Wolf Man")." In *Sigmund Freud: Case Histories II*, edited by A. Richards. London: Penguin.

————. 1984 [1912–1913]. "Totem and Taboo." In *Freud: The Origins of Religion*, edited by A. Richards. London: Penguin Books.

————. 1984[1920]. "Beyond the Pleasure Principle." Pp. 269–338 in *On Metapsychology: The Theory of Psychoanalysis*, edited by A. Richards. London: Penguin Books.

————. 1985 [1910]. "Leonardo DaVinci and a Memory of His Childhood." Pp. 151–229 in *Freud: Art and Literature*, edited by A. Richards. London: Penguin Books.

Freud, S., and J. Breuer. 1974 [1895]. *Studies on Hysteria*. London: Penguin Books.

Friedrich, P. 2001. "Ironic Irony." Pp. 224–252 in *Irony in Action: Anthropology, Practice, and the Moral Imagination*, edited by J. Fernandez and M. T. Huber. Chicago: University of Chicago Press.

Grunbaum, A. 1984. *The Foundations of Psychoanalysis*. Berkeley: University of California Press.

Hillman, J. 1983. *Healing Fiction*. Barrytown, N.Y.: Station Hill Press.

MacMillan, M. 1991. *Freud Evaluated: The Completed Arc*. New York: North-Holland.

Mahony, P. 1984. *Cries of the Wolf Man: History of Psychoanalysis, Monograph 1*. New York: International Universities Press.

————. 1996. *Freud's Dora: A Psychoanalytic, Historical and Textual Study*. New Haven: Yale University Press.

Micale, M. S. 1995. *Approaching Hysteria: Disease and Its Interpretations*. Princeton: Princeton University Press.

Miller, J. H. 1982. *Fiction and Repetition: Seven English Novels*. Cambridge: Harvard University Press.

Muecke, D. C. 1969. *The Compass of Irony*. London: Methuen.

————. 1982. *Irony and the Ironic*. London: Methuen.

Nehamas, A. 1998. *The Art of Living: Socratic Reflections from Plato to Foucault*. Berkeley: University of California Press.

Phillips, A. 1995. *Terrors and Experts*. Cambridge: Harvard University Press.

Rudnytsky, P. L. 1987. *Freud and Oedipus*. New York: Columbia University Press.

Schafer, R. 1992. *Retelling a Life*. New York: Basic Books.

Schorske, C. E. 1979. *Fin-de-siècle Vienna: Politics and Culture*. New York: Knopf (distributed by Random House).

Spence, D. 1982. *Narrative Truth and Historical Truth*. New York: Norton.

Thirlwall, C. 1833. "On the Irony of Sophocles." *The Philological Museum*, vol 2.

Chapter 6

SENILITY AND
IRONY'S AGE

Lawrence Cohen

I turned around, but Socrates was nowhere to be seen ...
Let him alone, said my informant; he has a way of stopping anywhere and
losing himself without any reason.

— Plato, *Symposium*

Between *Pralāpa* and Murder

There is a Sanskrit story of ancient provenance about an old priest named Aitasha
who, while reciting the speech of the sacrifice, begins to talk in a language no one
can recognize. This language has come down to us as Aitasha's *pralāpa*, his babble. The priest's son, worried about his father's inability to conduct the sacrifice

Notes for this chapter begin on page 132.

properly, prevents the old man from continuing. Aitasha is furious; he curses his son for murdering his speech.

This essay is concerned with the hearing of senile language, from Aitasha's *pralāpa* to modern dementia. If senility is the perception of troubling behavioral change in someone understood to be old (Cohen 1995), an anthropological inquiry into its incidence and effects might begin with the insight that this change is often something *heard*. "Listen to her!" I was frequently instructed in several years of fieldwork on senility in a north Indian town. Voice is central to the first European instances of physicians making sovereign claims of authority over old bodies with aberrant behavior: the appeals to the Prince and against the Inquisition of Renaissance doctors Reginald Scot and Johannes Weyer. Scot and Weyer offered an expert reinterpretation of the voices of accused witches as those of "doting old women" (Cohen 1998). At stake in many cases was what Alan Macfarlane (1970) classically described as shifts in ethics of care, in which demands for support by widows and other indigent women in particular came to be heard as threatening and troubling speech, as the curse. The question of the voice and of its possible or impossible coherence came to dominate my thinking. In this essay, I try to locate anthropological consideration of the senile voice in that space between *pralāpa* and murder, between diagnosis and displacement.

To think about how a senile voice is heard—and responded to—I turn to a discussion of irony developed by Paul Antze and Michael Lambek in conversation with the work of Alexander Nehamas on Socratic irony. In *The Art of Living*, Nehamas writes of Socrates' voice in the Platonic dialogues as meaning neither what it appears to say—if in a coded and provocative register suitable to pedagogy—nor the contrary to what it appears to say, but rather and simply meaning something *else*. For Nehamas, it is this opacity of Socrates' voice, combined with the integrity of his commitment to an ethics in the absence of a positive philosophy on which to base one's actions, that renders his voice and persona available as a model for others to constitute their own self-crafting practice of ethics, their own "art of living" (1998: 12, 57, 60, 67).

In the conversations that provoked the writing of this essay, Lambek and Antze have suggested the relevance of this reading of Socratic irony for thinking about the voice of the shamanic healer, the person possessed whose voice makes it possible for another to constitute a new kind of self, perhaps a new art of living. While the possibilities for rethinking not only possession healing but also the variety of contemporary psychotherapeutics through such an understanding of irony may be apparent, the use of such a conception in thinking about what I have termed senility is less obvious. Neither Aitasha nor his son make claims that the old man's voice means something *else*, that it points to some third possibility besides babble or proper ritual speech. Their fight appears dependent upon the failure of irony all around. Nor have the dominant figurations of dementia care since the rise of Alzheimer's as a clinical and popular concept in the 1970s and 1980s been ironic in their own claims upon senile bodies and voices.

In the face of my inability to meet Lambek and Antze's provocation head-on, I have constructed this essay as a series of sideways reflections on senility, old age, and irony. As these are reflections, I offer no single argument, and readers may be uncomfortable with such meandering fare. The reflections are organized around three assertions. The first is that there may be a kind of listening to senility that can be called ironic, and to which we might want to pay continued attention. Readers will note my shifting the locus of irony from an act of speaking to one of *listening*, a shift that is influenced by how I think one should approach senility. My work has stayed away from the hermeneutic project of fixing what a senile voice *really* intends, indexes, or means and has lingered on the question of how persons (including but not limited to the person so labeled) hear a senile voice, how they listen to it.

The second assertion, given that senility has since the late twentieth century been increasingly organized in metonymic correspondence with the brain and in some cases the gene, is that one might frame *as ironic* a kind of critical thinking that both draws on and yet troubles the 'biologization' of everything. Classic critiques of the shift into the biological as a process of medicalization—or more particularly, of "biomedicalization" (Lyman 1989)—often presume the coherence of some opposite move, some return to the 'social', against any apparent interest by clients or practitioners. Against these, a new kind of cultural critic has emerged, taking the biological 'seriously' but in oddly troped ways (see Zizek 2003 and the response by Lancaster 2003). The question may be how to think, and act, in the face of biomedicalization, and here a sense of ironic action may be useful. To be ironic in the face of biomedicalization may be to reimagine the work of the category and the pharmacy. Clarity as to what 'irony' is and is not here is critical. My colleague Paul Rabinow has called attention (personal communication) to the persistence of an easy irony in much critical science studies, a challenge parallel to his critique of Bourdieuvian *illusio* (1996), but what he is troubling is I think quite distinct from Socratic irony.

The third assertion is that classical formulations of irony—here I engage both Plato and Vico—are frequently constructed in reference to some problem of the aging of things. Alcibiades accuses Socrates' speech of *eirôneia* within his drunken lament in the *Symposium* (Plato 1928) that Socrates—who is always going after the youth—was leading him on, was cruelly playing at love. The status of Socrates' nonyouth, and its relation to old age, is in question within one of the critical texts framing Socratic irony as a contested ethical practice. Vico, of course, offers irony as the last of the four tropes in the progressive rationalization and disenchantment of the primitive poetics that inaugurates each historical era: it is the trope of the old age of history itself (1984 [1744]). How these two formulations taken together might relate to an anthropology of things over time seems worth reflection.

Irony as an Ethics of Listening

What makes a voice troubling to different listeners may not be a matter of meaning per se. Proper ritual speech—what Aitasha's son expected him to say—may lack any meaningful referent even when 'correctly' spoken (Staal 1989). But it is recognizable and exemplifies a particular order, in contrast to *pralāpa*, which threatens to destroy the orderly conduct of the sacrifice through its strangeness.

The issue is the same on the other side of meaning. The senile deformation of meaningful utterance is not necessarily a turn to meaninglessness. In many cases in my north Indian fieldwork, both the untroubled *and* the troubling speech of old persons was laden with meaningful referent. The dominant threat of a senile voice often lay precisely in its all-but-irrefutable claims of meaningfulness. For example, an old woman in what is now Kolkata screamed that her daughter-in-law had imprisoned her and was starving and beating her and begged passers-by to come to her rescue. What this old woman's voice disturbed were a series of orderings of bodies and relations in language: children's responsibilities to their parents, the inside of the household versus the outside of the street.

(In stressing a disturbance in language, I am not suggesting a *reduction* of the ways senility may trouble the old person in question or those around him or her to a matter of voice. In the example just given, the old woman repeatedly hid things and, in arguing or wandering, took up many hours of time that her son and daughter-in-law could not give to their work, themselves, or others. What I am noting is that voice served as the metonymic vehicle by which what was at stake in such a situation could be conveyed.)

In the case of both Aitasha and the old woman in Kolkata, a voice troubled when it turned the *order* of language—its relation to normative kinship, to space, or to the sacrifice—inside out. This essay is structuralist in taking this order of language, kinship, space, and sacrifice as an object of contemplation, one variant of the anthropologist's 'culture'. It is poststructuralist in reading such order as a dreamworld knowable at its moment of fragmentation and historical impossibility (Buck-Morss 2000) or through the often painful failures of positioned efforts to identify with it and frame one's desires accordingly (Trawick 1992). Senility does not so much turn the actual order of things inside out as trouble our desire for and identification with such an order.

When *Newsweek* in 1989 tried to illustrate what it took as the devastation Alzheimer's disease visited upon caregivers, it told the story of Frank from Boston, who along with his wife and daughter lived with his demented mother Ina. Ina says strange things, and the article details these and the threat they offer to Frank and family. As one sign of filial pathos, the writer describes Frank and one of his sisters staying up all night to wallpaper his mother's room. Why such an action is necessarily traumatic and why it specifically figures Ina's senility is not obvious. A clue comes in Frank's admission, after repeated probing by a journalist demanding trauma, that because of Ina ending up with him, his lifelong dream of going west, camping out, and sleeping on the ground has had to be put on hold. His mom aside, Frank has a job and a family and is not rushing off to live this variant of the great American dream. Ina makes life difficult for Frank and his wife, but it is less her disabling of the structure of everyday life than of Frank's dream of life (here, as the cowboy's westward odyssey) that conveys the force of senile trouble and that can transform nocturnal wallpapering into *grand guignol* (Kantrowitz 1989).

Senility thus can be framed as a voice that threatens—whether the threat is to everyday household norms or to the ritual constitution of cosmic order—through disordered speaking, which challenges the very continuity of culture. As such, senility may elicit a countervoice that positions the senile speaker as an exile from this order, whether as the nonperson ('he's no longer himself') that much contemporary Western counterspeech about Alzheimer's disease demands (Cohen 1995; Herskovits 1995) or as the willful subject of excessive desire that characterizes both early modern European discussions of dotage, folly, excessive choler, and witchcraft and numerous and distinct non-Western worlds (Cohen 1998: 72–79; Traphagan 2000). Sarah Lamb's discussion (2000) of the "biomorality" (Marriott 1976) of age and the frequent accusation against old persons of excessive attachment and desire in a Bengali village in the late 1980s offers a powerfully delineated example of the latter.

The work of these countervoices of diagnosis or accusation—and I am not implying a normative critique in identifying them as such—is usually to guarantee that senile voices are to be heard as radically exterior to the order of language, kinship, and culture. This radical removal of the voice from culture I will, after the story of Aitasha, term 'murdering the voice'. Again, I do not use 'murder' to imply a particular forensics or normative claim but rather to call attention to the external force that renders a senile voice impossible to hear, to suggest that it is never simply the voice in itself that is a priori incoherent.

I have elsewhere described support groups of the Alzheimer's Association in the United States in the mid-1980s where adult children and partners of senile persons were made to *iterate* their loved ones' likely Alzheimer's status as a disease in order to perform the clinical imperative that all previous norms of filial recognition and responsibility needed to be called into question (1998: 16–17, 55–58). In classic American twelve-step form, the support group was predicated upon the confession of one's loved one's status as a person with Alzheimer's. These children and partners heard their senile relations in a variety of ways, not all demanding diagnosis, the deferral of kinship norms, or institutionalization. The work of the group was to rationalize and routinize their listening into a uniform disease model, with institutionalization as its outcome.

In a classic piece of research on dementia, Colleen and Frank Johnson (1983) showed how a medical work-up centering on expert listening comprising the mental-status exam was utilized only when families had exhausted other means of listening and were ready for the institutionalization of a senile parent or partner. As with the Alzheimer's Association study, Johnson and Johnson's work focuses on a set of expert practices that function to remove a voice from the order of language and exhaust its relevance in the symptomatology and semiotics of disease.

There are other kinds of care, however, in and out of the clinic, which may involve a different relation to the senile voice, one I would term ironic. These other forms are not necessarily 'better' or 'worse', and I distrust my own possible romancing of them. Still, they merit attention.

I think, for example, of Deborah Hoffman's extraordinary 1994 film *Complaints of a Dutiful Daughter*, chronicling her mother's progressive dementia and Hoffman's efforts to help her mother and herself. The account is familiar: her mother's growing lapses of memory and loss of connection to their shared history is accompanied by moments of wandering, panic, and strange hoarding. In the beginning, Hoffman painfully holds her mother to account for this lost history, questioning her again and again, trying to find some familiar and shared marker, as if terrified of having to 'recognize' (as in the support groups described above) that this person is in some serious way no longer her mother.

But something happens beyond, or at least other than, such recognition. Rather than coming to realize that this person is in effect no longer herself, Hoffman comes instead to a recognition that her mother can no longer be bound to their shared history. As this latter recognition sharpens, the filmmaker can again *listen* to her mother. Her words freed from necessary correspondence to a specific history, the older woman has a newly coherent voice. Her speech is surprisingly no longer simply *pralāpa*. Within the ironic time of this *now*, beyond expected correspondences, unexpected recognitions occur for both women.[1]

I call this temporality ironic since within it words neither correspond to the expected referents of a shared history (that is, are coherent) nor are they necessarily radically beyond coherence. Senility heard ironically offers no redemptive or hidden speech, but neither does it of necessity reduce the voice to *pralāpa*.

Irony and Medicalization

If irony suggests a practice of signification in which speaking implies neither fealty to the subjectifying effects of a given language nor simply their antithesis, then the kinds of possibilities for irony in the face of senility extend beyond the question of listening. The context, again, is the reduction of senility in much of the world to dementia and specifically to Alzheimer's disease. The popular knowledge I grew up with and frequently saw confirmed—that adverse living conditions and in particular (in my world) the monotony of many old-age homes could make you senile—gave way under the age of Alzheimer's.

I might tell the story of a great-aunt living in a Montreal old-age home who spent the week with my family during the prescribed period of mourning after a funeral. Generally thought by my cousins and aunts who took care of her to be growing senile, this aunt, over the course of a week in the space of extended family, appeared to all to improve considerably in her memory and lack of confusion, a feat treated as wonderful, if inexplicable.

By an ironic engagement with medicalization, I mean the ability first to trouble the sufficiency of classifications. One of my college professors in the late 1970s told us of a study she had done in two matched nursing home wards, in which half the inmates were given frequent opportunities to make basic decisions regarding how to allocate their time and resources and half were subjected to the usual passive and total institutional treatment. The half that were allowed to make choices, she revealed, over several years turned out to live longer and with less evidence of cognitive impairment. This kind of research, coming just as the newly rediscovered ubiquity of Alzheimer's disease was becoming a feature of Western European and North American popular culture, was quickly forgotten in the 1980s when its author's apparent claim that senility was *not* caused by Alzheimer's but rather by the mindless conditions of institutional life seemed exaggerated and impossible.

Both the newly hegemonic ontogeny of dementia as Alzheimer's and such counterclaims operate through an either-or logic: senility is a matter either of the brain or of institutional settings—one must choose. Such a choice underestimates the power and value of biological reduction and implies a false dichotomy. Given the hegemony of this reduction, complex or hybrid ontogenies of senility are difficult in practice to sustain: despite my own sustained reflection on the topic, it was hard to engage family members in a different kind of thinking about senility. By an ironic engagement with classification, I do not imply a refusal, a turn to the antithesis of what the categories imply, a claim that aged great-aunts or others do not face the transformations that we today term the senile dementias. What I am suggesting is a way of engaging these categories against their metonymic tendency to stand for the whole of an ontogeny. That I failed in my initial efforts to achieve such an ironic voice suggests, as one might expect, that a Socratic art and ethic are not so easily achieved.

By an ironic relation to the pharmacy I engage one of the dominant features of a sociology of dementia today, the proliferation of caregiver-driven medication with new structures of marketing and publicity. An ironic approach to the reduction of medicine to pharmacology would neither dismiss nor uncritically embrace the usefulness of this new, and not so new, pharmacopoeia. It would never presume what an ethics of drug use would look like.

In the case of most dementia drugs, their hype vastly exceeds their promise. A suggestion by the sociologist Veena Das in reference to my work on the marketing of both high-end dementia drugs and old-age tonics has stayed with me: never to see the value of the drug only in terms of its efficacy, or lack thereof, but simultaneously to see it in terms of the work it does *as a gift*, from a loved one to an aging and often ailing person, as an acknowledgment of the senile voice in its mode of complaint.

Is Old Age Ironic?

I turn to the third and lengthiest of these sideways reflections: Is irony old? A funny question, perhaps, so I begin with what on the surface is a more sensible one: Is Socrates old? The answer may hinge on a play of oppositions:

ugly/beautiful, strong/weak, inside/outside, untimely/timely. As Nehamas notes, Socrates' depiction as Silenus, the externally ugly satyr hiding internal beauty, has been a central figure of his interpretation, from Alcibiades' accusation in the *Symposium* through the work of Montaigne and Nietzsche. Socrates is signifiably not young, if youth, as Alcibiades suggests, has fairness as its mark. Age, the younger man reports Socrates saying, is the time when "the mind begins to grow critical," and philosophers almost by definition cannot be young. Yet Alcibiades also reveals that Socrates' nonyouth is considerably hardier than the strength of much younger soldiers: at the end of the party, Socrates, who had come in wandering and redolent of senescent confusion, has drunk everyone else under the table and remains awake, alert, and intellectually agile. He is Nestor with the strength of Pericles. But even as he offers this juxtaposition, Alcibiades goes on to admit that no mythic reference seems to capture Socrates' age.

Socrates is old, in this confounding and demythologized sense of ugly but strong, but he is not old enough that his death can appear timely to his companions and followers. Though in the *Apology* (Plato 1969a) he is "like a father or an elder brother" to the leading men of Athens, and though if his accusers had "waited just a little while," he would have died "in the course of nature," his execution raises profound questions about the order of justice and about life and death. Socrates must reconcile his followers both to the impossibility of a meaningful life outside the law (in *Crito*, Plato 1969b) and to the possibility of approaching one's own death without fear or regret (in *Phaedo*, Plato 1969c). In this reconciliation, Socrates in effect achieves a death under the law but outside, if just barely, the order of nature. Despite his interest, in the opening of the *Republic*, in talking with the aged Cephalus to learn about the latter's somewhat frail if well-preserved old age as "a road that we too may have to tread," Socrates' own end lies elsewhere.

Historian Georges Minois, in his encyclopedic *Histoire de la Vieillesse en Occident de l'Antiquité à la Renaissance*, summarizes the 'Greek world' in terms of a "recherché incessante de la Beauté" that left old age a matter of sadness and malediction (1987: 71–72). Plato, Minois argues, is one of the few apologists for old age in this world, but the exalted position he offers the old in his ideal city is yet a testament to their abjection in the quotidian politics of the age (ibid.: 89–93): the dominant Greek image of the old is comic ugliness (ibid.: 81–84). Socrates' achievement in such a context is doubled: achieving an old age that is far from pitiable, Pericles in Nestor's body, something almost indescribable within the dominant mythos of aging; and achieving a death outside of the natural order of decrepitude, beyond old age, and yet within the law.

I will read the matter of Socrates' old age as an embodiment of Socratic irony, deferring for now the intriguing question of the relation of this irony to the law. At stake, ultimately, is a body that cannot easily be read within conventional binaries—this versus that—and their apparent guarantee of meaning. It is neither that Socrates' body as Alcibiades would have it is a Silenic dissimulation—ugly outside, beautiful in essence—nor that it contains in the instance of this concealment some secret truth, some ethic for those able to read the signs. It is only that Socrates' body, by turns not fair, not weak, aging uniquely, and evading age altogether, casts doubt on what it is to be or not be old, that it troubles the adequacy of any particular gerontology.

Socratic irony, for Nehamas, "does not always hide an unambiguous truth" (1998: 67). Socrates "appears more real than fictional" precisely because he is rendered by Plato as "incomprehensible and opaque" (ibid.: 91). This liminal register is elsewhere framed by Nehamas as a matter of sound: Socrates' irony is "the silence that envelops his life and character" (ibid.: 10, 12). And this silence enables latter-day philosophers to take Socrates as a model for an ethics as an 'art of living' without undue risk of their own engagement being reduced to mere imitation. Socratic irony, Nehamas notes after Kierkegaard, is a matter of infinite negativity (ibid.: 71). Socrates' body, refusing transparent or audible meaning within the binary old/young, points elsewhere, demands a different accounting.

The specificity of this 'elsewhere' varies, given what mode of reason and practice is being accounted for. Contemporary old age may be constituted as an assemblage (Rabinow 1999) of many such modes and moments: some of the more compelling recent accounts of old age have focused critically on the figures of perfectibility (Cole 1992) and the norm (Katz 1996) in what comes to constitute late life and their relation to new and ongoing incitements of capital (Featherstone and Wernick 1994). Against the perfectible, normalizing, or commodified regimes of age that these authors address, we might imagine the old age of a Socratic body and the demands that its silence and opacity place upon us. The challenge for scholars writing on late life today, in the face of the various welfare apparatuses caring, or not caring, for those we call the old, is not merely how to iterate the normative machinery constituting old age (Cohen 1994), but rather how to learn something new.

Irony as a figure of the last days is at least as old as Vico. Human history, in *The New Science*, suggests an arc of development and forgetting in which the imaginative identifications of humanity's childhood are condensed, reworked, and eventually set adrift, a cyclical progression through the sequential tropes of metaphor, metonym, synecdoche, and irony. Irony marks the fallen present as an epoch of historical senility in which the continual reworking of the root metaphors poetically anchoring a given world's language and myth have rendered the once enchanted and obvious relation of things to each other entirely contingent, the old metaphors forgotten; it is simultaneously an epoch in which such radical contingency holds out the possibility of a new poetic order taking hold.

What, if any, relation might there be between the irony of old age and this old age of irony? Vico's *recurso* troubles any linear sense of the last days: the incoherence of the disenchanted present provides the material and force for its reenchantment under a new dispensation of metaphor. Is a Socratic understanding of aging similarly to trouble its linear presumptions? Historian Thomas Cole's work chronicles the disenchantment of the life course over the past five hundred years, its shift from cyclic to linear form (1992). Is the purpose of an ironic reading to return to such a premodern understanding?

Much of the contemporary anthropology of old age seems to take its mission as precisely that. Old age has become devalued, and the discipline's mission is to return it to cultural preeminence through the heartfelt exploration of closely textured, gritty, bittersweet accounts of 'the life cycle'. I have argued that this gerontological anthropology has been dominated by two particular tropes—of anger ("old age is not being taken seriously as a topic, and I'm mad as hell about it!") and of ambiguity ("old age is a time of experience and debility, achievement and loss, honor and abjection, and, in the final analysis, all accounts of it will reflect this ambivalence") (Cohen 1994). Socratic irony must do more than shore up this anger or iterate vague appeals to ambiguity if it is to be a useful frame for rethinking old age.

The challenge is to push anthropology beyond normative iteration: old age as better or worse, or as some mixture of the two. One disciplinary figure worth reconsidering—particularly in reference to Vico's old age of irony—is the Frazerian figure of the dying and regenerated god-king (Cohen 1998: 288–289). *The Golden Bough* systematized a Victorian anxiety and desire for demythologization by organizing the state of nature around a particular feature of primitive error: the need to prevent the aging of the cosmos—dangerously identified with the aging of its sovereign—through killing an old king and replacing him with a younger successor. As for Vico, the coherence of things in a Frazerian universe becomes undone, if for very different reasons and within a significantly compressed time span—the life of the sovereign. The sovereign's old age threatens the continuity of life and culture, rooted in the necessary correspondence of the king's body with the commonwealth. The old body deforms this equation: it must be removed, in some sense 'killed'. Primitive thought, within such a Frazerian matrix, lacks irony.

Culture, in a sense, is the maintenance of timelessness (and thus, in Vico's sense, of the equivalences of metaphor) through the removal or erasure of signs of decay on bodies, such as those of sovereigns, that exemplify the whole. The Frazerian insight is to see violent *temporal* rupture at the heart of culture. These ruptures and their killing, like Socrates' old age, are just outside of nature yet within the law: they are outside of nature as decrepitude must be avoided, and they are within the law as this 'killing' *is not murder*. It is on the contrary essential to reason: people grow old, but the order of things must be extended.

Senility often troubles when the accusation of its disordering voice frames the necessity of such killing as a crime, as murder. Senility intensifies the Frazerian demand of erasure: one must kill, but against reason one stands accused of a crime. The solution is to get rid of the evidence. The means of displacement, the marking of a body as other and obsolete, are various.

One displaces through reproduction—by *becoming* one's parents or teachers. Such becoming may or may not allow for a coexistence of parent and adult child. In my 1980s fieldwork on old age in urban north India, I found that adult children coexisted with old women more easily than with old men within the space of an extended family, while old women not tied to a single household threatened far more than similarly unplaced old men. *One displaces through parody*—by framing the old body as a thing of infinitely exaggerated desire, whose voice can only be heard *in extremis*, like the pantaloons, bawds, and dotards of the Restoration theater. I have documented parodic reconstitutions of both old and senile voices in mainstream news media in the United States, as well as in expert medical discourse (1998: 47–60). *One displaces*, finally, *through incomprehension*—through hearing *nothing* in the lament or demand of the elder, refusing the specificity of a voice by hearing *only* its sickness, madness, or curse, or conversely, its hoary wisdom.

To hear ironically is neither simply to displace through willed incomprehension or some romantic or impossible alternative, nor to hold on to things as they are. It is not to escape from the burden of killing, but it is to discriminate between this burden and the accusation of murder, and thus it is not to hide the body and therefore not to be haunted by its ghostly presence as a speaking corpse. If killing is not murder, then perhaps there is a kind of listening that can yet transpire and an ethic of care that is not merely a redoubling of parricidal force. To hear ironically is to hear language and its correspondence and everyday work in unexpected ways.

Hoffman's film suggests that in listening ironically, the fact of killing in no way exhausts the possibilities of voice. Irony in Vico presents a challenge to the continuity of language, but at least in the first instance it seems to call for an act of displacement, as in Frazer: the return of youthful metaphor and the destruction of ironic consciousness. But against the doubled figure of the old and young sovereign, the former refusing to yield and the latter demanding his or her displacement, the figure of Socrates offers a different reading of irony's old age. Socrates stands on both sides of history, as it were. He is available for our own ethical work as we locate him in what for Vico was the preceding age of heroes. Socrates *does* embody the spirit of Pericles, Nestor, Achilles, and others, but while exemplifying the particular *arete* of each, he mixes them and troubles their expected reference in—through our listening—making himself a new man.

NOTES

1. That this dyad is a mother and daughter and my initial example of ironic failure was of a father (Aitasha) and his son may suggest the relevance of gender to the troping of senility. For Vico, the descent into irony follows the decline from a hypermasculine age of heroes into the present.

REFERENCES

Buck-Morss, Susan. 2000. *Dreamworld and Catastrophe: The Passing of Mass Utopia in East and West*. Cambridge: MIT Press.

Cohen, Lawrence. 1994. "Old Age: Cultural and Critical Perspectives." *Annual Review of Anthropology* 23:137–158.

———. 1995. "Toward an Anthropology of Senility: Anger, Weakness, and Alzheimer's in Banaras, India." *Medical Anthropology Quarterly* 9, no. 3:314–334.

———. 1998. *No Aging in India: Alzheimer's, the Bad Family, and Other Modern Things*. Berkeley: University of California Press.

Cole, Thomas R. 1992. *The Journey of Life: A Cultural History of Aging in America*. Cambridge: Cambridge University Press.

Featherstone, Mike, and Andrew Wernick. 1994. "Introduction." Pp. 1–15 in *Images of Aging: Cultural Representations of Later Life*, edited by Mike Featherstone and Andrew Wernick. London: Routledge.

Herskovits, Elizabeth. 1995. "Struggling over Subjectivity: Debates about the 'Self' and Alzheimer's Disease." *Medical Anthropology Quarterly* 9, no. 2:146–164.

Hoffman, Deborah. 1994. *Complaints of a Dutiful Daughter* [film]. New York: Women Make Movies.

Johnson, Colleen Leahy, and Frank A. Johnson. 1983. "A Micro-Analysis of 'Senility': The Responses of the Family and the Health Professionals." *Culture, Medicine, and Psychiatry* 7:77–96.

Kantrowitz, Barbara. 1989. "Trapped Inside Her Own World." *Newsweek*, 18 December.

Katz, Stephen. 1996. *Disciplining Old Age: The Formation of Gerontological Knowledge*. Charlottesville: University Press of Virginia.

Lamb, Sarah. 2000. *White Saris and Sweet Mangoes: Aging, Gender, and Body in North India*. Berkeley: University of California Press.

Lancaster, Roger. 2003. "Letters: Do Your Homework" [response to Slavoj Zizek]. *London Review of Books* 25, no. 12:4.

Lyman, Karen A. 1989. "Bringing the Social Back In: A Critique of the Biomedicalization of Dementia." *Gerontologist* 29, no. 5:597–605.

Macfarlane, Alan. 1970. *Witchcraft in Tudor and Stuart England: A Regional and Comparative Study*. New York: Harper and Row.

Marriott, Mckim. 1976. "Hindu Transactions: Diversity without Dualism." In *Transaction and Meaning: Directions in the Anthropology of Exchange and Symbolic Behavior*, edited by Bruce Kapferer. Philadelphia: Institute for the Study of Human Issues.

Minois, Georges. 1987. *Histoire de la Vieillesse en Occident de l'Antiquité à la Renaissance*. Paris: Fayard.

Nehamas, Alexander. 1998. *The Art of Living: Socratic Reflections from Plato to Foucault*. Berkeley: University of California Press.

Plato. 1928. *Symposium*. Pp. 333–393 in *The Works of Plato*, translated by Benjamin Jowett; edited by Irwin Edman. New York: Modern Library.

———. 1969a. *Apology*. Pp. 45–76 in *The Last Days of Socrates*, edited and translated by Hugh Tredennick. Harmondsworth: Penguin.

———. 1969b. *Crito*. Pp. 79–96 in *The Last Days of Socrates*, edited and translated by Hugh Tredennick. Harmondsworth: Penguin.

———. 1969c. *Phaedo*. Pp. 99–183 in *The Last Days of Socrates*, edited and translated by Hugh Tredennick. Harmondsworth: Penguin.

Rabinow, Paul. 1996. *Essays on the Anthropology of Reason*. Princeton: Princeton University Press.

———. 1999. *French DNA: Trouble in Purgatory*. Chicago: University of Chicago Press.

Staal, Frits. 1989. *Rules without Meaning: Ritual, Mantras, and the Human Sciences*. New York: P. Lang.

Traphagan, John W. 2000. *Taming Oblivion: Aging Bodies and the Fear of Senility in Japan*. New York: State University of New York Press.

Trawick, Margaret. 1992. *Notes on Love in a Tamil Family*. Berkeley: University of California Press.

Vico, Giambattista. 1984 [1744]. *The New Science, Third Edition*. Translated by Thomas Goddard Bergin and Max Harold Fisch. Paperback edition. Ithaca: Cornell University Press.

Zizek, Slavoj. 2003. "Bring Me My Philips Mental Jacket: Slavoj Zizek Welcomes the Prospect of Biogenetic Intervention." *London Review of Books* 25, no. 10:3, 5.

Afterword

Vincent Crapanzano

> What should we be without the sexual myth,
> The human revery or poem of death?
>
> — Wallace Stevens, *Men Made Out of Words*

It is a privilege to have been asked to write an afterword to this fine collection of essays on illness and irony. They offer a far more radical critique of anthropological practice than any one of their authors is likely to admit. In making this observation, I assume the privilege of the afterword but reject the definity it presumes. I prefer provocation. Hopefully, it will perpetuate the speculative thrust—the implication—of the essays. I will refrain from commenting specifically on any one of them, as a discussant at a conference or a critic might, for that would be an exploitation of the position of the writer of an afterword. I will, of course, refer to them from time to time. My emphasis will be on irony rather more than illness and suffering.[1]

It is by now a truism that our ethnographies and ethnologies are always limited by our social and cultural investment. However critically reflective we are, we can never attain to an investment-free vision of the way things are. Wherever there is insight, there is blindness. Wherever there is blindness, there is insight. We can never fully escape ethnocentrism. Indeed, were we able to do so, what would our anthropologies look like? How would we—or those others—read them? Could we—could they—read them without introducing bias? We aspire to an ideal that is perhaps more dangerous than the recognition of our deficiencies. All of this is a long way about to say that the implications of our assumptions about language and discourse are perhaps the most difficult to recognize and reckon with, not only because recognition and reckoning are themselves cast in language and its discursive forms and maneuvers, but because they themselves are subject to the whims of desire and the dictates of power, neither of which is immune to language and discourse. As Michael Lambek says, our biomedicine is subject to a literalist regime. I would go further: our science, certainly our anthropologies—those of North America, at least—are subject to such a regime. Though it is impossible to purify language of rhetoric, figuration, and generic constraint (the logical positivists notwith-standing), it is possible to recognize their implication—that is, if we do not sur-render to the preclusive regimes of reading and interpreting that support that literalism, those orientations, scientific or not. These regimes always risk stum-bling on what they have precluded. However we feel about the deconstruc-tionists, we must recognize the often hysterical defenses lodged against *their* attempt to read *our* texts from *their* perspective as symptoms of the disciplinary territorialism that those reading regimes bolster. I imagine the Azande would have reacted in much the same way to Evans-Pritchard's readings of their witchcraft scenarios, had they been privy to them and had they not been sub-ject to the discretion imposed by imperial arrangement.

Despite our ever growing sensitivity to the nuances of indigenous texts and discourse, our literalism—or, perhaps more accurately, our blindness to our lit-eralism—has impaired, if it has not precluded, our sensitivity to prevailing tropes in the cultures we study. More importantly, it has impeded an apprecia-tion of the status of language, discourse, and communication—and by exten-sion, social and political arrangements—indexed by those tropes. We must remember that hedging tropes such as irony call attention to, if they do not con-stitute, the way in which language, discourse, and communication are con-ceived of, evaluated, and interpreted. An American Christian Fundamentalist would look askance, if not with horror, at an ironic reading of Scripture. A Jesuit during the baroque era might have taken delight in the same ironic read-ing; he might have expounded on the artifice of language and the glory of God. One might find a pair of similar responses to an ironic reading of the Koran by one of today's Islamicists and a Sufi mystic. It seems clear that even if we were to assert that irony—that is, rhetorical or Socratic irony—always calls attention to the artifice of language and the world understanding constituted, or at least influenced, by that language, we would have to measure the effect of that irony in terms of the attitudes the society has toward artifice. As I argue in *Serving the Word* (2000), we have to give recognition to the moralization of signification.

The contributors to this collection all recognize the difficulty of defining irony, and though they are wont to quote one definition or another, they eschew any definitive definition. They do recognize a fundamental distinction between what they call tragic and rhetorical irony, the irony of Sophoclean tragedy and that of the Socratic maieutic. The first centers on the inexorable given, which is usually misapperceived (*méconnu*), if not ignored or denied; the second focuses on language, its foibles and artifice, and ultimately on the but partially language-embedded self. The first mode, Sophoclean irony, is essentially dramatic, and its drama, at least for the Greeks, rests on the recog-nition (*anagnoresis*) of the contingencies of human life, on the fated, and on the resistance to that recognition. Think of Oedipus's refusal to acknowledge the truth before him. "Oh Jocasta," he says when he learns from his mother that his father has been killed at a crossroads, "as I hear this from you, there comes upon me a wandering of the soul—I could run mad" (Sophocles 1954a: ll. 725–727). Think also of the slowness—the post-trance fuzziness—of Agave's recognition of her murder and dismemberment of her son Pentheus. The second mode of irony, the rhetorical, is, as Lambek puts it, an irony of commission. It is intentional or taken to be intentional. The contributors ignore, for the most part, the ambiguous relationship between irony and the absolute, irony and totalization, which preoccupied the German romantics, forcing some of them, like the Schlegels, to write in fragments rather than systematically. What is the relationship between irony and a foundational—an encapsulating—reality? Put in less idealist terms, how does the ironist hold a position? How can his or her ironic words index a world that is put into question by the very act of indexing it ironically? Can irony liberate us, as many have claimed, from the press of language? The press of reality?

Lambek recognizes the problems posed by inserting intention into any discussion of irony. What may seem to be intentionally ironic may, in fact, be the unwitting use of conventionally ironic turns of phrase, as depleted of ironic force as exhausted or 'dead' metaphors are of their metaphoric effectiveness. They—the metaphors—serve within our Edenic mythology of language as traces of a more vital language—one that was not subject to the split in signification and the resultant alienation of the word, the symbol, from its referent but instead rested on the evocative, indeed, the 'presentifying', the magical force of the Word. Of course, irony becomes in this mythology one of the signs of an often violent alienation—a symptom of decadence, a falling away, the Fall. The total preclusion of language's redemptive possibilities is, however, as impossible to contemplate as total world-ending. As Lawrence Cohen notes in his essay, even the seventeenth-century Italian philosopher Giovanni Battista Vico saw irony as a prerequisite for language's renewal. Although Cohen at times intimates a romantic, redemptive, or language-renascent role to irony, he stresses a violence inherent in language—in hearing ironically the words of the senescent. He writes (chapter 6):

> To hear ironically is neither simply to displace through willed incomprehension or some romantic or impossible alternative, nor to hold on to things as they are. It is not to escape from the burden of killing, but it is to discriminate between this burden and the accusation of murder, and thus it is not to hide the body and therefore not to be haunted by its ghostly presence as a speaking corpse. If killing is not murder, then perhaps there is a kind of listening that can yet transpire and an ethic of care that is not merely a redoubling of parricidal force. To hear ironically is to hear language and its correspondence and everyday work in unexpected ways.

Irony has certainly not lost its negative moral evaluation in Euro-American culture. It is frowned upon by language purists, literalists, and devotees of the moral rectitude of singular meaning—monovocality. Its deprecation has been exploited by those masters of irony, such as Oscar Wilde, who seek in it scandal. As Paul Antze notes in his essay, the meaning and negative evaluation of the *eirôn*, the ironist, as a deceiver or dissembler still color our appreciation of irony. We see in irony trickery, escapism, the refusal to take a part, a lack of commitment, passivism, resignation, skepticism, cynicism, nihilism, and—worst of all, in some powerful circles in the United States today—intellectualism.

It should be clear by now that one has to distinguish carefully between formal definitions of irony of the sort that grammarians make (e.g., the determinate negation of what is asserted in a proposition) and what one might call narrowly the ideology and axiology of irony, more generally of rhetoric and figuration, and still more generally of language and discourse. By the ideology and axiology of irony, rhetoric, figuration, language, and discourse, I mean the way speakers understand and evaluate, implicitly if not always explicitly, the use of irony, rhetoric, figuration, language, and discourse (Crapanzano 1992: 14ff.; Kroskrity 2002; Silverstein 1979) It is this ideology and axiology (however they are related to the grammar of the speaker's language and the possibilities it affords) that govern, to a point, ironic usage and attribution. They have an ambient effect.

This distinction is important, I believe, because how one understands irony and other rhetorical figures not only influences their usage but also how they relate to other discursive domains and normative orientations. I want first to note that I am uncomfortable with the separation of irony from other tropes and from moral and existential stances such as skepticism, cynicism, stoicism, and Epicureanism. In our contemporary understanding of irony, it is difficult to separate Socratic irony from skepticism and cynicism and Sophoclean irony from stoicism and even Epicureanism. Associated with these stances are moral values and attitudes that encompass courage and resignation, cowardice and escapism, which cannot be divorced from ironic usage; they both influence that usage and are influenced by the possibilities—the edge, the distance, the play—that usage affords. On what grounds, then, do we separate irony from its linguistically endorsed moral climate?

These moral and existential stances should, of course, be written under erasure (*sous râture*), for they reflect historically specific moral and philosophical presuppositions—those of Hellenistic and late Roman times, as they have been modified over the centuries—that are by no means universal. Indeed, there are other such attitudes, for instance, those of the Indian *saddhu*, the Palestinian martyr, or the Yemeni women of Zabad about whom Anne Meneley writes so sensitively. These women accept, if not easily, the will of God with patience, *sabr*, which can also mean forbearance and endurance but in an active rather than a passive manner. The shock (*sadma*) of a sudden contingency—the near death of a child, for example—not only puts them into a state of fear (*faja'a*), during which they behave in demented fashion, but it leads, often after therapeutic cauterization, to a reflective stance in which they come to recognize the ironies of fate, cast their fright in story form, and are able to laugh with hilarity at what has transpired. Can we say that these frightened women were not able to separate themselves, their bodily selves, from the victims of contingency? I wonder if there is not a parallel between cauterization, which frees them, through pain, from their fright, and the (burning) irony that follows, which gives them an edge on themselves and their fated world. There are, of course, those women who have suffered traumas of such magnitude that they cannot attain to a liberating ironic reflection. Or they are simply possessed of a weak heart (*qalb da'if*). They are caught, we might say after Freud (that is, in our insistent psychological idiom), in a melancholy that is resistant to the liberation that comes through mourning. They are not, in an idiom I prefer, able to cross, for whatever reasons, the fine line that divides the tragic from the comic. My idiomatic preference notwithstanding, I should note that laughter is itself a cultural construct that need not necessarily be related to the hilarious or the comic, but may be a sign of sadness, its recognition and that of the conditions that gave rise to it. Can it not be a symptom of sudden recognition and reversal, of the sort that Antze refers to in his discussion of irony in psychoanalysis? Psychoanalytic therapies are filled with laughter, and that laughter may be stimulated by what is manifestly not funny.

The consideration of the ideological and axiological dimensions of irony raises an important question that has not received the attention it deserves. Why should we conjoin rhetorical irony with tragic, or dramatic, irony? What justifies *their* conjunction—and not other conjunctions? Obviously, were I even capable of doing so, this would not be the place to give a philological or historical explanation. It is clear that the association of these two modes of 'irony', however it came about, has determined much of our thinking about each of them and their relationship. It seems that they are both concerned in one way or another with contingency. This is certainly clear in the case of tragic irony. Oedipus and Pentheus, Phaedra and Andromache (to mention two of Racine's heroines) have had to come to terms with powers greater than themselves, whether cast in cosmic terms as nemesis, the will of a god or gods, the workings of society, the intransigencies of character, or the force of passion to which they are at first blinded. (It is extraordinary how difficult it is to talk about tragedy without talking about blindness.) For rhetorical irony, the case for contingency is less clear. The rhetorical ironist calls attention to the artifice of language in a way, I suppose (though I think this is pushing it), that can be likened to the way the recognition of fate calls attention to the artifice—indeed, the presumption—of our world constructions. We are fatally condemned to language, to the inevitable misfit of that language to the world in which we find ourselves and which we know to be not immune to the effects of that misfitting language. We can set ourselves aside, as does the rhetorical ironist, to demonstrate, if not comment, through indirection if not silence, on the gap between world and language and the irony of the role of language in the construction of that world. We must not forget to include the gap in that construction. The ironists have to recognize that they themselves are entrapped in language, for language is the medium not only of their irony but also, through its reflexive capacity, of the distance they take from it. Ironies of ironies, we might say. Perhaps tragic irony can better be compared to meta-rhetorical irony than to rhetorical irony. More simply, we might say that what the two ironies have in common is entrapment.

However the position of the ironist is facilitated by the reflexivity of language, that reflexivity cannot determine the ironist's position and how it is construed. It certainly cannot determine the communicative etiquette of ironic usage. To me, at least, the determination of the ironist's position, the distance he or she is afforded, how that distance is evaluated, how effective—how authoritative—it is, how it indexes both intra- and extralinguistic contexts and personnel (including, if circularly, the ironist's) are of ethnographic import. We should note that most discussions of irony in literary circles do not take into account the way the ironist's position is determined, and if they do, they do so from within the text in terms of literary-textual strategies. The ironist is afforded, thereby, an unrealistic freedom. Rhetorical ironists, at least, are both within and without their texts, their conversations. Tragic heroes are, to speak figuratively, in their texts only—that is, perhaps, until the moment of recognition. Then, they achieve edge. (I am not speaking here of the tragic hero's audience, whether, complexly, in the text—the chorus, for example—or outside the text—in the theater.) The ironist's position is, as such, pivotal. It is subject to both extratextual—social and political constraints—and intratextual ones. The ironist is not, however, without a certain freedom to choose or not to choose an ironic attitude. Psychoanalysts, so favored in several of the contributors' essays, may assume the distance, the authority, the neutrality of the 'psychoanalyst' in making or not making an ironic intervention or, indeed, in restraining themselves from making such interventions. They may play upon their institutional authority, but they are restrained by that authority, both organizationally, in terms, say, of the ethics of the profession, and personally, in the way they wish to be understood as 'psychoanalysts'. Their 'decisions' to ironize or not are also determined by the micro-politics (read, inter alia, transference and countertransference) of the occasion. They are as subject to these indexical dramas as are their patients.[2]

I have used the textual metaphor here, but it is clearly insufficient to the task of understanding how the position of the ironist is determined. I suggest rather that we look at it in terms of interlocutory dynamics, whether they occur in actual conversations, are 'internalized' in self-reflection, are embedded in seemingly context-free written texts, or, following Lambek, are played out in spirit possession. The interlocutors are never simply exchanging information that is free from pragmatic (among other) implications. In exchanging such information, they are indexing themselves as worthy of making or receiving such information as well as indexing the authority of such information. This is particularly salient in languages in which the status of the information exchanged is marked by evidential particles. I should note that we have yet to consider the relationship between tropes such as irony and 'exotic' grammars like those of many Amerindian languages in which hedging and other text-evaluating locutions are grammatically required. Do they limit ironic expression? Or do they enrich it?

Most important, for our purposes, are the conversational strategies by which the interlocutors indicate at once their engagement with and disengagement from what they are saying and how what they are saying is to be interpreted—literally, figuratively, as the contrary of the literal, or in a conventionally stylized manner of one sort or another. It is within this space that the rhetorical ironist plays. It is rare, if not impossible, for irony to be conveyed by a single utterance taken out of context. Irony is always dependent on real or fancied interlocutors. This is why, I believe, definitions of irony such as 'the determinate negation of what is asserted in a proposition' fail to capture the ironic. This is especially clear if we drop 'determinate' from the definition, for 'determinate' calls forth an interlocutor who will or will not appreciate the speaker's determination or intention. Indeed, this definition of irony can be applied equally well to other modes of exchange, such as, for example, the children's game in which each of the players says the opposite of what he or she means until one of them is caught saying exactly what he or she means. A more serious example, because the stakes are high, is court speech, in which speakers may or may not say what they mean in order to shield themselves from responsibility for the 'real' message they want to convey. Courtiers in the court of Louis XVI or in the Moroccan court of Mohammed V found themselves in a continuous and tortuous hermeneutic bind as they had to appraise how to take what other courtiers were saying to them—that is, as literal, as the contrary of the literal, or, indeed, ironically.

I found myself in a similar hermeneutic bind as I talked to South African dissidents during apartheid who did not know me well enough to trust me. I was told, "Oh, no sir, there is no press censorship in South Africa. We do, of course, have to send any news story concerning shipping in the port of Cape Town to the port authority to make sure it is accurate." Yes, we can call such statements ironic, but though they may have had ironic import, they were mainly ways of protecting the speaker, if I should happen to have been a bugged spy, from whatever accusations the apartheid government would come up with—and they could come up with many. It was, in fact, my impression that for many of these dissidents, the determinate negation of what they asserted in their propositions had become so habitual as to lose any ironic import. It was as coded—as conventional—as the children's game I mentioned, but in a court of law, such as the South African, in which any but the literal meaning was either out-of-bounds or easily contested, it offered the speaker the comforting illusion of some legal protection. It is one of the ironies of the law that any legal system that takes literal meaning as the only permissible meaning in fact loses the truth—at least, those truths (the only real truths, the poet might say) that are expressed through indirection. My point here is that we have to be very careful of how we attribute irony to modes of communication that are structurally or dynamically similar to the ironic but are not marked as ironic (however irony is understood).

I would now like to raise the question of the audience. At least in my reading of the Oedipus cycle, but also of other Greek tragedies, the heroes are not given to rhetorical irony. Indeed, their appreciation of their situation is expressed in stately, existential terms. (I am obviously not using 'existential' here as the existentialists would understand it.) They are suddenly confronted with their fate; they come to understand how what is ordained is beyond their—or any—human control. In *Oedipus at Colonnus* (Sophocles 1954b: ll. 1414ff.), Antigone pleads with her brother Polyneices not to return to Thebes, where, as her father predicted and cursed, he would be killed by his brother Eteocles, as

Eteocles would be killed by him. In that marvelous conjunction of the social (shame), character (anger), and destiny, which Sophocles manages here as elsewhere in his tragedies, Polyneices refuses to—cannot—heed his sister's plea. "And do not try to hold me back," he tells Antigone,

> The dark road is before me; I must take it,
> Doomed by my father and his avenging Furies.

(ll. 1432–1434)

Polyneices is no ironist. He simply finds himself under obligation to do as he must. He does not appreciate the possibility that by not succumbing to anger or the power of shame, he might avoid what has been ordained. Or perhaps he knows better.

The audience is, of course, in a different position. They are not blinded. They know from the start—or are given hints of—what has been ordained. However they may respond in the depths of their souls, they simply witness what is being enacted. To me, at least, their resistance to doing more than witnessing (and vicariously, cathartically participating) is itself part of the tragedy, which they, given the constraints of theater, do not normally appreciate in ironic terms. They are fated, here by convention and self-constraint, not to interfere with the dramatic action of the tragedy. As such they—their refusal to intervene, their submission to convention—embody, or at least perpetuate, the hero's fate.[3] Suppose we were to extend this thought to ordinary conversationalists. They, too, witness what their interlocutors are saying and enacting. Though in most conversations the constraints are not as great as in the theater, the conversationalists are not free to intervene as they will. They are subject to prevailing conversational etiquette. They may transgress, but such transgressions are indelicate, if not dangerous. They may disrupt or even end the conversation. Conventional or indeed idiosyncratic restraint can, though it need not, produce an ironic edge to what is transpiring. One or the other or both interlocutors can assume the distance of an audience. What is said is no longer taken simply as an exchange of information or emotion but becomes a symptom of something else—a take on language, a drama, the display of character, an expression of passion, or the constitution or destruction of a position. I suppose it is something like this that Cohen refers to as "murdering the voice" when he speaks of the way in which the "demented" voice of the senescent is taken only as a sign of neurophysiological defect.

Cohen advocates that we learn to hear with irony the voice of the senile. We must not understand their words simply as symptoms of a physical ailment nor in terms of their ordinary meaning. Words "neither correspond to the expected referents of a shared history (that is, are coherent) nor are they necessarily radically beyond coherence." In discussing Deborah Hoffman's film, *Complaints of a Dutiful Daughter,* Cohen notes that once Hoffman recognized that her mother was no longer bound to a shared history, she discovered a new coherence in her mother's voice. Senility, he argues, "does not so much turn the actual order of things inside out as trouble our desire for and identification with such an order." No doubt like other radically different modes of speech—those of the psychotic, for example, or the holy fool—senile speech can threaten our sense of order, but, I would argue, beyond that threat is another, more potent one (at least in our society as we construe senescence): *it could happen to me.* Listening ironically cannot, I believe, be divorced in such cases from fear. The ironic listener may try to sidestep fear by standing aside, but however liberating such an ironic strategy is, it remains always a subterfuge.

There is, I believe, something dangerous in the assumption of ironic edge, for not only can it destroy (the illusion of) conversational bonding—the trust one has in one's interlocutor, his or her sincerity—but, more importantly, it can give rise to all sorts of inappropriate thoughts (from the unconscious, we say fashionably) that 'ought' to be immediately expunged. The psychoanalyst would understand the emergence of such thoughts in terms of the indexical dramas they refer to as transference and countertransference and, as I have argued elsewhere, interpret them meta-psychologically (technically, in the referential language required for meta-pragmatic depiction). Antze's exposition of the development of Freud's two ironic stances—the rhetorical and the dramatic—can be read as a story of their complementarity. The tales of Oedipus, of psycho-sexual development, and—the more idiosyncratic—of trauma and fixation give basis, however illusory, to the interpretations of ironic play. Can we extend this complementarity to other interlocutions, particularly those that demand intense self-reflection?

I want to suggest, extravagantly, that behind these two dangers—conversational disruption and the eruption of inappropriate thoughts—lies an even greater danger: the recognition that we can never really know what is going on in the mind of our interlocutors any more than they can ever really know what is going on in our minds.[4] Usually, we are shielded from this fear—this knowledge—of epistemic loneliness through our active (and conventional) engagement in the world in which we find ourselves. But from time to time, as when we are confronted with the senescent, the psychotic, those suffering in extremis, and the dying, we find our fear laid bare. We are perhaps in the position of an Oedipus at such times. But all of us do not have the courage of an Oedipus, who was able to see before blinding himself (an act that, ever since I first read Sophocles' tragedy in secondary school, has impressed me as a final—a tragic—failure of courage). We blind ourselves before we fully recognize. The Argentinean psychiatrists whom Andrew Lakoff writes about refused to delve into the subjectivity of their patients, either pragmatically justifying their stance by insisting on the efficacy of psycho-pharmaceuticals or, as the Lacanians did, understanding that subjectivity in abstract psychoanalytic terms. What is striking about the latter, at least as Lakoff describes it, is the psychiatrists' failure to appreciate Lacan's insistent, at time perverse, irony.

One can talk, as the Argentinean Lacanians did, of the need to take into account the patient's subjectivity, but to discuss this need is a far cry from being able to grasp that subjectivity. One must listen—hear ironically, as Cohen would have it, 'read' as the Lacanians would describe it—but subjectivity taken in the abstract, theoretically, at a step removed, can never catch those points that, however illusory they may be from within our epistemic horizons, however resistant to linguistic denomination, are the fulcra of our engagements with others that convince us of having somehow caught their subjectivity. One of the psychiatrists with whom Lakoff worked put it this way: "What one tries to read in the discourse of the patient [in psychoanalysis] is not the history of the patient, but the impressions of subjectivity in the history of the patient— these points of rupture in the story [*historia*], the posture of each one in front of his own story." Cohen would probably take issue with the insistence on the patient's own story. I would insist that the distancing inherent in this stance— this listening with the third ear—precludes intersubjective understanding. A Heideggerian such as Hans-Georg Gadamer (1975: 345ff.) would stress the blending of perspectives in authentic communication that comes with the recognition and bracketing of inevitably biased historical horizons. But what is this blending? Where does projection—mutual projection—end and under- standing arise? Two of my students once described how as children they had to 'translate' their mother's schizophrenic talk to their elders. They were not con- cerned with subjectivity but simply with getting a message, a desire, across, and this they apparently did with considerable success. We have, I suppose, to recognize ironically that our formulations of subjectivity and perhaps even communicative and interpretive efficacy are, by their very remove from what they aim to convey, destined to failure—and continuance. The reflexive capac- ity of language does not lead us, as I have said, to escape language altogether.

Conversational etiquette, including that governing ironic expression and attribution, masks, it would seem, this insistent possibility. Can we approach it in any but an ironic—a meta-ironic—fashion? Can we express such irony in ordinary conversational engagement? Probably not, for it would serve to dis- rupt conversational flow by, minimally, but not without pragmatic effect, changing the register of conversation. Two lovers are bantering: "You do not understand me." "No, *you* do not understand *me*. You have never understood me." "Oh, honey, no one ever understands anyone else. We are to each other black holes."

When and how we can be rhetorically ironic depends on conversational gen- res and conventions. Minimally, they frame self-expression. It is possible in cer- tain societies such as France to elaborate the ironic observations of your interlocutor in ordinary conversation, if those observations are directed toward the circumstances in which you find yourself. But if they are manifestly self- ironic, any elaboration you make will probably be considered indiscreet and is liable to produce a break not only in conversation but in friendship. Often, in my observation, North Americans who are freer in sharing their self-ironies make this mistake when they engage with their French counterparts. Among the Moroccan Arabs with whom I worked, the elaboration of an interlocutor's self-irony was possible so long as it was cast in broader existential terms, as, for example, the fate of mankind or the inscrutability of God's will. I wonder if the role of fate in the Zabadi women's self-understanding permitted, in a similar fashion, the mutual elaboration of their self-irony.

Lambek discusses the ironic stance in which Ali, one of his informants from Mayotte, found himself. Caught between the demands of the French army, which he had willingly joined when he was living in France, and those of his family, as given primary expression by his mother, which were opposed to his military service and especially to his being sent to the first Gulf War, the young man suffered from bouts of rheumatism that were severe enough for his eventual discharge. Ali seemed at times to understand his rheumatism ironically, as a way to escape not only the conflict between personal goals and familial obligations but also the threat of death, the admission of possible cowardice, and, no doubt, other factors. Lambek argues that the ironic situation in which Ali found himself (conducive, I suppose, to a prepossessing— indeed, a possessing—double-voicedness) permitted him, within severe limits, ironic recognition of the role of his illness. Though I am not sure I share Lambek's understanding of Ali's situation in terms of irony, I am reminded of many Moroccan cases in which conflict or ambivalence was resolved in terms of a command relayed in a dream (understood as a message from a supernatural agent, a *jinn* or, more often, a saint, or *siyyid*) or by an illness (most often being struck or possessed by a *jinn*) (Crapanzano 1992: 155–187, 239–259). Often, though not always, the dreamer or the possessed seemed to have an almost uncanny appreciation of the role of the spirit, saint, or illness in resolving the conflict—an appreciation that hovered on the recognition of his or her own role in the dream, the spirit attack, or the illness. I cannot, however, call this savvy ironic since there was finally no *full* recognition of the opportuneness of supernatural intervention or its possible relationship to individual motivation. Such cognizance would be precluded by the belief system. I was reminded, rather, of the *belle indifference* of the hysteric or the intuitiveness of the adolescent acting out what he or she cannot admit but somehow knows. To be caught in an ironic structure does not necessarily produce an ironic attitude. It may lead, as I believe it does in Ali's case, to something like unrecognized self-knowledge. Such knowledge merits study in its own terms.

I do not, however, want to deny the Moroccans who suffered from spirit possession or received dream-commands ironic possibility. Where the stakes were less high, they could be ironic. I am thinking of a Moroccan friend who joked about blind seers. How, he used to ask, can they see what will happen if they can't even see what is going on in front of them? Then one day he suffered a major crisis. One of his daughters had disappeared. She had, in fact, been kidnapped by a white-slaver. In desperation, he went to one of the blind seers to find out her whereabouts. He did not—he could not—ridicule any seers at this time, and naturally I could not remind him of how he had once made fun of them. Later, however, when his daughter had been recovered (no thanks to the seer), he spoke ironically of how his desperation had blinded him to the seer's blindness. Seers are worthless, he said, but sometimes you need them as worthless as they are. I should note that my friend, who was often spirit-possessed, could not treat his possession in ironic terms, though it had served to resolve conflicts in his life. He was at times savvy, nevertheless.[5]

Lambek says (ironically, I hope) that unlike their informants, as they portray them, anthropologists find themselves in a structurally ironic position—one, I would insist, that does not necessarily lead to an ironic attitude. We are certainly not immune to a moralizing etiquette of irony. To speak ironically of the people we work with is seen (though it need not be seen) as somehow demeaning. It posits us as superior. Of course, we are often subject to biting irony by the people we work with in the field, but we tend not to give this the attention it probably deserves in our cultural formulations. Usually, when ironies are expressed, they are expressed *dans les colisses* and not in publications. Janice Boddy's contribution is rare in this respect. She is cognizant of the irony in her study of the attempts to put an end to female circumcision in the Sudan. It is just possible, she suggests, that the Wolff sisters' efforts to gradually break the Sudanese of the custom by training midwives and encouraging less drastic operations would have been successful, whereas its immediate interdiction by British authorities, who put a stop to the Wolff sisters' approach, ended in complete failure. Irony is also implicit in Lakoff's discussion of the relationship between the proponents of psycho-pharmaceuticals and the Lacanians in a hospital in Buenos Aires: their differing approaches to therapy are—more, perhaps, than they themselves realize—a response to the political and bureaucratic conditions of a capitalist society (which, of course, they understand in a seemingly conventional ideological fashion).

My Moroccan friend and mentor Moulay Abedsalem, an illiterate shroud-maker, was one of the most trenchant ironists I know. His irony was directed at our failure to realize the insufficiency of language, its artifice. For Moulay Abedsalem, there was only one true language and that was of the Koran. All other language—that of daily conversation, that by which we attempt to make sense of our world and ourselves—was deficient, but its presumption of truth could arouse in us immodesty, arrogance, passion, anger, and false knowledge, including, he would say with a smile, the knowledge of the failings of our language. In other words, he recognized that what we have been calling Socratic, or rhetorical, irony was as subject to the artifice of language, to which we are blinded, as the heroes of Sophoclean tragedy were to their pretense before the powers of destiny. Moulay Abedsalem often spoke of death. He was an old man and, as a shroud-maker, had had much experience with the dying, the dead, and the mourning. For him, however he understood the afterlife, the fact of death was unyielding. It reminded him of our presumption.

I never spoke to Moulay Abedsalem about irony, but I know that had I, he would have said that death, as the inexorably contingent, the fated, over which we have no control, lurks behind every irony—substantively, we might say, in the case of tragic irony; through indirection, as the ultimate embodiment of negation (an oxymoron is necessary here) in the case of rhetorical irony. None of the contributors to this volume, despite their concern for illness, suffering, and even death, have thought to relate death to ironic possibility and the illusion at least of disengagement (some would say, liberation) that irony offers us from our embeddedness in language. This is, perhaps, the supreme irony. As Moulay Abedsalem always insisted and as I, in my own terms but under his influence, have argued here, we are so caught up in our language, its artifice, its manipulation, and (I would add) its moralization that we can only stumble over the obvious.

NOTES

1. I have written this afterword on short notice because I find the subject so important. Ever since my first fieldwork, among the Navajo, I have been fascinated by the use of irony, ironic-like tropes, and other hedges, including those figurative ones, such as the oxymoron, that call attention to the limits, if not the artifice, of language. I have often spoken of the need to consider them not only in those utterances and discourses that are declared to be characteristic of a particular culture, but also in the conversations and interviews we have with the people with whom we work. Not only are the latter culturally revealing, but they challenge the assumptions we make about the nature of our conversations. As I am writing from the countryside in Italy, far from any library, my references are limited. I am certain that much of what I have had to say in this afterword has been said elsewhere. To those who have said it, I apologize for not citing them.
2. For a discussion of transference and countertransference in terms of indexical dramas, see Crapanzano (1992: 115–135).
3. I am reminded of Richard Schechner's 'experimental' version of the *Bacchae, Dionysius 69*, which was performed by the Performance Group in New York City in 1968 and 1969. The performers had agreed that the play would end immediately if Dionysius failed to win what they called the "Dionysius Game," that is, if Pentheus was able to obtain whatever he wanted—in case in point, any woman or man in the audience—without Dionysius's help. One evening, when William Shepherd was playing Pentheus and "had refused Dionysius's help," he approached a woman in the audience who accepted his caresses and left the theater with him. The play ended, causing pandemonium in the audience, most of whom wanted their money back. On a second occasion, a group of students from Queens College, who had attended the play several times, decided to rescue Pentheus just as he was about to be murdered and dismembered. They jumped into the center of the theater—there was no stage—and carried him off. This time, Schechner decided to continue the play. He asked for a volunteer in the audience whom he would walk through the remainder of the play. A young man volunteered, and the performance was brought to completion with very considerable success. In both instances, thanks largely to Schechner's direction, which demanded audience participation, the conventionally passive role of the audience was so disturbed that they were able to interfere with the play's outcome—with Pentheus's fate. How are we to read 'fate' under these circumstances? Tragedy? See Schechner (1970) for details.
4. I should make it perfectly clear that there may be other societies that are not as dedicated to an epistemology that foregrounds solipsistic possibility.
5. See Kramer (1970) and Crapanzano (1992: 155–187) for more details.

REFERENCES

Crapanzano, Vincent. 1992. *Hermes' Dilemma and Hamlet's Desire.* Cambridge: Harvard University Press.

———. 2000. *Serving the Word: Literalism in America from the Pulpit to the Bench.* New York: New Press.

Gadamer, Hans-Georg. 1975. *Truth and Method.* New York: Seabury Press.

Kramer, Jane. 1970. *Honor to the Bride Like the Pigeon That Guards Its Grain under the Clove Tree.* New York: Farrar, Straus, and Giroux.

Kroskrity, Paul V. 2002. *Regimes of Language: Ideologies, Politics, and Identities.* Santa Fe: School of American Studies Press.

Silverstein, Michael. 1979. "Language Structure and Linguistic Ideology." Pp. 193–247 in *The Elements: A Parasession on Linguistic Units and Levels,* edited by P. Clyne, W. Hanks, and C. Hofbauer. Chicago: Chicago Linguistic Society.

Sophocles. 1954a. *Oedipus the King.* Pp. 11–76 in *Sophocles.* Vol. 1. Translated by David Grene. Chicago: University of Chicago Press.

———. 1954b. *Oedipus at Colonnus.* Pp. 77–156 in *Sophocles.* Vol. 1. Translated by Robert Fitzgerald. Chicago: University of Chicago Press.

Schechner, Richard, ed. 1970. *Dionysius in 69.* New York: Farrar, Strauss, and Giroux.

NOTES ON CONTRIBUTORS

Paul Antze teaches in the Division of Social Science and in the Graduate Programs in Anthropology and Social and Political Thought at York University, Toronto. His research interests include psychoanalysis, the anthropology of memory, trauma and dissociation, and the anthropological study of therapeutic movements. He is co-editor with Michael Lambek of *Tense Past: Cultural Essays in Trauma and Memory* (Routledge 1996). His essay "The Other Inside: Memory as Metaphor in Psychoanalysis" appeared recently in *Regimes of Memory*, edited by Susannah Radstone and Kate Hodgkins (Routledge 2003).

Janice Boddy is Professor of Anthropology at the University of Toronto. She has worked with Arabic-speaking Muslims in rural northern Sudan, investigating how gender roles and images come to be embodied both physically and in the objects and acts of everyday life. She is equally interested in the religious and ritual dimensions of health and in comparative understandings of the human body. Her latest research examines attempts by the British colonial state to reform Sudanese women's bodily practices. Publications include "Tacit Containment: Social Value, Embodiment, and Gender Practice in Northern Sudan," in *Religion and Sexuality in Cross-Cultural Perspective* (Routledge 2002), and *Aman: The Story of a Somali Girl* (co-author, Vintage 1994).

Lawrence Cohen is an Associate Professor in the Departments of Anthropology and of South and Southeast Asian Studies at the University of California, Berkeley. Since the 1998 publication of *No Aging in India: Alzheimer's, the Bad Family, and Other Modern Things*, he has been working on two forthcoming projects. *India Tonight: Homosex and the Political Secret* examines the relation between beauty and violence in contemporary India. *The Operation and Its Reason* links analyses of organ transplantation markets, state-sponsored sterilization, cataract surgical camps for the rural poor, and the elections of eunuchs to state office in a genealogy of the operation as a modern political form.

Vincent Crapanzano is Distinguished Professor of Comparative Literature and Anthropology at the Graduate Center of the City University of New York. His most recent books are *Hermes's Dilemma and Hamlet's Desire: On the Epistemology of Interpretation*; *Serving the Word: Literalism in America from the Pulpit to the Bench*, and *Imaginative Horizons: An Essay in Literary-Philosophical Anthropology*. He is currently writing a book on the rhetoric of personal transformation in life histories.

Andrew Lakoff is Assistant Professor of Sociology and Science Studies at the University of California, San Diego. He was a postdoctoral fellow at Harvard from 2000–2002. His forthcoming book, *Pharmaceutical Reason: Technology and the Human at the Modern Periphery* (Cambridge University Press), examines the role of the global circulation of pharmaceuticals in the spread of biological models of human behavior. He has published articles on visual technology and the behavioral sciences, on the history of attention deficit disorder, and on the placebo effect. His current research concerns the intersection of science, capitalism, and subjectivity in the development of new behavioral medications.

Michael Lambek teaches in the Department of Anthropology at the University of Toronto. He has written two books and numerous essays on Mayotte. Recent work includes *The Weight of the Past: Living with History in Mahajanga, Madagascar* (Palgrave 2002), *A Reader in the Anthropology of Religion* (Blackwell 2002), and "Fantasy in Practice: Projection and Introjection, or The Witch and the Spirit-Medium," which appeared in *Beyond Rationalism: Rethinking Magic, Witchcraft and Sorcery*, edited by Bruce Kapferer (Berghahn 2002 and *Social Analysis* 46, no. 3).

Anne Meneley is Associate Professor of Anthropology at Trent University. Her anthropological monograph *Tournaments of Value: Sociability and Hierarchy in a Yemeni Town* (University of Toronto Press 1996) has just been reprinted for the third time. She has published several articles about her research in Yemen, as well as pieces about her research on the production, circulation, and consumption of Tuscan extra-virgin olive oil. She is co-editing, with Don Kulick, a forthcoming volume entitled *Fat*, which explores fat as a substance and a corporeal reality. With Donna Young, she is co-editing a forthcoming volume, *Auto-Ethnographies of Academic Practices*, which explores the quotidian and often recondite aspects of contemporary academic labor.

Index

Related Titles of Interest from *Berghahn Books*

BEYOND RATIONALISM

Rethinking Magic, Witchcraft and Sorcery

Edited by **Bruce Kapferer**

This book seeks a reconsideration of the phenomenon of sorcery and related categories. The contributors to the volume explore the different perspectives on human sociality and social and political constitution that practices typically understood as sorcery, magic, and ritual reveal. In doing so, the authors are concerned to break away from the dictates of a Western externalist rationalist understanding of these phenomena without falling into the trap of mysticism. The essays address a diversity of ethnographic contexts in Africa, Asia, the Pacific, and the Americas.

From the Contents: B. Kapferer, *Introduction: Outside All Reason – Magic, Sorcery and Epistemology in Anthropology* – M. Brendbekken, *Beyond Vodou and Anthroposophy in the Dominican-Haitian Borderlands* – K.G. Telle, *The Smell of Death: Theft, Disgust and Ritual Practice in Central Lombok, Indonesia* – B. Kapferer, *Sorcery, Modernity and the Constitutive Imaginary: Hybridising Continuities* – K. Rio, *The Sorcerer as an Absented Third Person: Formations of Fear and Anger in Vanuatu* – R. Bastin, *Sorcerous Technologies and Religious Innovation in Sri Lanka* – R. Devisch, *Maleficent Fetishes and the Sensual Order of the Uncanny in South-West Congo* – M. Lambek, *Fantasy in Practice: Projection and Introjection, or the Witch and the Spirit-Medium* – Ø. Gulbrandsen, *The Discourse of 'Ritual Murder': Popular Reaction to Political Leaders in Botswana* – A. Feldman, *Strange Fruit: The South African Truth Commission and the Demonic Economies of Violence*.

Bruce Kapferer is Professor of Social Anthropology at the University of Bergen, Adjunct Professor at James Cook University, and Honorary Professor at University College London.

2003. 288 pages, 18 color and 11 b/w illus., bibliog., index
ISBN 1-57181-418-3 paperback

HEALING PERFORMANCES OF BALI

Between Darkness and Light

Angela Hobart

Contemporary Western societies have tended to proclaim a separation between the scientific and artistic, or the human and non-human. In Bali, these dimensions are intertwined as this study shows. Although the island is undergoing rapid change and modernization, the traditional medical system, which includes myth, movement, dialogue, comedy, and a spectacular masking tradition, has remained an integral part of Bali society. It is deeply embedded in a network of social relations that extends far beyond the parameters of the rituals themselves.

The healing performances discussed in this book take into account healing by spirit-mediums and scholarly healers, the masked ritual drama, and the shadow theater. These animated performances take place during the annual religious festival that is aimed at individual well-being as well as social regeneration, brought to life in this volume through rich illustrative material.

Angela Hobart is the coordinating lecturer at Goldsmiths' College on Intercultural Therapy (Medical Anthropology) and lectures at the British Museum on the Art and Culture of South East Asia. She also works as a psychodynamic therapist at the Medical Foundation for the Care of the Victims of Torture.

2003. 288 pages, 6 color and 30 b/w illus., bibliog., index
ISBN 1-57181-480-9 hardback

orders@berghahnbooks.com www.berghahnbooks.com